JUSTICE ON EARTH

Justice on Earth

Earthjustice and the people it has served

TOM TURNER

EARTHJUSTICE
Oakland, California

CHELSEA GREEN PUBLISHING COMPANY
White River Junction, Vermont

First Edition
10 9 8 7 6 5 4 3 2 1

Frontispiece photo: Lisianski Inlet, near the town of Pelican Bay, lies
across from the entrance to Glacier Bay at the north end of the
Tongass National Forest, Alaska. The land around the river mouth was
once scheduled for massive clear-cutting, halted by the efforts of citizens' groups and Earthjustice (see chapter 9). *Robert Glenn Ketchum*

This page: Native American fisherman releasing salmon, Columbia
River, Oregon. *Joel Sartore*

Page 9: Lush vegetation around Fisheating Creek, south Florida.
Earthjustice went to court to keep the creek open for public use
(see chapter 6). *James Valentine*

ISBN: 1-931498-31-8

Library of Congress Cataloguing-in-Publication Data is available
on request.

Editorial and production supervision by Diana Landau,
Parlandau Communications

Book and jacket design by Ingalls + Associates
Thomas Ingalls, art director
Sara Streifel, designer

Editorial services by Jacqueline Volin
Proofreading services by Melissa Leveton

Printed in Italy on recycled paper

Copies of this book may be purchased directly from Earthjustice.
Please call (800) 584-6460 or visit our Web site, www.earthjustice.org

Distributed to the trade by:
Chelsea Green Publishing Company
P.O. Box 428
White River Junction, Vermont 05001
(800) 639-4049
www.chelseagreen.com

As with all such enterprises, this book depended heavily on the kindness of friends and strangers alike. The following people consented to interviews, reviewed the manuscript, unearthed musty documents, gave guidance, or otherwise made the project possible. I thank them all but insist that any errors that remain in the text are mine alone.

Paul Achitoff, Irene Alexakos, Jim Angell, Denise Antolini, Don Bachman, Cindy Barkhurst, Heidi Barrett, David Baron, Craig Bell, Enrico Bighin, Brent Blackwelder, Bob Boone, Joe Brecher, William M. Brinton, Tim Bristol, David Brower, Anna Cederstav, Everett Ching, Mike Clark, Jim Connolly, Diane Curran, Susan Daggett, Peter Dobbins, Jeff Dose, Bob Dreher, Francis Eatherington, Bob Ekey, Carrie Foley, Howard Fox, Nancy Freeman, Patti Goldman, Alisa Gravitz, Daniel Greenberg, David Guest, Monique Harden, Herb Harris, Marty Hayden, Becky Hendry, Smiley Hendry, Susan Herring, Calvin Hoe, Charlene Hoe, Doug Honnold, John Hooper, Mark Hughes, Tom Ingalls, Toney Johnson, Eric Jorgensen, Mary Jorgensen, Matt Kirchhoff, Diana Landau, Melissa Leveton, Ann Maest, Roy Mardis, Michael Marriotte, Stephen Morris, Adriana Murillo, Richard Nelson, Buck Parker, Walt Patterson, Cara Pike, Kim Ramos, Mike Reagan, Katie Regnier, Charlie Reppun, Paul Reppun, Joe Sax, Florian Sever, Fern Shepard, Kapua Sproat, Andy Stahl, Sara Streifel, Norton Tompkins, Todd True, Bret Turner, Katy Turner, Ashlyn Van Pelt, Pat Veesart, Jacqueline Volin, Martin Wagner, Tom Waldo, Nathalie Walker, Michael Wall, Frazer Walton, Damon Whitehead, Louisa Willcox, Almeter Willis, Robert Wiygul, Essie Youngblood, Marjorie Ziegler, Ted Zukoski.

—T.T.

The Court of Last Resort

By Bill McKibben

Meet Erin Brockovich, minus the cleavage. This is the story of some of the country's last democrats, actually committed to the preposterous notion that people who aren't wealthy nonetheless have some value, that places might be important even if they aren't making money for anyone. And a hell of a story it is—one last-ditch battle after another, a series of Davids with writs for slingshots and precedents for stones.

From Louisiana to California, from D.C. to Oregon, from Hawai'i to Alaska, the plot is pretty much the same: local people start out behind the eight ball, facing rich corporations, corrupt politicians, slick PR agencies. They mount a furious fight, for their lives, their livelihoods, the places they love. And in the end, they manage to beat the odds, in part because they manage to find aggressive lawyers. Heroes, really—people like Diane Curran and Nathalie Walker, who managed to help fight off a nuclear facility planned for one of the poorest, blackest corners of the South. Or Paul Achitoff helping the small farmers of the windward side of O'ahu win back their water. Or—well, the list is long, and many of the names on it work for Earthjustice, the environmental law firm that began as an arm of the Sierra Club and still carries on with the fire of the late Dave Brower.

And these are stories that need telling. It's possible that baseball is still ahead, but criticizing lawyers comes in a pretty close second as a national pastime. Lawyers are greedy, wily, interested only in lining their pockets. They gum up the works, slow progress, raise the cost of doing business. They chase ambulances, and now they run sleazy commercials on late-night TV.

But as this book makes clear, there are still corners of the country, and corners of the courthouse, where they function as the only hope for people who would otherwise be overwhelmed by the sheer power of money. Where gumming up the works is an absolute necessity, because the skids have been greased. (And greased in a thoroughly bipartisan fashion, one should add—the single blackest hat in this book's long list of villains might well belong on the head of former Louisiana Democratic senator J. Bennett Johnston.) It shouldn't have to be this way; in a democratic country we should be able to control our destinies without going into court. And indeed, savvy organizers know not to call the lawyer first: there has to be a real, angry, empowered community already taking on the fight, a community that won't go to sleep while the wheels of litigation slowly turn.

These stories also make clear, albeit implicitly, how important it is to take part in the political process long before your community gets in trouble—if only to affect the quality of the judiciary. The best lawyer in the world is powerless before an ideologue on the bench, and increasingly that's what the lawyers of Earthjustice face. The situation is bad enough that going to court may not save the day that much longer. For the moment, though, these men and women are still holed up in the Alamo, fighting like hell for the rest of us.

If you're a tree hugger—well, you better hug a lawyer or two as well.

Location of Earthjustice cases corresponding to chapters in this book

② New World Mine and Yellowstone National Park
③ Forest Grove and Center Springs, Louisiana
④ Waiāhole Stream and the Waiāhole Ditch, Oʻahu, Hawaiʻi
⑤ Garcia River, California
⑥ Fisheating Creek, Florida
⑦ Umpqua River watershed, Oregon
⑧ Anacostia River, Washington, D.C.
⑨ Tongass National Forest, Alaska

🐢 Sea turtle, representing international trade issues discussed in Chapter 10

ENVIRONMENTAL LAW IN THE TWENTY-FIRST CENTURY

There are many ways to go about influencing the behavior of human beings: education, coercion, guilt, extortion, brainwashing, force, persuasion, bribery, reward, trickery, and deceit, to name a handful. There are fewer ways to go about changing the behavior of institutions, be they private corporations or government bureaucracies. One way is bribery and its legal counterpart, campaign contributions. Another is revolution, bloody and expensive. A third is to put farsighted, incorruptible, intelligent people into elective office: democracy. This is cumbersome, expensive, dangerously slow, and, as the election of 2000 showed, itself susceptible to manipulation and corruption.

A fourth is through use of the law by citizens—at least in countries such as the United States, where there is a strong and wise Constitution and where public servants and private citizens generally obey the law and the courts.

Earthjustice, which began life as the Sierra Club Legal Defense Fund in 1971 and adopted its new name in 1997, was established in part to encourage a change in the way corporations and agencies go about their business, to make their activities less damaging to the global life-support system that sustains us all. Whether the organization and its thousands of allies will ultimately succeed in stopping the destruction of the earth is a wide-open question. What one can say with certainty at this point is that, as frightening as the current situation is, without the efforts of these organizations and their millions of members and sympathizers, things would be far, far worse.

The 1989 book *Wild by Law* described a handful of the most important struggles the Legal Defense Fund had been involved in during its first two decades. The book outlined the opening-up of the legal system, the confirmation of the fact that citizens, under certain broad circumstances, have what lawyers call "standing to sue"—a right to take grievances to court, to request that the courts review and sometimes overrule the actions and regulations of agencies and corporations. Standing was first affirmed in a case involving Storm King on the Hudson River, then reaffirmed in a backhanded way in one involving Mineral King valley in the Sierra Nevada.

Indeed, the Mineral King case inspired a dissenting opinion from Justice William O. Douglas, who wrote that, in the best of all possible worlds, the valley itself should have

An early and persistent theme of environmental litigation was and is to protect public lands and their wildlife habitat from excessive logging, grazing, road building, mining, and recreational development. *Opposite:* This rock formation in the Bob Marshall Wilderness in Montana is known as the Chinese Wall; bear grass in the foreground. *Carr Clifton* been the lead plaintiff, represented by human beings who bore its best interests in mind. This, in turn, sparked the following rejoinder by John Naff in the *Journal of the American Bar Association* from 1972:

If Justice Douglas has his way—
    O come not that dreadful day—
We'll be sued by lakes and hills
    Seeking a redress of ills.
Great mountain peaks of name prestigious
    Will suddenly become litigious.
Our brooks will babble in the courts,
    Seeking damages for torts.
How can I rest beneath a tree
    If it may soon be suing me?
Or enjoy the playful porpoise
    While it's seeking habeas corpus?
Every beast within his paws
    Will clutch an order to show cause.
The courts, besieged on every hand,
    Will drown with suits by chunks of land.
Ah! But vengeance will be sweet
    Since this must be a two-way street.
I'll promptly sue my neighbor's tree
    for shedding all its leaves on me.

For better or worse, Justice Douglas's vision is a long way from being fulfilled.

In 1992, the Supreme Court, led by Justice Antonin Scalia, began chipping away at citizens' rights to redress environmental wrongs in the courts in a series of opinions that raised the barriers to standing slowly and ominously. The backsliding slowed at least temporarily with a decision in 2000 that helps ensure access to the courts will remain fairly open and straightforward for the time being.

Since the publication of *Wild by Law* a decade has passed into a new millennium, and it's time to take stock. In this second book, however, we're spending a little less time on the legal campaigns and a little more on all the rest of the myriad activities that go into an environmental crusade, particularly those of the organizations we work with and for. Some are tiny, almost accidental collections of people who band together to fend off an ill-advised project or reclaim what was taken from them. Others are more formal and permanent institutions. All work vigorously and selflessly for the common good.

The specialty of Earthjustice is litigation, both to block imminent disasters and to encourage long-term, systemic change. The organizations we work with have other specialties: Some concentrate on public lands nationally, some exist only to protect a single plot. Some work to save and restore wildlife. Some work to reform industries involved in logging, mining, ranching, or industrial activities that too often sully air and water to the detriment of nature and the public health. Some represent people who catch fish for a living. Some encourage whistleblowers to speak out and then defend them from retaliation. Some work to protect their communities from invasion by noxious factories or waste dumps, being unwilling to put up with an affluent society's effluvia to their own detriment.

Such organizations and individuals participate in a bewildering array of activities: mounting protest marches, writing letters to newspapers and legislators, speaking at schools and on radio and television, publishing books and magazines, conducting studies and producing reports, pressuring city councils to adopt sensible rules and regulations—

The suit that launched the Sierra Club Legal Defense Fund, now known as Earthjustice, was filed to block construction of a massive ski resort in Mineral King valley in California's Sierra Nevada range. The resort was not built, and Mineral King, with a few historic mining buildings, has been added to Sequoia National Park. *Carr Clifton*

and on and on. Earthjustice seeks to complement their activities when a little legal muscle is appropriate, and to be there for the long haul. Because if one thing's for certain, it's that only an effort sustained over many years will eventually carry the day in many of these battles.

A subtle change in subject matter between *Wild by Law* and this book reflects a change in the outside world. Where *Wild by Law* mainly recounted stories of efforts to protect pristine, or nearly pristine, landscapes and resources, this book speaks more often of restoration, of efforts to reclaim wounded lands and return them to a healthy condition for wildlife habitat, recreation, or other purposes. To that end it examines the monumental crusade to stop the mining giant Noranda from reopening an old, bleeding gold mine on the border of Yellowstone National Park. The land is now, thanks to this massive citizen effort, being restored to its pre-mining condition.

Likewise, on the Garcia River in northern California, we describe a broad-based effort to heal a river system badly damaged by logging, road building, and gravel mining over the past century. And from Hawai'i, we recount a campaign to restore water stolen from Windward O'ahu and piped to the center of the island to grow sugar, destroying taro farms and wreaking havoc on Native Hawaiian communities nearly a century ago.

South Florida has been an environmental battleground since its wetlands were drained for agriculture (see chapter 6). Here, baton rouge lichen decorates cypress trees in the Loxahatchee National Wildlife Refuge. *Carr Clifton*

THE ROLE OF LITIGATION

A widely quoted and misquoted observation goes more or less as follows: "We have not inherited the earth from our ancestors; we are borrowing it from our children." It has been attributed to our old friend Anonymous, described as a Native American saying, and carved into the façade of the National Aquarium. In fact, it was tossed off by David Brower in the course of an interview published in *Mother Earth News* in the early 1970s. Brower didn't even remember having said it until Lester Brown of the Worldwatch Institute later pointed it out to him. Regardless of its lineage, it is an excellent bit of wisdom that should inform everything society does that involves natural resources.

But what is the role of litigation in the picture? We offer here four observations to whet your appetite. One is from Craig Bell, a fishing guide and restoration expert working with Trout Unlimited on the Garcia River project (see chapter 5). He has been working to rescue the Garcia for two decades and more, and he has this to say: "We don't get much without litigation."

Biologist Michael Dombeck was chief of the Forest Service at the end of the Clinton presidency and the architect of the policy aimed at keeping roadless areas on the national forests roadless. He bluntly acknowledges how the litigation campaign carried on by Earthjustice and many other groups fundamentally changed the way his agency operated:

> Following World War II, we worked with the growing timber industry to help fulfill the national dream of providing families with single-family homes. Our timber harvests escalated for nearly a quarter of a century.
>
> Along the way, social values changed. Eventually, the changing times caught up with and overran us in a flood of controversy, lawsuits, and injunctions. We've learned that we must be responsive to new demands—demands for clean water, healthy habitat for fish and wildlife, recreation opportunities, and ecologically sustainable timber harvests.
>
> Today, we no longer manage public forests primarily for outputs of wood fiber, minerals, or animal unit-months of grazing. In ever-greater numbers, the American people are asking—demanding—that we focus less on what we take from the land and more on what we leave behind.

Joe Sax is a pioneer in the field of environmental law, having drafted at least one, litigated many cases, written about and analyzed many others, worked in government, and taught for many years at the law schools at Michigan and Berkeley. Sax spent three years as counselor to Interior Secretary Bruce Babbitt and notes the following:

> There are two purposes to litigation of this sort: To achieve tangible results—block a timber sale, get a species listed, stop a dam—and to discipline the agencies.
>
> Agency bureaucrats are well-meaning, but if they weren't worried about being brought into court, enforcement would be orders of magnitude less than it is.
>
> It is clear that concern on the part of federal agencies over these suits drives public enforcement. The outstanding example is the spotted owl litigation. It brought about dramatic change including an all-day meeting/hearing/summit called by and presided over by the president, which led to a new management scheme called Option 9. That never would have happened without those suits. It's the same all across the country: Either the presence of suits or fear that they may be filed drives the game. Agencies and private concerns worry that the courts might simply take over management of the forests and other resources.
>
> The Platte River is another good example. Fear of litigation drove Wyoming, Colorado, and Nebraska to the negotiating table along with irrigators, hydro[electricity] operators, and providers of residential water to hammer out a plan to conserve the river and its water.
>
> Litigation generates a crisis atmosphere that drives the parties to the negotiating table. Regulators tend to like it as well, since they can say to the regulated, "Look, if you won't deal with us, those environmental crazies will drag you into court and you'll lose all control. You never know what a judge will do. You're better off dealing with us. We're reasonable."

Jeff Dose, our fourth observer, is a Forest Service fish biologist in western Oregon in the drainage of the Umpqua River. He says, "No government agency has done anything good without being sued."

GAS VAPORS

Finally, there is the extended example of a case pursued by Howard Fox, an Earthjustice attorney who began as a volunteer in the late 1970s and in the 1990s took over the managing attorney spot in Washington, D.C. Fox has spent a large fraction of his career jousting with the Environmental Protection Agency, which, no matter who is in the White House, seems incapable of meeting deadlines imposed on it by Congress unless and until it is goaded by citizen-initiated litigation.

Pollution enhances the sunset above Phoenix even as it damages crops, trees, and lungs. One source of the problem—gasoline vapors that escape when gas tanks are being filled—is coming under control via a successful lawsuit against the Environmental Protection Agency. *Craig Wells*

While the Departments of the Interior and Agriculture are the principal agencies to manage and protect the nation's land, the EPA was created to control, abate, minimize, perhaps even eventually eliminate pollution. All kinds of pollution: air, water, ground, noise, visual, you name it. President Nixon created the agency by executive order, and Congress wrote its job description in a long series of laws beginning, more or less, with the Clean Air Act of 1970. Other laws outline the agency's responsibilities as regards water, toxic waste, hazardous chemicals, and myriad other dangers that beset the environment and public health.

One of those dangers is the fumes that escape from the gas tanks of cars and trucks when the gas cap is removed for refueling. As gas is burned and the tank slowly empties, gasoline evaporates and fills the growing airspace. When new fuel is pumped into the tank, the vapor is forced out. Perhaps you have smelled it.

This may sound trivial, but it is not. Fumes escaping from gas tanks are a major contributor to smog, which is created when hydrocarbons—like those gas fumes—interact with sunlight. And smog, as we all know, aggravates lung problems and damages crops and forests. Constituents of gasoline can cause cancer. The contribution of gas fumes to this problem is hardly a recent discovery.

The Clean Air Act amendments of 1977, among dozens of very specific mandates, directed the EPA to investigate methods for controlling gas-tank fumes. Two specific methods had been suggested, one that involves sucking the vapors back into the pump as the gasoline is being dispensed, the other a so-called onboard system that would capture the fumes inside the vehicle and use them as fuel.

The two methods set up an interesting contest. The oil industry, which owns a majority of the country's filling stations, and the independent operators, who own the rest, favored onboard recovery (because they wanted to avoid installing vapor recovery systems on their nozzles); the auto industry favored the gas-pump option (for the opposite reason).

In the 1977 Clean Air Act amendments, Congress ordered EPA specifically to study the onboard option and, if it looked feasible and desirable, to issue regulations requiring auto manufacturers to equip cars with onboard devices. This prompted EPA to study the matter, and in 1980, at the tail end of the Carter administration, it allowed as how the onboard systems looked like a good bet.

Then the Reagan team took the field and, much the way the second George Bush was undertaking his new job as this was being written, dozens of proposals and regulations were rescinded, delayed, or suspended. In the case of the onboard standards, a delay of four years was announced—allegedly to give a boost to the then-ailing auto industry.

In 1984 EPA resumed its study, and in 1987 (these things take time) it announced that onboard systems were best. Environmentalists and public-health watchdogs saw this as a good thing. If onboard systems were made mandatory, that would mean that air quality would improve everywhere, not just the places where the gas pumps were outfitted with vapor recovery devices.

With that announcement, however, EPA washed its hands of the matter. No regulations were forthcoming.

Congress passed yet another set of amendments to the Clean Air Act in 1990, the most extensive and specific such legislation ever enacted. President Bush senior deemed them worthy and signed them into law. This time Congress left nothing to chance regarding vapor recovery. It explicitly gave EPA one year to promulgate regulations that would require all new cars to be equipped with onboard systems, starting with new cars built in about 1995. The law was signed on November 15, 1990.

The one-year deadline for issuance of the regulations passed with no action. Then, on March 13, 1992, four days before the presidential primary in Michigan, President Bush spoke to the Economic Club of Detroit. It was only the primary, but he was clearly running for reelection as Democrats vied for the chance to challenge him, Ross Perot rallied his libertarian enthusiasts, and Pat Buchanan took pot-shots from the right. The economy was in a tailspin, especially the auto industry.

The president was desperate to ignite his supporters. So on that day in Detroit, even though he had signed the law himself, he announced that EPA would not after all be requiring onboard vapor recovery equipment. EPA made it official two weeks later. It looked like a sop to the auto industry. It also looked illegal. Howard Fox filed suit on behalf of the Natural Resources Defense Council and the Center for Auto Safety. In the

Redwood Creek, California. When Redwood National Park was established in the late 1960s, it was left vulnerable to landslides caused by logging operations upslope and upstream from the park. Litigation helped persuade Congress to double the size of the park to protect it adequately.
Carr Clifton

strange bedfellows department, they were joined by the American Petroleum Institute and two oil companies. The defendant, EPA, was joined by the Motor Vehicle Manufacturers Association and a few other groups.

Fox filed suit in federal court in Virginia, but the judge wanted nothing to do with the case. He said that since EPA had officially announced that its final decision was to do nothing, the lawyers should take their case directly to the court of appeals in Washington, D.C. They did.

Back inside the Beltway, the EPA continued to resist, telling the Court of Appeals that one particular onboard design raised safety concerns. But the evidence didn't support this claim, and in any event there were other designs available for development. Moreover, onboard systems would absorb flammable vapors, thus preventing dozens of service station fires each year. EPA hadn't accounted for those benefits. For their part, the auto manufacturers argued that they were caught in a Catch-22: if the regulations required the onboard devices but EPA eventually deemed them unsafe, they'd be stuck with cars they couldn't sell. The appeals court wasn't having any of this. It ruled unanimously that the law meant what the law said. EPA issued the regulations in 1994, and the situation feared by the automakers never materialized. To the contrary, onboard vapor recovery systems are now standard equipment on cars and light trucks and buses throughout the country.

As mentioned at the outset, Howard Fox and a few other lawyers have contested scores of missed deadlines under the Clean Air Act. One might expect that the government would one day simply issue its regulations on time and avoid the lawsuits, but there's little evidence that that will happen. As Fox explained, the agency is often slowed down by its own paralysis-by-analysis approach, and by lobbying from affected industries or states—or their surrogates in Congress or the administration. "The voices urging EPA away from

Colorado River, Canyonlands National Park, Utah. In the 1960s and 1970s, it looked as if the Southwest would be stripped of its coal, which would then be transported to huge power plants to create electricity and pollution. Many plants were built. Many more were not. The battles will go on as long as the coal is there and our appetite for power continues to grow. *Carr Clifton*

its core public-health and environmental mission are numerous and well funded, and unfortunately they often sway the agency," Fox said.

At the end of the day, there is a strong advantage to having a court order or a consent-decree settlement signed by a judge: if EPA blows another deadline, it must answer to the law.

EPA is just one of many agencies and private entities that Earthjustice and its allies watch over. Each has its own personality and way of operating; all are susceptible to outside pressure from politicians and vested interests. In subsequent chapters we will explore campaigns waged against the Forest Service, a large Florida landowner, the sugar industry in Hawai'i, a Canadian mining company, an international energy consortium, and the city of Washington, D.C., among others. The stories are as diverse as the participants, but the objective is generally the same: to respect Dave Brower's observation that we, the present generation, have an obligation to preserve the earth intact for those yet to come.

In his majority opinion in *Marbury vs. Madison* in 1803, the case that established the courts as equal in power to the executive and legislative branches and made possible all the litigation discussed herein, Chief Justice John Marshall wrote: "The very essence of civil liberty certainly consists in the right of every individual to claim protection of the laws whenever he receives an injury. One of the first duties of government is to afford that protection."

Earthjustice and its kindred organizations are here to see that individuals are able to enjoy and exercise that right, and that government executes the duties required of it by the law and the Constitution.

THE CASE OF THE SPRING IN THE ROAD

Rumors started reaching Cooke City in the late 1980s. The Canadian mining giant Noranda was buying up claims on Henderson and Fisher Mountains and the valley between them, a couple of miles and three thousand vertical feet above the town.

Cooke City is in the extreme south of Montana, just two-and-a-half miles from the northern boundary of Yellowstone National Park. A hamlet with a year-round population of no more than a thousand, it began as a camp established about 1870 by miners lured by the gold in the mountains directly above. It sits next to Soda Butte Creek, which ambles downhill to join the Lamar River and, pretty soon, the Yellowstone River. In 1880, the town was named for Jay Cooke, the owner of the Northern Pacific Railroad. The miners hoped by this flattery to lure a rail spur to the area. It didn't work.

By the 1980s, there remained old workings above the town that had been mined on and off since 1870 but abandoned for good in the 1950s. The old pits and mine portals—entrances to horizontal tunnels known as adits—plus various vent holes and seeps still leaked rust-colored water into the creeks, and an old pile of tailings taken from the McClaren mine up the mountain squatted ominously right next to the town, dribbling its own historic poisons into Soda Butte Creek. Traces of the acids could be measured inside Yellowstone National Park downstream. For years, grizzled fellows with picks had been snooping around the old mines—known as the New World Mining District—hoping to strike it rich. Most people in Cooke City figured they were hobby miners and hoped they would strike out.

Jim Barrett, a young carpenter and artist, moved to Cooke City from Detroit in 1973, captivated by the high-mountain beauty of the Beartooths, which loom over the town. He remembers running into a Noranda fellow in a Cooke City bar in 1989 or so and asking him if they were having any luck. "Oh yes, there's gold up there," the man said. "We've just found a big seam."

The news spread quickly. Pretty soon it was Topic A at the Cooke City store, run by Ralph and Sue Glidden, who had been summer residents of Cooke City for twenty years. They invited another Noranda man home for dinner. He confirmed that a major deposit of gold-bearing ore had been located.

Opposite: Winter on Soda Butte Creek, in the Lamar Valley, Wyoming. Lamar Valley in Yellowstone National Park was one of three major watersheds threatened by a proposal to reopen a large gold and silver mine above Cooke City, Montana, just north of the park. *Carr Clifton*

Miners J. F. Curley, Horn Miller, and Joe Brown of Cooke City, Montana, c. 1880s. *National Park Service*

In 1990, the rumor became official fact. A Noranda subsidiary called Crown Butte Mines submitted an "Application for a Hard Rock Operating Permit and Proposed Plan of Operation" to the Forest Service and the Montana Department of State Lands. The application described a year-round operation to take vast amounts of ore—1,200 to 1,800 tons a day, or about 540,000 tons a year, for ten to fifteen years—from both new and old mines. The ore would be processed on site using liquid cyanide, and the wastes disposed of in a gigantic pit in a high-altitude creek and wetland much favored by moose. It would be a major industrial development, with a camp to house 175 miners, and would change the character of Cooke City, not to mention the New World Mining District, forever. As will be noted shortly, several corporate entities were involved in the project, but for our purposes we shall refer to them interchangeably as Crown Butte or Noranda.

The application ran to fourteen volumes and took up about three feet of shelf space. A new lode had been discovered—within twenty-five, maybe fifty, feet of where the miners had finally given up in the 1950s, rumor had it—and modern technology would make it profitable to return to the old diggings.

GETTING ORGANIZED

Soon the phone in the Gliddens' store rang. It was Richard Parks, a representative of the Northern Plains Resources Council over in Gardiner, Montana, just north of the Mammoth entrance to the park. He said he'd heard about the mining project. What did the people in Cooke City think about it? Were they inclined to fight it? If so, he'd be happy to come over and give them some pointers. The Northern Plains Resources Council is in business to do just that. Parks was one of its community organizers, on call to help small communities get themselves organized to defend their resources and way of life. He made the trip to Cooke City, where the Gliddens and Jim Barrett had assembled a dozen or so people who were alarmed at the prospect of a vast mining operation virtually over their heads. Parks explained the rudiments of organizing, and the group decided to give it a go. They declared themselves the Beartooth Alliance and elected as their first president a summertime carpenter and wintertime ski guide named Wade King.

King was chosen partly because he lived in Cooke City year-round, as most summer residents did not. He was also a likely candidate because he already had a healthy dislike of the Forest Service on account of his having been refused permission to install a yurt to house skiers on national forest land—a yurt that would sit lightly on top of the snow in winter and be removed when the snow melted, a virtually no-impact project that didn't fit into any of the Forest Service's rules and regulations. The idea that the agency might bless a large industrial installation when it wouldn't give him the time of day made him livid.

They set out to write simple bylaws and objectives and invited neighbors and visitors to join their crusade, including a young summertime visitor who had just been lured back from Nebraska for yearlong residence. Heidi married Jim Barrett and shortly thereafter became the first employee of the Beartooth Alliance.

Pretty soon they had a visit from Louisa Willcox, a young woman from Bozeman who had helped create the Greater Yellowstone Coalition in 1983 to save Yellowstone and its surroundings from bad management and overexuberant development in the park, and out-of-control logging, mining, grazing, road building, ski development, and various other insults nearby. Willcox suggested that GYC might join the crusade.

Soon the Cooke City people had to face the fundamental matter of what they actually wanted. In the early days of the Beartooth Alliance, most members, in a perfectly under-standable desire to be practical and reasonable, argued that they should insist only that if the mines were reopened, they be the cleanest, most efficient, least intrusive mines in the world. Others argued that the only good mine under these circumstances was no mine. The absolutist position, quietly urged by the people from GYC, slowly gained favor.

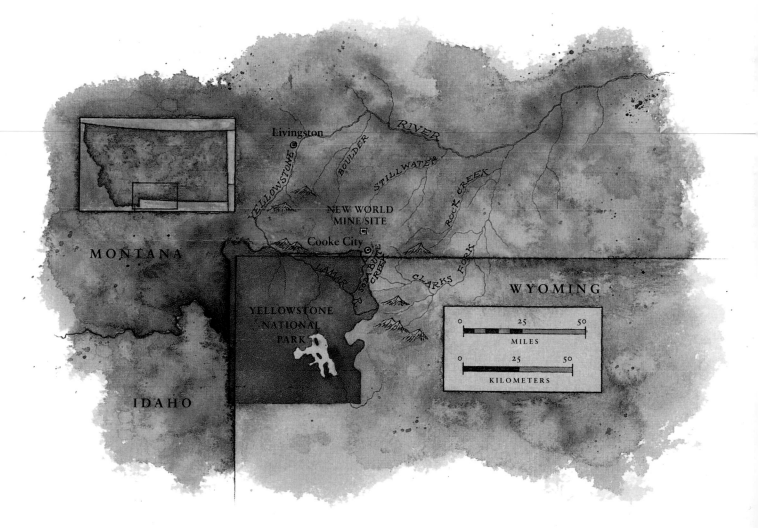

By the time GYC signed on officially, the position was clear: Both groups would insist that permission to resume mining must be denied. Period. No compromise.

For GYC, however, that wasn't as easy as it may sound. Ed Lewis was the director of the organization then, and he remembers a period of deep soul searching. "We knew if we took on this fight it would be long, it would take a lot of money, and it would drain effort from other activities. Plus, as we kept reminding ourselves, no group of citizens anywhere had ever beaten a mine proposal before. Never.

"We did a careful assessment. We figured there was no point in getting involved unless we were willing to make a total commitment. It was a tough decision.

"There were several ways to look at the matter. In one way, it was a local problem. It wasn't a pristine area; the opposition was a huge, wealthy corporation. On the other hand it is a very critical site, the headwaters of three separate tributaries to the Yellowstone River, important wildlife habitat, and the potential for causing a major disaster for Yellowstone park was huge. And there's the matter of a community's having a say in its own future."

The GYC board met. "In the end, we couldn't duck it," Lewis remembers. "I think everyone knew we didn't have a choice." They began to raise money and to look around for geologists, chemists, economists, and biologists to help them build a case against the mine. And lawyers to investigate any legal challenges that might be available. To that end, Andy Andrews, a Minnesota attorney and member of the GYC board, had a discussion with Doug Honnold of the Sierra Club Legal Defense Fund (the name had not yet changed to Earthjustice) on the general topic of whether the mine might be vulnerable

Street scene in the early days of Cooke City. The Cooke City Store, run by mine opponents Ralph and Sue Glidden, is decorated with reminders of the town's frontier past. *National Park Service*

to legal attack based on the federal Clean Water Act. Honnold thought it might work but said it would be expensive, since experts would be needed.

"How much do you need?" asked Andrews.

Honnold thought maybe thirty thousand dollars.

"When do you need it?"

No answer.

"How about next week?"

Within ten days Andrews had raised seventy thousand dollars for the upcoming legal battle—almost all of it from individuals. "Without Andy we would never have gotten off the ground," Honnold remembers.

COOKE CITY AND THE MINE

I visited the New World Mining District on September 6, 2000, in the company of Don Bachman of the Greater Yellowstone Coalition, a tall, weathered man the other side of sixty but looking at least ten years younger. He grew up in San Mateo, California, son of a career Forest Service employee. He studied forestry at the University of Oregon but never quite finished his degree. Bachman has lived all over, including several years in Crested Butte, Colorado, which was involved in an epic battle with the Amax mining company. Amax wanted to decapitate a mountain behind the town in order to get at the molybdenum beneath it. Don remembers an Amax representative's telling the people of Crested Butte they should be grateful: "Removing the mountaintop will give you eight more minutes of daylight every day."

Above: Miners and smelter crew at Republic Smelter in Cooke City, c. 1880s. *National Park Service. Below:* The lichen-encrusted remains of an old miner's shack on Henderson Mountain, above the mine site. *Tom Turner*

"The only miner with a sense of humor I ever met," Bachman says.

It was raining when we arrived in Cooke City, at about 10:30 in the morning. We checked in at the store with Ralph and Sue Glidden, who were winding down, getting ready to make their annual trip to Arizona for the winter. Winter at Cooke City and the mine site lasts about nine months, and most years see at least twenty-five feet of snow. The average annual temperature is said to be six degrees below freezing. There are twenty-three frost-free days in an average year. Operating a mine up there would be an incredibly difficult undertaking, requiring a fleet of snowplows on duty round the clock, to men-

Wild wolf in Yellowstone National Park. Wildlife conservation groups have collaborated with the U.S. Fish and Wildlife Service and the National Park Service to restore this important native predator to the Yellowstone ecosystem. Pollution from the mine and its waste pit could have imperiled water in the streams used by park wildlife.
Joel Sartore

tion only one of many necessities. "The scars you see today are from old pick-and-shovel mining activities," Don Bachman says. "The Noranda proposal was something else altogether. There's absolutely nothing romantic about modern mining. Nothing."

As Ed Lewis said, the mining district sits at the headwaters of three major tributaries of the Yellowstone River. One is Soda Butte Creek, which flows south past Cooke City and into the park, joining the Lamar River, which in turn joins the Yellowstone below its Grand Canyon. Daisy Creek flows down the back side of Fisher Mountain and through the Absaroka–Beartooth Wilderness in the Gallatin National Forest, where it empties into the Stillwater River, which joins the Yellowstone a hundred miles downstream from the park. Last is Fisher Creek, in the most danger from the mining proposal. It flows east through the Shoshone National Forest then south into Wyoming, where it joins the Clarks Fork of the Yellowstone—a congressionally protected Wild and Scenic River, the only one in the state. The Clarks Fork then returns to Montana and empties into the Yellowstone River near Billings, a hundred-odd miles from its headwaters. The mine site is habitat for moose, elk, bighorn sheep, grizzly bears, squirrels, and many other creatures.

ALL THAT GLITTERS

Mining, by its nature, is a very destructive activity. As George Wuerthner wrote in *Wilderness* magazine in 1992, "Mining produces twice as much hazardous waste per year as all other sources combined." At best, it involves sifting dust and nuggets from streambeds or boring holes into mountains. At worst, it involves stripping away the surface of mountains, hillsides, or valleys, soaking crushed ore with poisons such as cyanide, and leaving open pools of fiercely noxious liquid tailings, which seep slowly into streams and aquifers. Or their containment systems may fail altogether, sending cascades of death downhill, killing fish and threatening people. There is no such thing as a clean mine, though some pollute less than others.

We as a society accept the environmental impact of these mines because of the metals and fuels they produce. In truth, we as a society have little say in the matter. Mining decisions are made primarily by the people who command the companies that search for, extract, and profit from the minerals wrenched from the earth, and by government regulators whose objective is to assist the miners before it is to protect the natural environment. Still, society as we know it would not exist without steel, aluminum, copper, molybdenum, and scores more metals.

But would it exist without gold? Perhaps it could. Gold is used primarily for jewelry. Eighty percent of it. That's a legitimate use, but perhaps not one that justifies leaving a half-million suppurating sores throughout the West. It is also used to cap teeth, though modern synthetic materials can now do that job just as well and more cheaply. It used to be used for money, but has not been for many decades.

One principal problem with gold is that it is nearly always found in the company of fool's gold, iron pyrite. When the pyrite is disturbed, put into contact with air and water, it produces sulfuric acid. Herein lies the most difficult problem associated with gold mining and the cause of the garish orange creeks that trickle from abandoned pits and adits. If the natural rocks in the streambed are alkaline, the acid is swiftly neutralized. If not, the acidity can remain lethal for many miles downstream. The mining industry is quick to point out that this process can happen naturally, and here and there it does: glaciers can disturb gold-bearing ore, as can earthquakes and natural erosion. Noranda would argue that the acid drainage in the New World District was the result of natural processes, a topic we shall explore in more detail presently. As with so many things, this is a

Peaks around Soda Butte Creek during late-winter melting. *Carr Clifton*

matter of scale and of speed. Small natural acid seeps are one thing. Huge human-made wounds are entirely another.

Cleaning up old mines is a difficult, expensive process. Shafts and adits can be filled and plugged, but rainwater can still seep down through the old tailings and end up in groundwater. Tailings and waste rock can be isolated, at least in theory, and sealed off from the elements forever.

But we get ahead of ourselves.

THE SPECTER OF SUMMITVILLE

For Cooke City and Yellowstone, the year 1992 would prove pivotal. First, the Forest Service, with considerable fanfare, issued an award to Noranda for some modest reclamation efforts it had undertaken up at the mine site. Reclamation efforts had been begun by a Forest Service employee named Ray Brown twenty years before, without a great deal of success. Noranda people recontoured a couple of wounded hillsides, planted a few seeds, and the Forest Service

Above: Acid-laced water flows off the McLaren tailings pile next to Cooke City and empties into Soda Butte Creek just beyond the edge of the photograph. *Tom Turner. Below:* Fisher Creek, tinted with acid from seeps and old mine adits. The pipes are culverts made from thick cast iron; conventional galvanized culverts would be eaten through by the acid within months. *Tom Turner*

applauded. Later, it would be revealed that the reclamation activities had involved work in a wetland, for which the company had no permit. In fact, the activities for which the company had been honored were illegal, which was not lost on the mine opponents, who sensed, correctly, that the Forest Service would be no impartial party in the subsequent debate. The Army Corps of Engineers, which regulates wetlands, let the company off the hook by issuing an after-the-fact permit. "Sometimes it's better to ask for forgiveness than permission," a Noranda representative told the newspapers.

Soon after the award ceremony, Noranda announced that it had changed its proposal and would no longer use cyanide in a heap-leach operation high on the mountain. The lode it had found under Henderson Mountain was so concentrated, said Noranda, that it

would not bother to reopen the old workings. The Beartooth Alliance and GYC figured it was mainly a public relations gesture to defuse the opposition. Ann Maest, a chemist who will join our story soon, said that in fact the concentration of sulfite found with the Henderson deposit was so high—25 percent—that the heap-leach process would have been impossible to employ.

The General Mining Law of 1872

An extremely difficult problem that gave the GYC pause as it debated whether to jump into the battle was the General Mining Law of 1872, famously born the same year as Yellowstone National Park. It was enacted in part to spur development of the West by essentially giving land to miners who could prove there were economically viable deposits of minerals on or beneath it. In a sense, it was an after-the-fact ratification of the California gold rush, a free-for-all where miners swarmed the Sierra Nevada and grabbed nuggets and dust wherever they could find some. Those miners had invented the concept of mining districts to bring some order to the scene and minimize fights and claim jumping.

Originally the 1872 law governed all mineral deposits. In 1920, the Mineral Leasing Act split off fossil fuels—coal, oil, natural gas—and imposed a royalty on companies that pump or mine those substances from beneath public lands.

So-called hard-rock minerals—gold, silver, lead, copper, molybdenum, and several others—remain under the aegis of the 1872 law. Stake a valid claim and you can mine without paying a penny in royalties, or buy the land outright for $2.50 an acre if the claim is for a placer deposit (one found in a streambed) or $5.00 an acre if the claim is for a below-ground lode. There are well over a half-million abandoned mines in the United States, four thousand in the greater Yellowstone ecosystem alone. Many are contributing significant amounts of pollution to local lakes, rivers, and streams. If the mess isn't too horrible, you can sell your land to a developer who wants to put in a golf course or a ski resort. Many people have been made wealthy by the General Mining Law of 1872, not all of them from mining. Attempts have been made repeatedly over the years to repeal or amend the law and in the early 1990s came fairly close to victory, but the mining industry has powerful allies in Congress and has so far staved off major reform of the statute.

The Forest Service, in the view of many people, including Don Bachman, uses the law as a shield to hide behind when criticized for allowing mining where there shouldn't be mining. "There is a deep-rooted mineral culture in the agency, isolated from other branches. It's particularly strong in the Gallatin National Forest. They wanted the mine real bad, barely covered their enthusiasm."

Meanwhile, a few hundred miles to the south—in the San Juan Mountains of Colorado, near the headwaters of another storied American river, the Rio Grande—a catastrophe was playing out that held eerie similarities to the more dire predictions being voiced about the Crown Butte mine.

The Summitville Mine, operated by Galactic Resources (like Noranda a Canadian company), also was situated high in the mountains and had a long winter with frigid temperatures. It too produced silver, copper, and gold and had been mined with pick and shovel since the 1870s. Both areas suffer severe and frequent avalanches and are riddled with earthquake faults. The Summitville Mine operated from 1986 until 1992, using cyanide to dissolve gold from crushed ore, just as Noranda had first proposed at New World. The Summitville Mine was plagued with difficulties caused by the weather, the elevation, and shoddy construction. The first leak occurred on the mine's sixth day of operation. Many others followed. Over the next six years, repeated leaks wiped out all life in the river for seventeen miles and contaminated water that downstream farmers used for irrigation.

Then, in 1992, Galactic Resources went abruptly bankrupt and walked away from the site, leaving behind a pitifully tiny reclamation bond of $4.7 million. The Environmental Protection Agency sent inspectors to the site, who discovered that the pit, holding

Gold nugget. A chief problem with mining gold is that it is rarely found in pure form like this but usually in combination with iron pyrite, which produces sulfuric acid when it comes in contact with air and water during the mining process. *Mark A. Schneider/Photo Researchers* millions of gallons of cyanide-laced water, was dangerously close to overflowing. For a time, the agency was spending thirty-three thousand dollars a day to prevent an even worse disaster. EPA put the site on the list of places to be cleaned up under provisions of the Superfund. As of the late 1990s, the cleanup bill stood at nearly $150 million, and the job wasn't finished.

In addition to the physical parallels between New World and Summitville, Noranda had set up a series of curtains between itself and the corporation that would actually operate the mine and be responsible for cleaning up any problems. The parent company of Galactic had done the same, and when Galactic went belly-up there were no other corporate entities to hang responsibility on.

Next, up north in Canada, the government of British Columbia took a nearly unprecedented step that gave mine opponents a great boost: it refused permission, sought by a company called Geddes Resources, to mine gold at a site known as Windy Craggy, at the headwaters of the Tatshenshini River, which passes through the Alaska panhandle on its way to the Pacific Ocean. The concerns were exactly those at the New World site and Summitville: high concentrations of acid-producing sulfites, harsh weather conditions, great danger of earthquakes. If the Canadians could forgo a bit of gold to protect a natural treasure, why not the Americans?

Finally, in 1992 there appeared in *Environmental Science and Technology* magazine an article entitled "Metals in Water: Determining Natural Background Concentrations in Mineralized Areas." It argued that in certain locations, acid drainage is the result of glaciation, earthquakes, and other natural phenomena. The article quickly became the seminal reference for mining geologists and others to cite. It would also loom large in the coming legal fight over the New World Mine.

RECRUITING THE MEDIA

In the autumn of 1992, the GYC people decided to try the direct approach and sent a delegation to Toronto to meet with the Noranda overlords and talk them into abandoning their proposal. The delegation consisted of Ed Lewis, Louisa Willcox, and Dwight Minton, a GYC board member and head of the Arm and Hammer Company, which operated several mines in Wyoming. They figured the Noranda people would be impressed by a fellow miner asking them to walk away from the New World District.

They weren't. As Willcox later reported, all they wanted to talk about was baseball. The Blue Jays were playing the Atlanta Braves in the World Series, on the verge of taking the championship north of the border for the first time. Ted Turner, owner of the Braves, also served on the GYC board. What kind of a guy is Ted? they wanted to know. Ed Lewis remembers a cordial meeting and thought they had at least succeeded in impressing the Noranda people with their seriousness, their commitment. The three returned to Bozeman.

There, they consulted with their public-relations specialist, Bob Ekey. Ekey had worked as a reporter for the *Billings (Montana) Gazette* for fifteen years before joining GYC and becoming a full-time advocate. He put together an elaborate plan for winning

Opposite: A pack train wends its way through the Absaroka–Beartooth Wilderness: 900,000 acres of mountains, glaciers, lakes, and meadows stretching from northern Wyoming into southern Montana. *Michael K. Nichols/NGS Image Collection*

the hearts and minds of the public. It was based loosely on the advice rangers give people who encounter grizzly bears: try to look bigger than you are.

"The mining proposal, all fourteen volumes, gave us a wealth of material to attack," Ekey says. The plan was to release two stories each week to papers in the immediate vicinity of the park. They would conduct polls, then release the results. They would criticize the proposal's lack of attention to grizzly bears and other wildlife. They commissioned an independent economic study of the project; it suggested that the net value of the gold might be far lower than the company claimed. They painted lurid word pictures of the tailings pond, which would cover an area the size of seventy football fields, have a hundred-foot-tall earthen dam to hold back the force of gravity, and sit in an area prone to avalanches and violent earthquakes—no surprise, as it was right next to Yellowstone, the biggest and most active geothermal area on the planet.

They took TV crews to the mine site. When the weather was too bad, they provided videotape of shafts and adits and garish orange streams and pointed out that mining in that sort of weather would be risky and dangerous. The stories ran everywhere.

They visited the McLaren tailings pile, cheek-by-jowl with Cooke City—an ugly wasteland still bleeding poison into Soda Butte Creek. The new tailings pond up on the mountain would be twenty times as big. At one point, Noranda assured the public that it would clean up the McLaren pile as part of the overall project. A man from Camjak, a company

Grizzly bear on a rock wall in Yellowstone National Park. The park ecosystem is one of the few places in the lower 48 states where this legendary predator survives. *Joel Sartore*

in Great Falls, telephoned GYC and spoke to a young man named Brian Kuehl. "We own those tailings," he said, "and we've never spoken to Noranda."

"Would you put that in writing?" Kuehl asked. He would and did. Kuehl immediately gave the story to the papers.

GYC had people buy stock in Noranda and go to shareholders meetings. At one point the *Toronto Globe and Mail* ran a story on the annual meeting of Noranda. Nearly the whole piece was about the New World Mine protesters. In the fourteenth paragraph came the news that Noranda had just posted record profits.

Ekey and company disseminated news of Summitville and of the Tatshenshini. The objective was first to win over the regional papers, in part to make sure that no local politicians came out in favor of the mines. It worked. The volume of press coverage was staggering. There were stories nearly every week in every paper, often two or three, and more on radio and television. Soon papers started to compete to break new stories. They ran a barrage of editorials denouncing the project.

An old mine adit above Fisher Creek, source of acid for a hundred years. *Tom Turner*

Representative Pat Williams, a Montana Democrat, worried publicly, and soon his colleague, Senator Max Baucus, expressed his concerns in a letter made public in the spring of 1993. Wyoming's senators, including the witty and avuncular Alan Simpson, put their fingers to the wind and decided Noranda would have to fight this battle on its own. Wyoming's junior senator, Craig Thomas, announced his own reservations, as did Wyoming's governor, Jim Geringer. Even the normally antienvironment Representative Barbara Cubin of Wyoming and Senator Conrad Burns of Montana took a pass.

In the end, the only major political figure in the region to support the mine application was Montana governor Mark Racicot.

Hoteliers in Gardiner put anti-mine brochures in every room, every night.

Noranda, meanwhile, was waging a vociferous campaign accusing GYC of spreading misinformation. The object of the company's scorn was a brochure produced by the coalition in the early stages of the struggle that spoke of the company's plan to use cyanide to extract gold, silver, and copper from the raw ore. The old brochures were still circulating, and Noranda did its best to smear GYC with accusations of spreading false information. So much for the goodwill engendered in Toronto.

Once the regional papers were on board and the politicians neutralized, the plan was to take the story national, using clippings of news stories and editorials to get the national press interested. And the way to impress on the national media the importance of the story was to emphasize the threat to Yellowstone. This the coalition knew from polls and focus groups. Of all the arguments against the mine project, the ones that most stirred public passions were the threats to the park and to streams and fish. The other argu-

Old Faithful Geyser commemorative stamp, National Parks Issue, 1934. *Thomas Ingalls collection*

ments—about industrializing a beautiful, high-mountain valley, or destroying Cooke City—were legitimate, but Yellowstone was sacred and was much in people's minds, owing to the fires that had swept through the park in 1988. One fire, in fact, had stopped a few yards from our tale's central town and inspired some to call it "Cooked City." In any event, it was Yellowstone that would arouse the public.

A REAL PUBLIC HEARING

Meanwhile, after demanding five rounds of revisions to the mine-permit application, the Forest Service and the Montana Department of State Lands declared Crown Butte's application complete in April 1993, thereby formally launching the environmental-impact-statement process.

But rather than calling formal public hearings on the application, as is customary, the Forest Service opted for what it called "open houses" to take public comment. GYC and the Beartooth Alliance objected loudly and publicly, pointing out that the open houses were often rowdy free-for-alls and, worse, that the Forest Service kept no formal records of the testimony. Since the agency wouldn't, they hired a court reporter themselves and called their own public hearing, for July 13, in Bozeman, on the campus of Montana State University. Three hundred people attended. One supported the mine. The newspapers loved it.

At approximately the same time as the people's hearing was being held, the legal battle began in earnest. The situation was difficult. Noranda owned the mining claims or leased them from others. The 1872 law virtually guaranteed the owners the right to mine their land if they chose to do so. Some other angle would have to be found. Doug Honnold, taking a lead from Andy Andrews, had an idea.

Honnold had been working with Earthjustice since the early 1980s, first in Denver, then in 1992 opening an office in Bozeman to concentrate on the greater Yellowstone ecosystem and to be closer to Louisa Willcox, whom he would soon marry. He had worked to rein in overdevelopment of the park, to protect grizzly bears and other creatures, to bring oil and gas development under control, and in general to preserve the lands on all sides of the park.

For this battle, Honnold was convinced that the Clean Water Act could provide a chink

---

THE FIRST NATIONAL PARK?

Some say—and countless pieces of propaganda declare—that Yellowstone is the world's first national park. We would like to take a moment to interpolate a point for the historical record.

The first two tracts of land set aside for the people of the United States, to be preserved forever for themselves and for the pleasure and understanding they could give to those people, were Yosemite Valley and the nearby Mariposa Grove of giant sequoias. It was the first national park in everything but name.

The Yosemite Reserve was created in 1864. Yellowstone National Park was created in 1872. Both required acts of Congress and approval by the president. Care for Yosemite was assigned to California. Care for Yellowstone was retained by the federal government. So although Yellowstone may seem, at first glance, to be the first "national" park, that's only because neither Wyoming nor Montana existed in 1872. End of sermon.

Above: Twilight over the Absaroka Range. *Galen Rowell/Mountain Light. Below:* A series of editorials written by Bob Semple in the *New York Times* helped keep the mine issue before the public and earned Semple a Pulitzer Prize.

via which one could break through Noranda's armor. A key provision of that law forbids the discharge of pollutants into lakes, streams, wetlands, or other water bodies without a permit. The permits are generally issued by the states and must comply with state standards that, in turn, must fit within federal guidelines. Discharges made without permits are illegal and can result in fines that run to tens of thousands of dollars per day, per violation. It seemed logical to Honnold that the acid- and metal-laden waters bleeding into the three creeks in the New World Mining District were discharges that should require permits. If he could demonstrate that Noranda and its subsidiaries were in violation of the Clean Water Act and subject to stiff penalties, maybe there was a chance of raising the stakes so high that Noranda would walk away from the project.

In July 1993, as required by law, Honnold formally notified Noranda that it had sixty days to stop its illegal discharges into the creeks or it would face a federal lawsuit. Noranda responded by hiring a significant fraction of the legal talent in Montana, plus reinforcements from South Dakota and from headquarters in Toronto, and hunkered down for a war of attrition.

No Mines Near Yellowstone

A calamity threatens Yellowstone, the crown jewel of the American park system. Administration officials say their hands are tied by archaic laws and that there is nothing they can do. But if people like Secretary of Vice President A remembered as a of the country's seek ways to sto beginning with a s ested parties and legislation.

The threat aris ate, Noranda Inc. mountain that sits a miles from the par

from Federal land and to take title to that land for a few dollars an acre.

The law does not provide for stringent "suitability" review to determine whether the site is

Mr. Clinton Acts on Yellowstone

President Clinton is vacationing this year in western Wyoming, playing golf and reveling in the wonders of Grand Teton and Yellowstone national parks. Last Friday, too late for the evening news shows, he took a crucial first step toward protecting Yellowstone and much of the adjacent wilderness from an environmental catastrophe.

This disaster-in-waiting is the proposed New World mine, which a Canadian conglomerate, Nor-

The most controversial aspect of the project is a proposed tailings impoundment — a deep reservoir the size of 70 football fields — where the company would store acid wastes. Reputable geologists say that given the region's extreme weather and history of earthquakes, any such structure is bound to crack at some point in the future.

The reservoir would be built on 56 acres of wetlands that lie under the jurisdiction of the Army ermit to where to le alter- dent has orced to peration

dent has

Canceling the New World Mine

A United Nations committee has now designated Yellowstone National Park as a "world heritage site in danger" largely because a Canadian conglomerate wants to build a huge gold, silver and copper mine less than three miles from the park's borders. The designation carries no legal weight, but it adds an international voice to the virtually unanimous chorus of opposition to the mine, which includes President Clinton. Nobody seems to want this mine except Noranda, the Canadian company, and its American subsidiary, Crown Butte, which has title to the mine site and has so far invested about $35 million in this project.

After listening patiently to the company's safety pitch, this page is convinced that the proposed New World Mine is a disaster-in-waiting that could ruin one of America's leading ecosystems. Reputa-

safe on a permanent basis. The claim defies science and common sense. Unfortunately, the lead Federal agency in the E.I.S. process is not Secretary Bruce Babbitt's Interior Department; but the Agriculture Department's Forest Service, which controls most of the land near the mine. The service has an unfortunate history of favoring commercial values over environmental values, and its key negotiators are sounding the same tune now. Mr. Clinton should not be timid about muscling these negotiators to give full weight to the views of other Federal agencies, including the National Park Service, which think the mine is a terrible idea.

There is, however, a cleaner, quicker way to end the controversy. That is for Noranda to walk away from the project. It could cede the site to the Federal Government and win large tax credits or

Fisherman in the Lamar River, Yellowstone National Park. The Lamar River watershed would have been directly affected by runoff from resumed mining operations. Public sentiment about Yellowstone was one of the chief tools used by mine opponents in their efforts.
Carr Clifton

The suit was filed on September 16 at the federal courthouse in Billings. Plaintiffs were the Beartooth Alliance, Greater Yellowstone Coalition, Northern Plains Resources Council, Sierra Club, Montana Wildlife Federation, Gallatin Wildlife Association, Northwest Wyoming Resource Council, Wyoming Outdoor Council, and Wyoming Wildlife Federation. Defendants were Crown Butte Mines, Crown Butte Resources, Noranda Minerals Corporation, Noranda Exploration, and Noranda Incorporated. The reason for listing them all will become clear presently.

Sometimes obvious things are the most difficult to prove. Anyone looking at orange water flowing out of an old mine shaft would assume that mining had something to do with the problem, but such assumptions are not enough to take to court. Honnold and his new colleague, attorney Susan Daggett, would have to prove that the pollution was the direct result of historic mining activity, and not the result of natural processes, as Noranda maintained. The best way to do that would be to gather evidence from undisturbed areas in the same neck of the woods—water that, they presumed, would be relatively free of contamination.

They engaged the services of geochemist Ann Maest, who was in private practice after a career that had wound from the U.S. Geological Survey through the Environmental Defense Fund. She had worked with Earthjustice attorney Maria Savasta Kennedy on an acid mine problem in the California foothills and came highly recommended.

Maest, Willcox, Heidi Barrett, and several others visited the mine site in mid-1994. Maest instructed her volunteer water samplers in the proper technique for gathering, labeling, and sealing samples. They set out a plan for sampling from several small streams that flow down Henderson Mountain through undisturbed areas and into the heavily damaged Fisher Creek.

In preparation both for the sampling exercise and for the trial itself, Honnold, with Maest at his side, had taken the deposition of Donald Runnells. Runnells is the geologist who had coauthored the article "Metals in Water," mentioned previously. First Runnells was asked if he had visited the New World site. He had not. Then they turned to *Environmental Science and Technology*.

Runnells's article cited more than two dozen studies from all over the world in which chemists had measured significant levels of metals and high acidification in streams flowing through areas known to contain minerals but where there had been no mining. One by one, Honnold asked Runnells about the studies. Had he seen the site himself? Had he confirmed that collecting and analysis had been carried out according to standard protocols? Had there been strict quality control? Do you know for sure there had been no mining activity near the site? In each case, the answer was "no" or "I don't know." Then came the bombshell, one of what Honnold calls the case's "Perry Mason moments."

The one study Runnells did know about firsthand was one he had conducted at Baghdad, Arizona, above an open-pit copper mine. Honnold was probing to determine exactly where the samples had come from. A short extract from the deposition follows:

Black bear *(Ursus americanus)*, drawing by Dugald Stermer

Donald Runnells: I was on an access road that was coming down into the pit.
Doug Honnold: I'm trying to visualize. You took a sample from a spring that was above the open pit or upgradient of the open pit?
Runnells: That's correct.
Honnold: Was there a road upgradient from the spring?
Runnells: Yes. This was on a road.
Honnold: The spring itself was on a road?
Runnells: Yes.
Honnold: Do you know how the road was created?
Runnells: It was a bulldozer road, access road with a bulldozer … The spring was in the middle of the road.

In other words, water trickling from a spring that had had a road bulldozed through it was being held up as natural, as coming from an undisturbed site.

Maest remembers being stunned. "I was amazed to find

that this paper, relied on by me and many others as the seminal work on naturally occurring acid drainage, had no scientific basis whatsoever."

A large part of Noranda's legal argument evaporated like snow on a hot skillet.

The second arm of Noranda's argument was based on a paper published in the 1920s, which reported that there was elemental copper in two bogs on the site, and ferricrete— the red-orange stain—on rocks in the creek. These were further proof, the company would argue, that the acid drainage that caused both deposits was perfectly natural. To counter this argument, Honnold had tests run to measure the age of both deposits and discovered that they were either very old (eight to twelve thousand years, caused by glaciers) or very young (within a century or so, the time when mining had been going on). In other words, the ferricrete was the result either of glacial activity thousands of years before or of mining within roughly a century—not a natural, continuous phenomenon.

And when Maest's stream samples came in to be analyzed, the mine opponents found what they'd been hoping for: relatively clean water supporting healthy populations of aquatic life. No fish, owing to the tiny size of the streams and their steepness, but plenty of insects and other creatures. They felt pretty good, but there was a long way to go.

WHEN IN DOUBT, LOWER THE STANDARDS

Noranda was caught in a lovely Catch-22. It was breaking a federal law by discharging pollutants without a permit, and it couldn't get a permit because the water entering Fisher Creek, Daisy Creek, and Soda Butte Creek exceeded Montana water-quality standards. Its logical move, then, which turns out to be a standard technique, was to get the state to lower the standards and make the problem disappear.

Accordingly, in August 1994, lawyers for Crown Butte Mines petitioned the Montana Board of Environmental Review to lower its water-quality standards for the streams in question. This was handled on the sly, with no public participation. Jim Angell, the third attorney in the Bozeman office of Earthjustice, remembers, "We started hearing rumors of secret meetings, and we and our clients worried that the state would quietly change the standards and award a permit, yank the rug out from under us." Angell filed suit under Montana's open-meetings law, demanding that the meetings be opened to the public. The state quickly caved in and promised to hold no more secret meetings.

Subsequently, it did hold at least one public meeting, at which a scientist in the employ of Noranda averred that there had never been any aquatic life in Fisher Creek because of natural contamination, and therefore the standards should be adjusted to reflect that situation. This claim was duly—and dramatically—countered by Ken Cummins and Peg Wilzbach, a married pair of world-famous fish biologists who had owned a cabin on Fisher Creek for many years and had spent many summers staring through face masks, studying fish and other species in the creek. Another Perry Mason moment.

In preparing their case, Honnold and Daggett decided to try a long-odds ploy known in the trade as "piercing the corporate veil." They would ask the court to rule not only that Crown Butte Mines was liable for penalties for illegal discharges, but that its parents—Crown Butte Resources, Noranda Minerals, and Noranda Inc. itself—were liable as well. Without keeping the parent entities in the game, a successful verdict might provide an empty victory: a judgment against a paper entity with no resources of its own. The lawyers had surveyed the literature and found a law review article indicating that the strategy occasionally worked when the defendant was a small, privately held company. Piercing the veil of a large, wealthy multinational was all but unheard of. They decided to try anyway.

And that, Honnold says, led to some sleepless, terror-filled nights. He and Daggett estimated that they had spent around a quarter-million dollars in hard cash, and had put in more than two million dollars' worth of time (had they been paid at commercial rates). Noranda, meanwhile, had hired three law firms in Montana, another in North Dakota, and employed a stable of attorneys at headquarters in Toronto. The two environmental lawyers calculated that Noranda had probably spent at least a half million on expenses and racked up at least six million in attorney time.

We recite those numbers because if you file suit under the Clean Water Act for penalties against a private company and lose, the defendant can come after you for its overall legal expenses. If Honnold and Daggett were to lose this case, nearly all the environmental organizations they represented could face bankruptcy.

Around the same time, the nation at large began hearing about the story. Some magazines published by environmental organizations had printed stories, but no mainstream paper did so until Timothy Egan, the *New York Times* correspondent in Seattle, pub-

Elk herd in hot springs mist, Yellowstone National Park. Elk are one of the park's signature big animals. *Galen Rowell/ Mountain Light*

lished a Sunday front-page article on September 14, 1994. The Greater Yellowstone Coalition plan to take the story national was under way.

Egan's article was a good introduction, but it focused on the economics of the mine, leaving out much of the story, in particular the threat to Yellowstone park. Mike Clark of GYC immediately sent a letter to the editor of the *Times*, which was published a few days later. It sketched out some of the concerns Egan's piece had omitted. That same morning the GYC phone rang. It was Bob Semple, a *Times* editorial writer, wanting to learn more.

Semple spent at least an hour on the phone that morning with Bob Ekey and Louisa Willcox, soaking up information and arguments. Two weeks later appeared the first of eight editorials the *Times* would publish on the battle, a brilliant series of opinion pieces that would earn Semple the Pulitzer Prize.

"A calamity threatens Yellowstone, the crown jewel of the American park system," he thundered in one of them. "Stopping this mine is priority number one."

ENTER THE CLINTONS

Yet another prong of the opponents' strategy was launched the following February, when a round-robin letter, signed by the GYC, the Beartooth Alliance, and a wide variety of regional and national conservation organizations, was sent to the World Heritage Committee outlining the mine's threat to Yellowstone and requesting an investigation. World Heritage sites

Former President Bill Clinton, Hillary Rodham Clinton, and their daughter, Chelsea, visited Yellowstone in August 1996 for the official signing of the agreement precluding further mining activity at the New World Mine site. *Mike Theiler/Reuters/ Landov*

are an international group of important natural and cultural areas so designated by the United Nations after being nominated by the home country. The committee examined the letter and wrote its own, to George Frampton, assistant secretary of the interior, asking for more information.

Then came the bombing of the federal office building in Oklahoma City, April 19, 1995. Newspapers carried accounts of militias and cults holed up all over Montana, Idaho, and Wyoming, armed to the teeth, waiting none too patiently for black helicopters to arrive. The White House decided to dispatch the president to hold one of his folksy town meetings to show that there were normal people in the Northern Rockies, living normal lives. The site chosen was Billings, Montana.

Sue Glidden heard the news on the radio. About seventy people would be invited to attend the meeting and ask their questions of the president. Listeners were invited to submit questions they would like to ask the president. Heidi Barrett quickly sent off her suggestion: What could the president do to help them stave off the ruination of Yellowstone?

She got the call and was one of only a dozen or so people who got to ask their questions. Mr. Clinton was evidently aware of the matter and promised to fight to save the park. "George Stephanopoulos wrote later that that trip was very nearly cancelled," Sue remembers. "I hate to think what might have happened if it had been."

Two months later, the Clintons were scheduled to go to Jackson Hole, Wyoming, just south of Yellowstone, for a vacation. On August 14, 1995, Bob Semple published his fifth editorial, this time urging the president to visit the mine site:

> Later this month, President Clinton will vacation on a ranch near Jackson Hole, Wyo. Here is a modest suggestion for him. The President should take a short flight in one of his military helicopters to the upper reaches of Henderson Mountain in Montana, just over the Wyoming border. There he will discover a beautiful and fragile wilderness. He will also see the proposed site of a huge gold, silver and copper mine that a Canadian conglomerate wants to build.
>
> This mine and its lethal wastes will threaten not only Yellowstone National Park, which lies three miles away, but also the adjacent wilderness. This is a catastrophe-in-waiting.

Bald eagle *(Haliaeetus leucocephalus)*, drawing by Dugald Stermer

Bob Ekey, meanwhile, headed toward Jackson Hole himself, sensing an opportunity to steer the White House press corps toward the story. The newspaper reporters weren't interested, but radio was desperate for stories. Ekey was happy to oblige. Then the Jackson Hole papers began urging the president to visit the mine site. At the daily news conferences the answer to the question of whether Mr. Clinton would visit the site slowly shifted from no, to maybe, then finally to yes. He boarded a helicopter on August 25 with the first lady and Mike Finley, the superintendent of Yellowstone National Park and a firm opponent of the mine, and took off.

"We heard later that when three big Hueys flew over Cooke City, there were people dancing in the streets," Ekey remembers. The weather was difficult. Clouds obscured the ground. They circled once, twice, and were about to give up when the clouds broke and they got a perfect view of the valley where the mine and tailings pond would go. They returned to the Lamar Valley. As they alighted from the chopper the president turned to Hillary. "I'm going to do the withdrawal," he said. And he immediately announced that he was instructing the Forest Service to withdraw all unclaimed land in the district and keep it under federal control for at least two years. Not a great deal of unclaimed land was left in the mining district, but environmental groups had urged the president to withdraw what was left to stop Noranda or other interests from claiming the land and using it for buildings and other infrastructure.

The withdrawal order, however, had to be printed in the *Federal Register*. Before that could happen, Crown Butte filed thirty-eight new claims, mostly for possible mill sites. The newspapers read that as a deliberate insult to the president and published several searing editorials accompanied by extremely rude cartoons, one of which showed a man from the company baring his backside to Mr. Clinton. More bad press, including an editorial in Noranda's hometown paper, the *Toronto Globe and Mail*, urged the company to leave Yellowstone in peace.

ON TO COURT

On September 8, 1995, the combatants in the lawsuit assembled in federal court in Billings, presided over by Judge Jack Shanstrom. Honnold and Daggett were at the plaintiffs' table. A phalanx of lawyers for the various incarnations of Noranda filled the defense table. Honnold systematically demolished Noranda's arguments and said that the Clean Water Act itself was under siege. "If granted, [Noranda's] arguments would not only allow these mining companies to go scot-free in this case, they would undermine the very foundations of the Clean Water Act, resulting in massive, unregulated pollution," Honnold told the court.

In fact, he argued, what Noranda is saying is that, if there's even a tiny trace of naturally occurring acid or metal in the streams, those substances are not pollutants no matter how much is added as a result of human disturbance. "In other words," Honnold said,

> these very mining companies could dump any amount of these minerals into Fisher and Daisy Creeks—say, whole truckloads—without any regulation under the Clean Water Act...
>
> The mining companies ask this court to go where no court has ever ventured, to reject twenty years of agency interpretation and federal court case law, and develop a new rule that would exempt not just these mining companies at this site from the Clean Water Act but would eliminate the application of the Clean Water Act in every place where some pollutants are naturally present in some trace amount.
>
> It is a breathtaking proposal. It makes no sense legally or biologically... The arrogance of this approach is chilling. It should be soundly, thoroughly rejected by this court.

With that, he took a deep breath and asked the judge to issue a summary judgment—a declaration that the plaintiffs had won their case and there was no need to conduct a trial on whether Noranda had violated the law. If Judge Shanstrom ruled for the conser-

Opposite: The American bison was nearly extirpated in the nineteenth century. The animals that took refuge in Yellowstone were the only survivors and saved the species from extinction. *Galen Rowell/Mountain Light*

vation groups, a trial would be scheduled to determine the extent of Noranda's financial liability. Noranda's lawyers then presented their case, and Judge Shanstrom withdrew to ponder and decide.

THE COURT SPEAKS

On September 9, 1995, a delegation from the World Heritage Committee arrived to investigate whether Yellowstone was really threatened by the project. They stayed five days, explored extensively, and left looking grim. Three months later they would report that the park was indeed "in danger."

On October 10, Judge Shanstrom handed down a decision in the lawsuit. He found that the old mine workings were indeed polluting waters of the United States in violation of the Clean Water Act and that the company was liable. It would have to apply for permits for the discharges, and by implication would have to conduct a massive restoration project before it would have any hope of receiving such permits. The judge also pierced the corporate veil, holding Crown Butte Minerals liable and refusing to let Noranda Inc. off the hook. He said he would set a date for the next phase of the proceedings soon, a hearing to determine the amount of the fine the companies would have to pay. The plaintiffs calculated that Noranda could face a fine in excess of $150 million.

Honnold, Daggett, and Angell were ecstatic, as were their clients. It seemed highly unlikely that the company would be willing or able to cough up that amount of money on top of the massive investment it would require to bring the pollution under control and then put a whole new mining operation in place.

"Then, and only then," Bob Ekey remembers, "did Noranda begin to get scared."

Honnold adds, "We found out later that Noranda's lawyers had assured the company there was no way they could lose this lawsuit. No way." The lawsuit, and the ruling from Judge Shanstrom that it sparked, had finally got the company's attention as nothing else had. Its representatives began to make noises about trying to find a way to settle the case and avoid the potentially huge fines.

Over the next ten months Honnold, Mike Clark, Ray Clark of the president's Council on Environmental Quality, and former senator Birch Bayh—representing Noranda—conducted extensive and quite secret negotiations in Washington. It was touch and go, as such things tend to be, with the talks threatening to break down time and again. Honnold gives much credit to Mr. Bayh, who stopped Noranda from walking out more than once. "I think it was a cultural clash," Honnold remembers. "There were virtually no environmental laws in Canada then; corporations were almost never held liable for environmental damage they might inflict. They were not used to being questioned."

In the end, however, a deal was struck, and the White House decided to make it a top-drawer event. Several hundred people, including all the principal players, gathered in the Lamar Valley on August 12, 1996, the day the Republican convention opened to nominate Mr. Clinton's next rival, Senator Bob Dole. After several hours of waiting, the guests heard the far-off thump of helicopters. The president, first lady, and a large entourage emerged from the choppers. All gathered for the announcement of the agreement, which Doug Honnold, a Justice Department lawyer, and a Noranda official signed on the back bumper of a rented Ryder pickup truck.

By the terms of the agreement, Noranda would relinquish its lands and mining claims in the New World District and withdraw its request for permission to mine there. In return, the United States would pay the company $65 million, $22.5 million of which would be used to clean up historic pollution, the balance to reimburse the company for its prior investment.

The environmentalists made their way up Henderson Mountain to toast their victory with warm champagne and listen as Brian Kuehl exorcised bad spirits with his violin.

Three months later, Congress played its part and appropriated the necessary funds, and the following June a consent decree was lodged with the court, tying up the legal loose ends. Yellowstone, Cooke City, the Absaroka–Beartooth Wilderness, and all the streams and rivers could breathe easy.

As of late 2000, reclamation efforts were well under way. They will take a long time, because the job is difficult and the conditions demanding and no one knows if $22.5 million will be enough to finish the job. But when they eventually succeed, and the extraordinary site is returned to its pre-1870 glory, it should provide a great lift to those who hope that someday many more of the old mines that scar so much of the West will be reclaimed as well.

Gray wolf *(Canis lupus)*, drawing by Dugald Stermer

CHAPTER THREE

NO NUKES IN CLAIBORNE PARISH

Way back at the far corner of the African-American section of the graveyard across the road from the Forest Grove Christian Methodist Episcopal Church in rural Louisiana is the grave of Joshua Willis. He was born in 1792, fought in the War of 1812, and died in 1826 of causes unrevealed. His is a neat little mystery. Few slaves, if any, fought in that war. Few slaves were named Joshua. Was Joshua Willis an exceptional slave? Or was he one of very few whites buried in the slaves' part of the cemetery? Is he the ancestor of Almeter Willis's husband, or the owner of Almeter's husband's ancestors? We'll never know.

There are dozens of Willises in that graveyard, plenty still living in Forest Grove. One of them, Almeter Willis, is as gentle, dignified, gracious, and soft-spoken a person as you could ever hope to meet. Her five children have all graduated from college. One is a psychiatrist, one a pediatrician, one a nurse, one a school administrator, one a chemist. A devoted corps of grandkids is growing steadily. Almeter retired from her job teaching grade school a couple of years before we met . She'd done her time, and there was the uranium plant to fight.

With the issuance of the Emancipation Proclamation in 1862 and the end of the Civil War and ratification of the Thirteenth Amendment to the Constitution in 1865, close to four million slaves were freed, ending the most shameful chapter in American history. As the former slaves began to exercise their new and precious freedom, they established new communities, often near the plantations and the masters they had served, sometimes a comfortable distance away. One of the thousands of new communities of freed slaves was in northwestern Louisiana, a tiny cluster of simple homes known as Forest Grove.

This part of Louisiana, about sixty miles east of Shreveport, had been part of the vast cotton-growing region of the South. The village was in Claiborne Parish, as Louisianans call their counties, a reflection of the Catholic heritage of the state. All Louisiana was once French and mainly Catholic. Now, in a religious sense, it's two states: Bible Belt Protestant in the north, Catholic in the south.

The Claiborne Parish seat is the town of Homer, named for the poet and established in 1850. In 1910, a second small community, Center Springs, was established a mile or so from Forest Grove. In the 1920s, oil was discovered in the parish, and, for a time, Claiborne produced more oil than any other parish in the state. People prospered enough

Opposite: "X" marks the spot where the Louisiana Energy Services uranium enrichment plant would have been built. The road connects the communities of Center Springs and Forest Grove in northwestern Louisiana. *Tom Turner*

to build many grand homes in Homer, and in the 1950s they built Lake Claiborne next to the town by erecting a dam that stores the runoff from five or six small creeks. The burghers of Homer built their retirement homes on the lakeshore, and life was good.

But not everyone shared in the prosperity. Statistically, Claiborne Parish was one of the very poorest in the United States. The African-Americans may have been freed, but they were by no means brought into the mainstream of parish life, in Claiborne or anywhere else in the South. In the country, for that matter. The people of Forest Grove and Center Springs farmed their fields, reared their children, and went to their churches, associating very little with the white folk in Homer, a scant five miles away. It's not that they were hostile to one another; there simply wasn't any social contact to speak of.

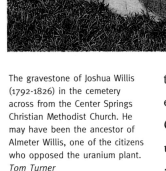

The gravestone of Joshua Willis (1792-1826) in the cemetery across from the Center Springs Christian Methodist Church. He may have been the ancestor of Almeter Willis, one of the citizens who opposed the uranium plant.
Tom Turner

A proposal to build a large industrial facility halfway between the two small communities would change all that, change the face of Claiborne Parish forever.

"As Clean as a Dairy"

Whereas the New World Mine opponents eliminated local officials from the debate by making it politically impossible for them to support the mine (see chapter 2), the people of Forest Grove and Center Springs had one of the country's most powerful politicians—and virtually the entire local political establishment—lined up against them before they even heard about the disaster that was planned for their neighborhood.

The politician was Louisiana's senior senator, J. Bennett Johnston. Johnston was born and reared in Shreveport, Caddo Parish; earned a law degree from Louisiana State University; served in the army and the Louisiana House and Senate; then went to Washington to the U.S. Senate, where he served four terms, retiring in 1997. By the end of his tenure, he was chairman of the Senate Energy and Natural Resources Committee. He was a Democrat of the Louisiana persuasion, a champion of the petroleum and nuclear industries—by all accounts, the man you wanted on your side if you had an energy project you wanted built. He scored poorly on report cards issued by both the League of Conservation Voters and the American Civil Liberties Union and, upon his retirement from the Senate, went to work as a lobbyist for, among others, Combustion Engineering, the Alliance for Competitive Electricity, Edison International, and the Nuclear Energy Institute.

The project that would rattle Homer and environs as never before was announced in front of the Homer courthouse on June 9, 1989, by the senator, representatives from a new company called Louisiana Energy Services, and various officials from the town of Homer and Claiborne Parish. It was described as a "chemical plant." Senator Johnston and his allies painted a picture of virtual salvation: a modern installation costing $750 million that would provide hundreds of badly needed jobs and bring oceans of tax revenue to the town's coffers. No dangerous material would be stored at the site. "It will be as clean as a dairy," Johnston assured the crowd. He didn't say precisely where the plant would be situated, because that decision hadn't yet been reached; the plant's sponsors still had to decide among six sites quietly nominated by Homer's leaders. The announcement was followed by a free barbecue for the entire town, courtesy of LES.

"We thought the free barbecue was a little strange," remembers Toney Johnson, a Homer appraiser and real estate broker and a fourth-generation Homerian, who had listened carefully to the senator's announcement. "Other towns in Louisiana and elsewhere were spending huge amounts of money to lure prospective project developers to their areas. We should have been more suspicious that LES was willing to spend big bucks to persuade us that its plant was something we should be happy about."

And spend big bucks they did, later sending twenty Homer residents on junkets to England and the Netherlands to see how clean, safe, and beautiful similar plants there were. The guests on the expeditions were the leading lights of Homer.

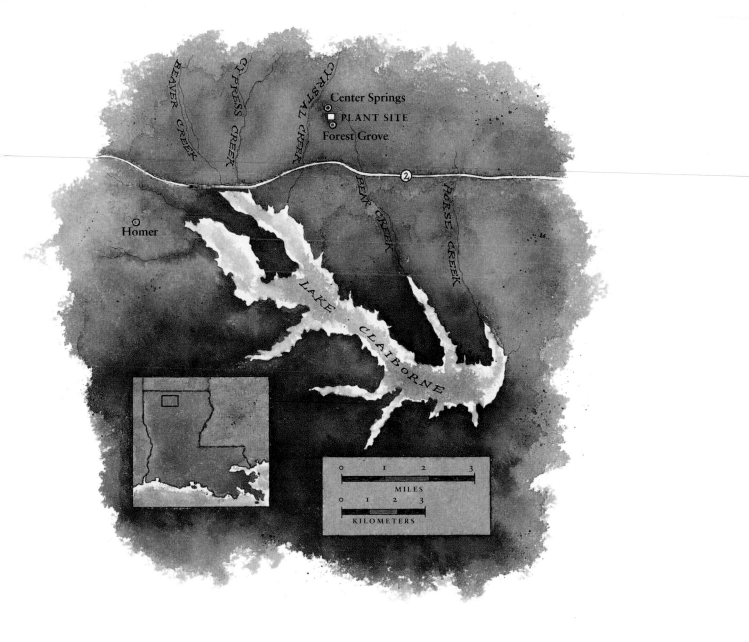

The final decision on the site was made in August and announced to the world on November 3, 1989. The plant would be built about five miles from the Homer courthouse, midway between Forest Grove and Center Springs. The residents of those communities,

Toney Johnson (left) and Willie Brooks. The predominantly African-American communities of Forest Grove and Center Springs were supported in their long struggle by many citizens of mainly white Homer, who took risks in doing so. *Daniel Lincoln*

who would be able to see the plant's fence from their porches, hadn't been consulted.

And, as the ordinary residents of Homer, Forest Grove, and Center Springs would find in the coming months, Senator Johnston had not been altogether forthcoming in his effusions over the facility. The proposed plant would enrich uranium for use as fuel in nuclear power plants. It would contribute nothing to the tax base for at least a decade because of a state incentive package enacted to lure industry to Louisiana. It would involve the storage of tens of thousands of tons of toxic and radioactive waste on site more or less forever. Most of the jobs would be filled by outsiders. In addition, treated liquid waste from the operation would be discharged into Bluegill Pond, a tiny body of water on the plant site, from there to make its way via Crystal Creek to Lake Claiborne.

Finally, they learned that the country road that runs the mile from Forest Grove to Center Springs, which is used steadily by people both in automobiles and on foot, would be closed: the uranium plant would be built squarely on the road, the entire facility covering some 450 acres. It was the road closure that first caught the attention of the two tiny communities.

The residents began asking one another about this grand new project. Why hadn't they been consulted? Were the promoters hiding something? What would building the plant mean for their communities, their lives? They decided to call a public meeting. It was held at the Center Springs church.

There was a big turnout from the people who lived nearby, all of whom are black. Elmira Wafer of the congregation invited Toney Johnson, who had written a letter to the *Claiborne Guardian-Journal* complaining that Senator Johnston had lied when he described the plant and its alleged benefits. Norton Tompkins, a retired chemical engineer and aluminum company executive, heard about the meeting and invited himself. A handful of people on the LES payroll showed up as well, sensing an opportunity to praise the proposal and defuse the opposition. The opposition, however, was not about to be defused.

The LES representatives tried to derail the meeting and stop any critics from speaking. They were politely told to back off. Speaker after speaker lamented the impending closure of the road, the danger that radioactive and toxic wastes might pose, the risk of a release of deadly gas. Eventually, they resolved to declare themselves a new organization pledged to fight the plant.

"We decided that since the project promoters had chosen a name whose initials could be pronounced—LES—we should do the same. We settled on CANT: Citizens Against Nuclear Trash," Toney Johnson remembers.

MORE QUESTIONS THAN ANSWERS

While it was the road closure that had alarmed the residents of Forest Grove and Center Springs, it was the danger of discharges into Crystal Creek that caught the attention of Norton and Gerry Tompkins. That, and the repeated assertion by LES that Lake Claiborne had been built for flood control, suggesting that some minor contamination was not worth worrying about. In fact, the lake had been built for recreation and was considered a potential source of drinking water should growth require a new one.

Norton is a native of Homer who, after a career spent in California, Texas, Jamaica, and elsewhere, returned with his wife, Gerry, to build a retirement home on the shore of Lake Claiborne, tend his garden, and go fishing.

"The charter that paved the way for building the reservoir and governs its management has a provision that forbids the discharge of anything nasty into the lake. That should have stopped this plant in a New York minute," he says. But the company hired the head of the local water district as a consultant, and he forgot about the rules. It was among the first of many questionable maneuvers the backers of the plant would execute. Tompkins would become the treasurer for CANT, not that it had any assets to manage.

Norton Tompkins confers with Beth Murphy and Jody Santos of *The Visionaries*, a documentary series aired on public television. The uranium plant struggle was featured in one episode. *Tom Turner*

Another minor but telling detail was revealed in the course of the struggle: The plot of land eventually nominated as the plant site belonged to Avalyn LeSage and her son, Joe LeSage, a Shreveport attorney and longtime friend and associate of Senator Johnston. Joe LeSage sold the land to LES for $536,461.80: about three times the going rate. The LeSages then had a year to sell the timber on the place, which they did for $296,088.

As if that weren't enough, LES hired the senator's former chief of staff, Charlie McBride, as its lobbyist in Washington. The sheriff of Claiborne Parish was J. R. "Snap" Oakes, whose son was on the senator's staff. Mr. Oakes, who would eventually become a federal marshal, quietly invited Homer's most influential people—the ones who would enjoy an all-expense-paid ten-day holiday in Europe—to intimate gatherings where the wonders and delights of the project were explained to them and their support was secured. At no time during this period was a single resident of the communities adjacent to the proposed site invited to attend one of the soirees. After all, they were all poor, nearly all black. Was that a coincidence? It was a question that would be asked, and tentatively answered, in the crucible of litigation in the years to come.

There were two general partners in what would eventually be called Louisiana Energy Services: URENCO Investments and Claiborne Fuels. There were also eight limited partners: Graystone Corporation (a creation of Northern States Power Company of Minnesota), Louisiana Power and Light, BNFL Enrichment (British Nuclear Fuels, Ltd), GnV (part of the government of Germany), UCN Deelnemingen (99 percent owned by the Dutch government), Claiborne Energy Services (owned by Duke Power of North Carolina), Le Paz Inc. (owned by Graystone), and Micogen Limited III (owned by Fluor Daniel of California).

URENCO, in turn, is made up of three companies, one Dutch, one British, one German. Claiborne Fuels is owned by Fluor Daniel, an engineering company ("Our mission is to assist clients in attaining a competitive advantage by delivering quality services of unmatched value"), which did the early planning on the plant, itself officially called the Claiborne Enrichment Center. Indeed, it was Fluor Daniel that did the research that led to the selection of the site between Forest Grove and Center Springs, a study that would figure prominently in the struggle. As it turned out, the three U.S. utilities were simply window dressing, enlisted to help secure the permit. They all planned to drop out of the project once the permit was issued. They were brought in because URENCO doubted that such a permit would be issued to a wholly foreign-owned enterprise.

KEEPING IT PRIVATE

Given the military ancestry of atomic power and its usefulness in weapons—and therefore its appeal to terrorists—uranium enrichment in the United States has been the exclusive province of the federal government. This would change with the Claiborne Enrichment Center proposal. It envisioned building a centrifuge enrichment facility, far more energy efficient than the gaseous-diffusion plants then in use (see sidebar), but so much better at producing bomb-grade uranium that the Stockholm International Peace Research Institute had called for outlawing the process as far back as 1983. It would produce 870 metric tons of slightly enriched uranium hexafluoride each year. It would also produce 3,800 metric tons of depleted uranium tailings—the U-238 discarded to increase the concentration of U-235. What exactly would be done with this toxic and radioactive trash was a bit of a mystery. It did raise questions about the "clean as a dairy" promise from Senator Johnston.

The owners of the plant, as enumerated previously, included domestic electric utilities and energy companies, plus foreign governments and companies. In order to get around the prohibition on private enrichment facilities in the United States, Senator Johnston set about to amend the Atomic Energy Act of 1954. Quietly.

In a technique that has become more and more popular in recent years, the good senator did not make any public noise over his little bill. In fact, he said nothing at all, but rather, in the spring of 1991, as a member of the senate delegation to a conference committee appointed to reconcile two versions of a "Balanced Budget Downpayment Act," he added simple language that relaxed the federal ban on private enrichment of uranium.

There was no announcement to the press, no public hearings. Assured that this was non-controversial housekeeping, the conferees accepted the language, and the Atomic Energy Act was changed.

Meanwhile, back in Homer, Toney Johnson's sister, Beth Griggs, had taken it upon herself to find help in Washington. She got in contact with Critical Mass Energy Project, a Ralph Nader-sponsored group, which provided some basic background information on uranium enrichment. Her contact at Critical Mass, however, was about to move on and suggested that she approach Michael Marriotte of the Nuclear Information Resources Service, a self-appointed watchdog of the nuclear industry and its government overseers established in 1978. Marriotte agreed to meet with CANT in Homer and, in early 1990, joined the anti-LES forces.

Toney Johnson, the appraiser and real estate broker, meanwhile, was suffering from the fallout of the savings and loan scandal that had rocked the country. As a result of the hullabaloo, Toney and his colleagues had to attend seminars concerning real estate financing and federal regulations. Many trips to New Orleans were required.

ATOMIC CENTRIFUGE

Natural uranium is plentiful but not suitable as power-plant fuel until it goes through a complicated process called "enrichment." Natural ore consists of two isotopes, uranium-235 and uranium-238. When bombarded with neutrons, U-235 will split into two smaller atoms, releasing a great deal of heat, which can be used to boil water, spin turbines, and generate electricity. It can also be used to cause immense explosions, like the one that destroyed Hiroshima. To be useful in the generation of electricity—or for making atom bombs—uranium must be enriched; that is, the concentration of U-235 must be increased from its natural .7 percent to about 4 percent for nuclear power plants. For bombs and missiles, it is enriched to as much as 97 percent. The process is the same, which is why the government has not allowed any private firms to go into the enrichment business.

The enrichment can be accomplished in at least two ways. The one employed exclusively in the United States is known as "gaseous diffusion." Uranium hexafluoride gas is pumped through thin membranes of metal, with the U-235 passing through at a fractionally faster rate than the U-238. In a second technology, developed in Europe, uranium hexafluoride is spun in thousands of small centrifuges, with the heavier molecules of U-238 separating themselves from the lighter U-235.

Both technologies are intricate and expensive. Once the required enrichment is achieved, the uranium is converted to powdered uranium dioxide, molded into small pellets, baked, and inserted into metal tubes called fuel rods that are less than a half inch in diameter and more than twelve feet long. They are then transported to nuclear power plants for electricity production. (Readers wishing to understand more of this complicated and controversial process are encouraged to check the bibliography for *Nuclear Power*, by Walt Patterson.)

The plant proposed for Center Springs and Forest Grove would have received solid uranium hexafluoride, heated it until it turned into gas, then carried out the enrichment. UO8 (uranium oxide) is a fiercely caustic substance in its gaseous form.

On one of those trips, Johnson remembers, he got to talking with an attorney and the subject of the uranium plant came up. "Are you fighting that plant?" the lawyer asked. "Yes, I am," answered Johnson. "I wish you luck," said the lawyer. "Senator Johnston was at the Petroleum Club last week and said he'd got a bill through the Senate that would speed up the licensing of the plant." His bill provided that there would be no public hearings and no environmental impact study.

It made sense. Time was very important. The contracts the utilities had with the federal uranium enrichment facilities were due to expire in 1998. For LES to have a chance to crack the American uranium market, it would have to be operating at close to full capacity by that time, which meant that construction would have to begin soon. There had been no news reports about the bill. None.

Johnson telephoned his congressman, Jim McCrery, and spoke to a staff member, asking whether this bill had come before the House yet. The staffer had not heard of it and couldn't find reference to it anywhere. "If it's here, I'll find it," the staffer said, and promised to call Johnson back. The next day, he telephoned. He had called the Nuclear Regulatory Commission to inquire about the bill. It turned out to be a paragraph or two that had been sandwiched in the middle of a routine bill designed to give a couple of federally owned islands in Lake Superior to the state of Minnesota for use as recreation sites. A day or so later, a story ran in the *Washington Post* outlining Senator Johnston's attempt to grease the skids for his pet project.

CANT member Juanita Hamilton takes a stand next to the Louisiana Energy Services signpost at the proposed location. *Daniel Lincoln*

This, in turn, caught the eye of Representative George Miller, who had assumed the role of de facto chairman of the House Interior Subcommittee on Energy and the Environment for the ailing Morris Udall. A member of his staff called Michael Marriotte of NIRS for background, and he described the Homer connection. Congressman Miller called a hearing to ventilate the mustiness surrounding the legislation.

FIASCO IN FIESTAWARE

Senator Johnston offered to come testify, which senators seldom do before House committees. Also invited were representatives from the Nuclear Regulatory Commission, LES, the Department of Energy, and the U.S. Public Interest Research Group. Michael Marriotte suggested that someone from CANT appear as well. The committee staff balked, arguing that the bill was simply procedural and did not concern the LES plant.

"Fine," said Marriotte. "We'll bring a busload of black kids up from Homer and hold a press conference on the Capitol steps during your hearing." The committee relented. Toney Johnson caught a red-eye for Washington.

Senator Johnston testified first. He tried to suggest that his bill had little to do with

Schoolkids from Homer and the nearby communities join a CANT rally against the uranium plant in April 1990. *Claiborne Guardian-Journal*

the LES plant proposal, that it was simply a minor rewrite of the rules governing the regulation of such plants. He suggested that because an enrichment plant was not a reactor and did not involve fission products (the fragments left behind when an atom of U-235 or another molecule breaks in two) or high-level radiation, it should not have to meet the same standards as a reactor.

Then he set out to demonstrate just how benign the LES plant would be. He had brought with him a Geiger counter, a .50-caliber bullet made from depleted uranium, a uranium fuel pellet, a reddish dinner plate, and a microphone. Someone else carried the pellet. (The senator may be wily, but he isn't stupid.) He held the Geiger counter in the air with the microphone next to it. Small clicking could be heard, coming, the senator said, from the granite walls of the hearing room. Then he held the bullet next to the Geiger counter, which emitted more modest clicks. Then the fuel pellet, which chattered loudly. Finally, he held the dinner plate next to the device, which produced a loud welter of clicks.

"You can buy this plate in any supermarket," the senator told the representatives seated behind the big curving desk above him. The message was clear: the uranium pellet was less radioactive than an ordinary dinner plate. He neglected to mention that the LES plant would produce not fuel pellets but uranium hexafluoride gas. Had he brought a canister of that gas and released it into the hearing room, it would likely have killed everyone on the spot.

And just how ordinary was the dinner plate?

Michael Marriotte and Jim Werner of the Natural Resources Defense Council were seated at the back of the hearing room, chuckling quietly. They knew that it must be an example of the infamous Fiestaware that had been decorated with a uranium-based glaze sometime before 1944, when the line was discontinued. The use of uranium and lead in glazes was subsequently outlawed. The congressmen and -women must know that Senator Johnston was trying to bamboozle them, mustn't they?

When the hearing adjourned, Marriotte dashed back to his office and telephoned his contact on Miller's staff. It appeared that the committee members were not aware of the Fiestaware scandal, and they would certainly not be amused to learn that they'd been misled by a fellow legislator.

Marriotte, Toney Johnson, and others then started telephoning reporters, describing Senator Johnston's Fiestaware stunt. They mailed a videotape of the senator testifying to Susanne Dozier, a reporter for the Shreveport television station KTBS. She cornered the senator in Shreveport the next day and asked him, on camera, if it was true that he had claimed that a Fiestaware plate was ordinary and safe.

"I never said that," Senator Johnston replied.

The story ran on the TV news in Shreveport that evening, first with Johnston saying "I never said that," followed by Johnston saying that very thing. Johnston—embroiled in a reelection campaign—suddenly became very quiet. The reporter was fired. Several other news outlets in Louisiana carried the story, not including Johnston's hometown paper in Shreveport. One doesn't embarrass a powerful senator in his hometown; not in Louisiana. Congress eventually enacted a bill that shortened the licensing process for the plant but required an environmental impact statement and public hearings.

During the hearing before the Subcommittee on Energy and the Environment, the senator had observed that there was no need to make matters complicated. "These are poor country people," he said. "They don't want to deal with lawyers."

Toney Johnson, speaking later at the same hearing, contradicted him: "We'll deal with lawyers if that's what it takes to stop this plant."

Fiestaware pitcher, c. 1930s. A uranium-based glaze used on some early Fiestaware was radioactive; the maker later discontinued it. A Fiestaware plate was brandished at a congressional hearing as evidence that the plant proposed for Claiborne Parish would be less radioactive than an "ordinary" dinner plate. *Collection David Reardon, photo Rick Gerharter*

The Opposition Digs In

An early service Marriotte provided was to introduce the CANT people to Diane Curran, an attorney who had labored in the antinuclear vineyards for many years, having battled the Seabrook reactor in New Hampshire, helped the Union of Concerned Scientists get the unsafe Yankee Rowe reactor shut down, and participated in the proceedings that closed the Sequoyah uranium processing plant in Oklahoma. The last was especially relevant: An accident at Sequoyah had resulted in the escape of the same uranium hexafluoride gas that would be processed at the LES plant. One person was killed; many were injured. Curran was well versed in the labyrinthine procedures of the Nuclear Regulatory Commission, which seem to have been written to discourage public participation in its deliberations.

(The episode at the Sequoyah plant was referred to as an "event," by the way. The nuclear industry does not have accidents, as Toney Johnson found later when he began investigating what this proposal was really all about; only "events.")

On behalf of CANT, Johnson signed an agreement to pay Curran a hundred dollars an hour to represent CANT before the Nuclear Regulatory Commission. CANT had no money. LES had sent five-hundred-dollar checks to the Forest Grove and Center Springs churches in the early going as an olive branch. The churches sent them back. "For us to accept checks from somebody who we consider our enemy would be a conflict of interest," Alean Jones, another member of CANT, told the *Shreveport Times*. "If we had cashed the checks, no sooner than they had cleared the bank they would have publicized it and said we are friends, which we are not."

Norton Tompkins sent grant applications to close to a dozen charitable foundations. Some of the foundations asked for evidence of community support for this effort, so Miss Essie Youngblood, the matriarch of Center Springs, who devoted her modest means to the fight and was to go without a new dress for ten years, rounded up several local families who pledged to come up with a hundred dollars each, every month, to fight the plant. These were not, please remember, in any sense wealthy people.

Curran and Marriotte put their heads together and drafted a series of what the NRC calls "contentions": reasons, in this case, why the commission should not approve the LES permit application. This was but the first step in a drawn-out process that would involve writing briefs, eliciting expert testimony, commissioning economic analyses, and eventually arguing in a live hearing before a three-member panel of administrative law judges.

Curran, however, could not handle the case alone. They turned to Nathalie Walker of Earthjustice's New Orleans office to share the load. The New Orleans office had opened a couple of months earlier, with a dual mission of protecting the Gulf Coast's vanishing wetlands and assisting community groups battling to achieve what was emerging as a new concern: environmental justice. The expression generally refers to the fact that chemical factories, waste dumps, incinerators, and other major sources of pollution tend to be built in and near minority and low-income communities. The Homer proposal reeked of environmental injustice. Walker knew that taking on this fight would be a major commitment, and indeed, it would eventually consume much of her life for nearly a decade. Her first step was to visit Homer and meet the people of CANT.

"I was impressed with their commitment, their passion, and their problem," Walker remembers. She was, however, an outsider, and it took time for the CANT people to accept her. Roy Mardis, one of the original CANT members, a lay minister and pillar of the two communities, admitted later that he was worried about Nathalie at first. "I wondered if she might be a spy. I had doubts and fears. But she began making suggestions about how we might fight the plant that made sense. And spirit shines through. You could sense her anger about what was being done to us. She was never not there." Marriotte, meanwhile, was quietly making trouble for LES, trying in every way possible to throw up roadblocks. "Delay worked in our favor," he remembers. "We were always trying to broaden the story because we were sure a couple hundred people in rural Louisiana could not stop such a project. We sent letters to Wall Street brokerages, urging them not to invest in the project because it was a bad gamble.

"We went to Minnesota and North Carolina to ask if any ratepayer funds were being invested in the project, and actually succeeded in forcing Duke Power to refund money to its ratepayers. We also squeezed from Northern States Power and Duke Power admissions that they would abandon the project once it had received its license, which added much power to the argument that the plant was a risky financial enterprise."

Marriotte met with the chairman of the NRC, Ivan Selin, who told him in confidence that he considered the project "economically ludicrous."

Resentment, particularly against the white members of CANT, ran deep among some people in Homer. Toney Johnson asked his CPA firm to draw up papers to establish tax-deductibility for CANT. The accountant refused. Pretty soon the bank stopped sending Toney out to appraise buildings it was considering lending money against. Johnson very nearly lost his business but managed to hang on. As of fall 2000, three years after the end of the fight, the bank still had frozen him out.

CANT leader Roy Mardis and his family. *Daniel Lincoln*

"We were ostracized by people we went to grade school with," Norton remembers. One day Norton's wife, Gerry, got an anonymous call at home. "I just saw your husband in the grocery store hugging a black woman next to the salt," the caller reported.

"Next time I hugged her harder just to aggravate 'em," was Norton's reaction. And the police even got into the act, following people home from meetings of CANT. "I worried about being set up," Roy Mardis says, "being framed." Toney Johnson was threatened with a beating.

In the spring of 1991, Norton Tompkins and Roy Mardis went to Washington, D.C., for a seminar on LES and other nuclear projects. Diane Curran took them to meet Arjun Makhijani of the International Institute for Energy and Environmental Research. Makhijani listened sympathetically to their story and offered to help. A few months later a call came to CANT from Dan Rather's office: CBS News was interested in the story. Soon reporter Bob Faw came to Homer and started asking questions, taking pictures, interviewing people from CANT and LES. The piece was aired as an "Eye on America" segment. It was decidedly sympathetic to the people of Forest Grove and Center Springs. "That's when attempts at intimidation began to fade," Toney Johnson remembers. LES didn't need bad press from the national media. Homer was on the map in a way it wasn't quite sure it wanted to be.

"We know that LES took at least three public opinion surveys," Johnson adds. "But they never released the results of any of them. We figured opposition to the plant was far broader than anyone would let on, but people were scared to come out and take a position in public."

In November 1993, LES submitted its draft environmental impact statement and permit application to the NRC. Neither document mentioned Forest Grove or Center Springs. Two months later, President Clinton signed Executive Order 12898, which ordered all federal agencies to make achieving environmental justice part of their mission by paying careful attention to identifying and addressing the adverse human health and environmental effects of their programs, policies, and activities on minority and low-income communities. The Nuclear Regulatory Commission pointed out that, as an independent agency, it was not bound by executive orders—but agreed to abide by it anyway.

The following September the final environmental study was released. It still mentioned neither Forest Grove nor Center Springs, prompting Michael Marriotte to issue a press release headlined,

NRC ADOPTS RUSSIAN-STYLE NUCLEAR LICENSING TECHNIQUES—
TWO MINORITY COMMUNITIES VANISH FROM LES DRAFT EIS

The text went on to charge, "The removal of the most affected areas from this report reminds us of nothing so much as the KGB removing contaminated Soviet areas from the map. We are embarrassed by our government…This charade has gone on long enough."

Once the permit application had been filed, one of Almeter Willis's daughters—the chemist—took a look at it. "Do you know what they're going to make at this plant?" she asked her mother. And she explained about uranium and radioactivity and the rest. Almeter and Miss Essie Youngblood set out to teach themselves all about uranium enrichment, plowing through technical papers and books, learning about isotopes and kilowatt hours, an unusual but necessary way to spend their retirement.

"We'd already become a little suspicious," Almeter said later. "If that plant was going to be as good as they claimed, they'd have put it in Homer instead of out here."

Nathalie Walker and Diane Curran filed papers with the NRC for a formal challenge to the environmental study and the permit application.

BILL OF PARTICULARS

The petition submitted by Walker and Curran on behalf of CANT contained several allegations. First, it alleged that the environmental impact statement was deficient in that it failed to analyze the alternative of not building the plant at all. Since, for all intents and purposes, the writers of the EIS assumed that Forest Grove and Center Springs did not exist, it was no wonder they had neglected to examine any benefits that might accrue to the people in the two communities by not building the plant.

Second, CANT challenged both the financing of the plant—especially the likelihood that there would be enough money to clean up the site once the plant became too irradiated to be of further use—and the need for the enriched uranium that would be produced, given the glut of enriched uranium on the world market.

Finally came the most incendiary allegation: that the site had been chosen, in part, because nearby residents were poor and black—and therefore invisible.

The petition recited the facts. Of the 150 people of Forest Grove and the 100 of Center Springs, around 97 percent are African-American. There are no stores, schools, medical clinics, or businesses in either community. Many houses have no running water and their occupants rely on wells. Claiborne Parish is one of the poorest regions in the country. Thirty percent of the population overall, and nearly 60 percent of the black population, lives below the poverty line. Half the blacks in the parish earn less than ten thousand dollars per year; one-third earn less than five thousand. Nearly 60 percent have less than a high-school education. The petition argued that ignoring the impact the plant would have on these nearby residents—the use of the road, for one thing—was a violation of the National Environmental Policy Act.

But what really got to the core of the matter was the manner in which the site was selected in the first place. Fluor Daniel had started with a map of the contiguous United States. To minimize transportation costs, it would make sense to situate the plant as near as possible to the facilities that would manufacture the uranium hexafluoride (UF6) that the plant would enrich and to the fuel fabrication facilities to which the enriched uranium would be shipped.

The suppliers of UF6 were in Illinois and Oklahoma. Six potential customers were scattered from Hanford, Washington, to Columbia, South Carolina, to Windsor, Connecticut. Fluor Daniel figured where the halfway point between the hexafluoride plants was—the point is referred to as the "centroid"—and drew a circle with a radius of six hundred miles on the map. The centroid was not far from Kansas City. Then they pinpointed the centroid of the customers' locations—this landed near Indianapolis—and drew another circle. Where the circles overlapped was where they would concentrate the search, an oval that stretched from Minnesota to the Texas panhandle, Pennsylvania to Oklahoma.

Next they considered, in order:

Earthquakes. The centrifuge equipment is expensive and delicate, and they didn't want to run the risk of having it damaged by an earthquake.

Winds. Wind could also damage the facility. Note, please, that the concern with both earthquakes and wind was for the plant, not for any damage a quake- or wind-caused accident might inflict on the neighbors.

Weighing these factors, they settled on northern Louisiana. It passed all the physical screens, and Louisiana Power and Light, which would have an interest in the project, could help them gain an entrée to the region. The Fluor Daniel report cites a few other factors that made the region attractive, such as plenty of workers experienced in chemical plants to recruit from. Louisiana is a right-to-work state with low labor costs. Land is cheap. Certain new businesses are exempt from ad valorem taxes for ten years (an exemption that can easily be renewed in perpetuity) and are also exempt from state and local sales taxes (which Senator Johnston forgot to mention when talking about the great windfall the plant would bring in taxes to Claiborne Parish).

Next, the Fluor Daniel people invited several towns in northern Louisiana that were within forty-five miles of Interstate 20 to nominate sites. The communities were told that the facility would be a chemical plant, that it would occupy between three hundred and a thousand acres. A square site would be best, with easy access but not too close to population centers. More than a hundred sites were proposed by twenty-one cities and towns.

Applying the criteria outlined, Fluor Daniel winnowed the list to forty-six sites. A Fluor Daniel consultant went touring, meeting with "community leaders" and landowners, although said leaders were not necessarily the people who would bear the brunt of the plant's construction and operation.

Further winnowing got the number of candidate sites down to thirty-three, in and near eight communities. They then picked the most congenial community, Homer, and set out to pick the best site from the six Homer had to offer. Here the desirable features were the site's distance from other facilities, the ability to keep unwanted intruders off the grounds, a low risk of flood, plenty of available electricity, solid local support, a sparse nearby population, and a few others. Weighing all these factors, Fluor Daniel recommended a site exactly halfway between Forest Grove and Center Springs. Despite the

The owner of this land sold it to Louisiana Energy Services at a tidy profit, then logged off the trees that stood on it, pocketing a substantial windfall. The plant would have stood in the center of the picture. *Tom Turner*

desire to have "community leaders" behind the project and strong local support, the Fluor Daniel people never felt the need to speak to a single person who lived near the site. Not one.

The Fluor Daniel report is sober and straightforward, or so it reads unless the reader is someone like Bob Bullard.

Dr. Robert Bullard is a sociologist and director of the Environmental Justice Resource Center at Clark Atlanta University. He has written extensively on how and why so many noxious facilities happen to be built adjacent to poor and minority communities, and he coined the phrase *environmental racism* in the 1980s. In 1991, Bullard had spoken at the first People of Color Environmental Conference in Washington, D.C. Among the attendees was Earthjustice's community liaison director in New Orleans, Sharon Carr Harrington. Now, at Nathalie Walker's request, Harrington approached Bullard about serving as an expert in the LES case. He agreed.

Bullard examined in excruciating detail the process Fluor Daniel had used to choose the site for the plant. What he found was shocking. Based on four major considerations, Bullard charged that the site-selection process was both biased and racially discriminatory. He did not charge that the individuals who selected the site were racists themselves, but that the process was a result of ingrained institutional racism. Whether racism was a motive is difficult to prove; the result is not, and that's all that matters in the end. Here's what he found.

    ◆ At Bullard's request, and with financial support from the Lawyers' Committee on Civil Rights—which also underwrote the cost of the many depositions Walker and Curran would conduct—the American Civil Liberties Union of Virginia looked at the racial makeup of people living within one mile of seventy-eight sites that Fluor Daniel had considered seriously for the uranium plant. The African American population made up 28 percent of the total. When the number of sites was whittled to thirty-seven, the black concentration rose to 37 percent. When the number of sites fell to six, the black population rose to 65 percent. When the final decision was made, the number—the population of Forest Grove and Center Springs—became 97 percent.

    ◆ One of the site-selection criteria was "low adjacent population within a 2-mile radius." On close questioning during a deposition it was revealed that the individual who visited the final six sites near Homer, Larry Engwall, had conducted what he called an "eyeball assessment," driving his car up a couple of dirt roads. Many houses had boards over their windows. He assumed the houses were abandoned, but as Dr. Bullard pointed out in his testimony, the people simply couldn't afford to replace broken glass.

Engwall had estimated the population adjacent to the plant to be about ten people. The actual number is about 250. In assessing another of the Homer finalist sites, meanwhile, Engwall had fiddled with the numbers to make a location near Lake Claiborne and its well-to-do residents appear far more populous than it really was. He conceded during his deposition, "we just felt opinion-wise, people would probably not want this plant to be close to their pride and joy of their lake where they go fishing." At this point, Diane Curran noted later, "we had what we needed to win."

⬦ Another of the siting criteria gave preference to places not within five miles of schools, hospitals, or nursing homes. This again would single out poor, rural areas, whether deliberately or not.

⬦ Finally, as has been alluded to, Bullard described as discriminatory the fact that the alleged "community support" for the project was based on support from opinion leaders in Homer, five miles from the proposed site, many of whom could expect to profit from the project in one way or another. Residents adjacent to the property had not been consulted, and no one from these communities served in the town government of Homer.

These factors, according to Bullard, amounted to institutional racism and discrimination, which violate the National Environmental Policy Act and Executive Order 12898.

The plant's sponsors stoutly denied the allegations. The staff of the Nuclear Regulatory Commission said they didn't see any evidence of racial discrimination in Bullard's report, but they did not rebut Bullard's factual findings. A formal hearing was arranged to look into the allegations that Walker and Curran had raised on behalf of CANT.

SHOWDOWN IN SHREVEPORT

The hearing was held in the J. Bennett Johnston Courthouse, a grand edifice in Shreveport, in March 1995. It was conducted by the Atomic Safety and Licensing Board, a three-person unit of the Nuclear Regulatory Commission. It lasted a week. It was a triangular proceeding: LES was arguing in favor of its proposal, CANT was arguing against it, and the staff of the NRC was not a formal participant—but was firmly in LES's corner. The courtroom was packed with CANT members and sympathizers—many of them children—who made the sixty-five-mile journey to the courtroom and back again every day on buses specially rented for the occasion. Miss Essie Youngblood sat in the front row every day, listening intently, wearing a bumper-sticker around her head that said "Keep Claiborne Parish Nuclear Free."

"I was so proud to be working with them," Walker remembers. "They made just incredible sacrifices." And, as Norton Tompkins notes, not a single one of the junketeers bothered to attend the sessions. The only supporters of the plant at the hearings were paid employees of LES or one of its partners. Indeed, at one point LES's lawyer admitted to Tompkins, "You've got something on your side that I don't. Loyalty."

Economists testified about the financing of the project. Energy experts debated the need for the plant. And Bob Bullard talked about racial discrimination. Board members asked lots of questions, then retired to contemplate their decision.

It took a while. On December 3, 1996, the board ruled that LES had not adequately demonstrated that there was a need for the project or that it was financially qualified to take it on, and that the NRC staff had not done an adequate analysis of the impacts of simply not building the plant. Five months later, it ruled on the environmental justice allegations. Its members clearly were deeply moved by the arguments presented by witnesses for CANT, particularly Bob Bullard. The ruling said, in various ways, again and again: "This statistical evidence very strongly suggests that racial considerations played a part in the site selection process...The possibility that racial considerations played a part in the site selection cannot be passed off as mere coincidence...It is not our intent to impugn the integrity of the Applicant's witnesses. Rather, our point is simply that this and similar testimony of the Applicant's witnesses does not adequately rebut the Intervenor's [that is, CANT's] statistical evidence...We find [Dr. Bullard] both credible and convincing."

Then the magic words: "The Applicant's requested authorization for a combined construction permit and operating license is hereby denied."

LES immediately appealed to the full Nuclear Regulatory Commission.

By this time the anti-LES coalition had swelled to impressive proportions. Lending their considerable weight to the battle were Greenpeace, the League of Women Voters, the Gulf Coast Tenants Association, the Louisiana Environmental Action Network, Public Citizen, the Southern Christian Leadership Conference, the Sierra Club, the U.S. Public Interest Research Group, Global Response, the Environmental Health Network, and the NAACP.

Almeter Willis, Roy Mardis, Toney Johnson, and Norton Tompkins get ready to be filmed inside the Center Springs church for the *Visionaries* documentary. Sound man Scott Carey is on the left; Geoffrey Hahn is at right. *Tom Turner*

This coalition swung into action, soliciting statements of support for CANT from all quarters. Members of Congress and civil rights leaders wrote to the NRC, urging it to endorse the findings of the licensing board. Another letter arrived signed by representatives of 182 environmental groups from eighteen countries. The Working Assets telephone company urged its customers to sound off to the commission. It is unlikely the NRC had ever been lobbied so hard by so many members of the public.

The commission did its own contemplation, combing the briefs, depositions, and transcripts. It then bespoke itself, again in a bifurcated fashion. On December 18, 1997, it said that though some questions still needed answering and guarantees should be made, it thought the financing of the project looked reasonably solid. Then, on April 3, 1998, it dropped the hammer. While it reversed the board's rejection of the permit on the basis of no need for the project, it said the staff would have to reconsider the no-action alternative. Most important, although it rejected the contention of racial discrimination, it affirmed the "disparate impact" ruling. In this case, the commission found that the closing of the road between Forest Grove and Center Springs, and the likely harm to nearby property values, would fall unfairly on the people closest to the site and was therefore illegal.

Just about everybody in CANT will tell you that the Lord guided them every step of the way in fighting the uranium plant.
Tom Turner

The celebration party was held in the parking lot of the Forest Grove church, a festive but muted affair, since CANT's members did not want to rub anyone's noses in their stunning victory. A coffin, representing the project, was serenaded by a Dixieland band playing funeral dirges.

But stunning the victory certainly was. For the first time in the history of the Nuclear Regulatory Commission, a citizen-group effort had resulted in the agency's denying a permit application for a new project, and for the first time, a federal agency had formally embraced the principle of environmental justice as a determining factor in its decision making. LES, having been stung by the CBS news report and the torrent of publicity that accompanied the battle, eventually decided against proceeding and withdrew its permit application in April 1998, soon after the commission issued its second ruling.

As of early 2002, the project was dead. Not just with respect to Homer, Forest Grove, and Center Springs, but anywhere else. It made prophetic the words of Ed Davis of the American Nuclear Energy Council, who had been quoted by the *Washington Post* saying, "If we can't build that plant in Louisiana, we can't build any nuclear plant anywhere."

CANT had incorporated and registered as a nonprofit organization with the Internal Revenue Service so it could apply for grants to pay for buses to haul members to the hearings and demonstrations, for stamps and photocopying, and for legal expenses incurred by Diane Curran. Nathalie Walker didn't bill CANT for anything. When LES finally threw in the towel, Norton Tompkins tallied the sheet: CANT, over a period of about seven years, had raised $165,000, spent $149,000, and had $16,000 left in the bank. LES had admitted to spending at least $32 million on the project and had 450 acres of cutover land to show for it, land worth maybe $25,000. The fight won, CANT dissolved, giving $5,000 to Earthjustice, $5,000 to Michael Marriotte's organization, and $3,000 each to the Forest Grove and Center Springs churches, "the people who helped us the most," in Tompkins's words.

For the members of CANT, life goes on, but not quite as before. Roy Mardis was elected to the Claiborne Parish Police Jury (the county board of supervisors). Almeter Willis served two terms on the school board. Two other members, Scott "Doc" Roberson and Susan Herring, were elected to the Homer Town Council. Herring, after her stint, became editor of the Homer newspaper, the *Guardian-Journal*. Two more CANT members served on the town council as well. Homer even elected a black mayor, David Aubrey, the first in its history.

Miss Essie Youngblood finally bought herself a new dress. Everything she had had gone into the fight. Was it worth it?

"We worked together. We loved each other. We still do. It's a bond that will last forever," Miss Essie says.

CHAPTER FOUR

RETURN OF THE WINDWARD WATERS

When the first humans arrived in Hawai'i fifteen hundred years or so ago, they carried with them a variety of plants and animals—two by two, like Noah, one may suppose—to plant or raise wherever they ended up. They could not possibly have known that two of the plants—sugarcane and taro—would wind up mortal enemies, the one threatening to destroy a way of life and an ecosystem, the other the best hope of saving both.

Most scholars now believe that the first wave of settlers came from the Marquesas Islands in what is now French Polynesia. In addition to sugar and taro, they probably brought pigs, chickens, dogs, bananas, breadfruit, and various medicinal plants. A second wave of immigrants is thought to have come perhaps five hundred years later, from Tahiti, also carrying plants and animals. Westerners, beginning in the late sixteenth century, brought with them cattle, pigs, sheep, goats, and deer and released them to be fruitful and multiply. Although it would take centuries before the damage became obvious—and largely irreversible—the alien animals and plants began to alter the primeval ecosystems of Hawai'i as soon as the first settlers arrived.

Islands are unusually vulnerable to outside influences, especially islands as isolated as the Hawaiian chain, which is the most remote major island group anywhere in the world, well over two thousand miles from the nearest continent. Being so far removed from other land masses, the plants and animals of Hawai'i are largely endemic—unique to the islands. And the diversity of animal species is very limited. While dozens of species of birds evolved on the islands, there were but two mammals: the Hawaiian monk seal and the Hawaiian hoary bat. With no natural predators to help them evolve defenses, native Hawaiian plants and birds were unable to fend off the exotic animals that set about munching on the vegetation the birds depended on for food, and ill-equipped to fight off the diseases the alien invaders brought with them. Hunting took a heavy toll as well. The result has been that at least half of the bird species that existed on the islands when Captain Cook visited in 1778 are now extinct, and most of those that survive do so only barely.

Another example of natural Hawai'i's uniqueness is its streams. They are small by mainland standards, flowing not very far before they reach the coast and therefore not having vast catchments to drain. Indeed, perhaps to make them sound large and impressive, Hawaiians measure the flow of their streams in millions of gallons per day (or, mgd).

Opposite: Kane'ohe Bay, Windward O'ahu. Waiāhole Stream rushes down the mountain, watering taro fields on its way to the bay. Water that once produced only sugar is now rebuilding a way of life. *Douglas Peebles*

On the mainland, the more commonly used measure is cubic feet per second, frequently shortened to cfs or cusecs. As we shall see, a heroic battle has lately been fought out over the fate of approximately twenty-eight million gallons per day on Windward O'ahu. Twenty-eight million gallons a day is equivalent to 43 cusecs and change. (By comparison, the Northwest's Snake River, about which so much fighting has occurred on behalf of salmon restoration, runs more than 50,000 cusecs on average.) Still, on a small island, 28 mgd can make all the difference to several watersheds.

In any event, there remain just nine species that are native to Hawai'i's streams. Five are fish, two are mollusks, and two are related to shrimp. Two of the fish—all are species of 'o'opu, or gobi—grow to a size big enough for humans to eat, as does one of the mollusks and one of the shrimp.

That is, if you can find any.

All the species are "amphidromous": they are born in fresh water and migrate almost immediately—within forty-eight hours—downstream to the coast, out through the estuary if there is one, and into the open ocean, where they become part of the mélange of tiny creatures collectively called plankton. There they remain for three to five months, at which point they dash back to fresh water. The stream need not be their birth stream as with salmon and steelhead, but it must be reasonably clean, voluminous, and cool.

Diversion of many of the streams on all the major islands has impaired all three of those features, with the result that the native species in those streams are exceedingly rare. In addition, exotic species of fish—imported either on purpose, for sport, or by accident—compete with the natives for food and carry parasites against which the natives have no defense. The combination of insults has nearly wiped out native species in many streams.

Native Stream Animals of Hawai'i. This painting by O'ahu artist Patrick Ching depicts five species of *'o'opu* as well as their post-larval stage *(hinana)* and the remaining crustacean and mollusk species that survive in windward O'ahu streams. *Patrick Ching, © Hawaii Division of Aquatic Resources*

When the species return to fresh water, a profound change takes place almost immediately. In the case of the *'o'opu* returning to fresh water, the change is magical. Kaipo Faris is a boat repairman who has taken it upon himself (as a volunteer) to gather data on water chemistry and temperature for two or three Windward streams; as he describes it, "When the *'o'opu* return to the mouth of Waiāhole Stream they are transparent. All you can see is two tiny black dots, the eyes. But within minutes their skin begins to take on color, and within a few hours they look like fish. We catch the *'o'opu* as they arrive and watch the transformation. It's amazing."

There is a catch, however. If the fish sense that the stream is polluted—which they evidently are able to do—or if the temperature is too high, it's too late to turn back to sea. If they do so, they will die. So at some of the streams, the returning fishlets just mill around the mouth until they perish.

Another profound effect of stream diversion has been on the human culture that depended on stream waters not just for fishing but also for agriculture. Rainfall varies dramatically from the windward to the leeward side of the islands—thus Native Hawaiians tended to settle around the windward streams, where water was abundant. Here, for centuries, the primary crop they cultivated was taro, at least until their fateful encounter with western society in the late eighteenth century.

THE PERFECT PLANT

Taro is a vegetable. It is also a way of life. Taro probably originated in Southeast Asia and was spread throughout the tropics by settlers. The best taro, the "hardest" taro, which lasts longest, grows in *lo'i*—small patches divided by low berms and canals called *'auwai*—amply irrigated with cold running water, much the way rice grows.

The corm is boiled or steamed (raw, it is poisonous), scraped clean, sliced, and eaten or pounded into the viscous, vaguely purple, heroically sticky concoction called poi. The leaves—called lu'au, like the feast—taste a good deal like spinach. The corm is high in fiber and carbohydrates, low in fat (it has less fat than rice), and is said to be good for diabetics and people with high blood pressure. Worldwide, it is the staple food for more people than either potatoes or rice. It is a crashing irony that, as a state, Hawai'i is the healthiest in the union, while Native Hawaiians, who have succumbed to the lure of french fries and sweetened drinks, are the least-healthy identifiable group in the country. If taro could be reintroduced to the Hawaiian diet in a big way, the health benefits would be enormous.

But that's just the practical part of the story. According to Hawaiian lore, when the sky father and the earth mother mated, their first offspring was taro—known as *kalo* in Hawaiian—and their second child was a human. Thus, taro is a sacred being, to be revered and honored, a sibling to us all.

Boy standing in taro field, location unknown, c. 1890s. Most likely photographed by J. J. Williams. *Hawaiian Historical Society*

HARD TARO AND THIRSTY CANE

When Captain Cook landed on the island of Hawai'i in 1778, he estimated that there were around two hundred thousand acres of taro *lo'i* scattered around the damper regions of the islands. (See sidebar.) By the time the movement to restore streams and native wildlife gained a foothold in the early 1990s, the number had dwindled to a meager four

Kaneʻohe Bay, looking north. The bay's fisheries were badly damaged by diversion of water to the leeward side of the mountains to water sugarcane fields.
Douglas Peebles

hundred acres or fewer. On Oʻahu there were but fifty acres in taro where, as recently as 1935, there had been a thousand. The land was still fertile, and people still liked to eat taro and poi. The trouble was, no water. It had been stolen—not too strong a word—and diverted in order to water other crops, mainly sugar.

In a sense, the trouble began with the onset of the gold rush in California and, not long after that, the Civil War. Gold miners needed food, including sugar, and it was easier to ship it from Hawaiʻi than to haul it by wagon from Florida and other sugar-growing states. And when the Civil War erupted, Union states would not, or could not, buy their sugar from the Confederacy. Entrepreneurs, many of them descendants of the missionaries who followed Cook to the islands, began to plan a sugary future for the Hawaiian Islands.

The thievery previously referred to was already well under way. American traders and colonists had been pressuring the Hawaiian monarchy to become more "democratic," by which they meant adopting the western system of private land ownership, then unknown in the Islands. They prevailed upon King Kamehameha III to issue an edict known as the Great Mahele of 1848, which instituted a system of land ownership. Within thirty years, westerners owned 80 percent of the private land in Hawaiʻi. Ordinary Hawaiian people were virtually landless.

Next, the sugar traders engineered a stunning deal between the monarchy and the United States government called the American Reciprocity Act of 1874: in exchange for a cancellation of all duties on sugar imports, Hawaiʻi would give the United States permanent permission to use Pearl Harbor as a navy base. The sugar barons now had the skids greased for a lucrative enterprise. All they had to do was find room to expand their operations. They realized that the central plains of several of the islands would be ideal sites for cane plantations, only they did not receive much rainfall. Such streams as they had were meager, and the groundwater beneath them, if any, would be expensive to deliver to the fields.

And sugar is an incredibly water-intensive crop. One pound of granulated cane sugar requires four thousand pounds—or, five hundred gallons—of water to produce. A hundred-acre field of cane takes a million gallons of water a day to irrigate, which means dousing the field with approximately three inches of water a day. That's more than a thousand inches a year. Rainy Seattle gets not quite forty inches in an average year. In its heyday, sugar was estimated to consume fully 60 percent of the fresh water in Hawai'i .

So, these visionaries turned their attention to the windward, eastern, rainy side of the islands, where it can rain eighty inches or more a year and the population was relatively sparse. Most of the people there were of Native Hawaiian descent, working their taro fields, fishing the estuaries and the open ocean, minding their own business. The budding sugar barons thought, If only we could deliver that wonderful water to the leeward fields, we could grow a lot of sugar and make a lot of money. As is all too typical in the history of such projects, they paid no attention to the effect such diversions would have on the streams—let alone the people who depended on those streams for their livelihood and culture.

The Waiāhole Ditch, the subject of this tale, was not the first of the great Hawaiian water-diversion projects, but at the time it was begun it was "the most ambitious tunnel project yet undertaken in the Territory of Hawai'i," according to Carol Wilcox in *Sugar Water*, an excellent account of water and sugar in the islands. The project would also

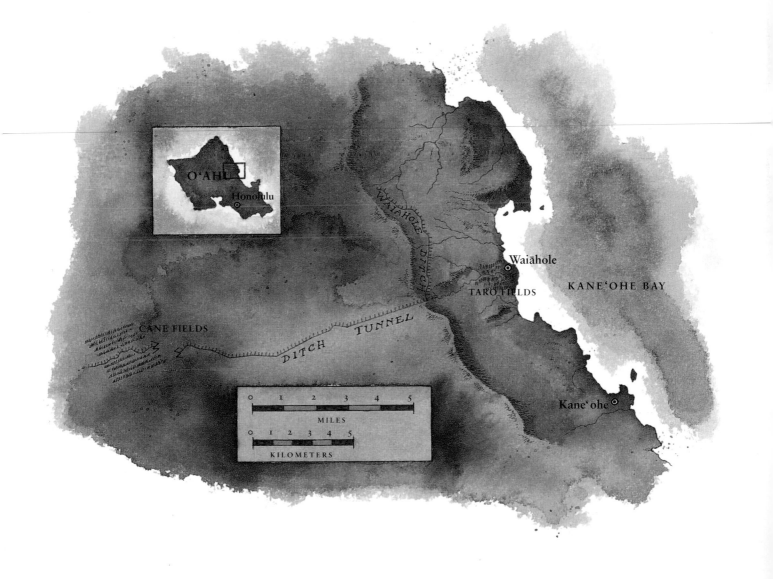

become, through a series of political developments driven by a doughty band of Native Hawaiian activists, environmentalists, righteous bureaucrats, and visionary jurists, the most prominent and the most controversial water dispute ever to wend its way through the Hawaiian legal system.

THE WAIĀHOLE DITCH

Waiāhole is a tiny community on the windward side of O'ahu. It is one of a string of small settlements perched next to the streams that empty into Kane'ohe Bay, the island's largest. Waiāhole Stream was a major waterway by island standards, carrying roughly thirty million gallons per day to the estuary before the diversions began. When that happened, the flow in Waiāhole Stream plummeted to three million gallons a day.

The Waiāhole Ditch was built in the 1910s and, in fact, is not a ditch, just as the other plumbing systems that honeycomb the islands are not ditches but agglomerations of tunnels and flumes and siphons and penstocks and reservoirs. The Waiāhole system captured runoff from several streams in the Kane'ohe watershed, sent it through the Ko'olau Range of mountains in a three-mile-long tunnel, then delivered the water to the 'Ewa plain, in central O'ahu.

Ditch construction began in 1913 and immediately ran into trouble. The necessary equipment was late, so the workers dug by hand at first, being lucky if they could advance two feet a day with their tunnel, which was roughly seven feet square. Not far into the mountain, they encountered and breached the first of a series of so-called dikes, ultrahard and impermeable membranes of rock that divided the otherwise porous mountains into water-filled chambers: The mountain was, in fact, a lava sponge that stored rainwater and released it slowly through springs and into the streams that course down the range. Thus, although the ditch had been expected to gather and transport surface runoff from the east side of the mountains, in fact the water it eventually delivered was more groundwater than surface water, and over the following decades it slowly drained millions upon millions of gallons of stored water that had nourished Windward streams for millennia. This emptying of the mountain was the most profound effect the Waiāhole Ditch would have on the streams on the east side of Oʻahu, and the most difficult to reverse.

The capacity of the Waiāhole Ditch was a hundred million gallons per day, but the amount it actually delivered to the ʻEwa plain and its acres of emerald-green sugarcane averaged about 30 mgd. Thirty million gallons per day that could no longer be used to grow taro or support aquatic life on the windward side of the island, that would no longer nourish the once productive Kaneʻohe Bay, a nursery for many species of oceangoing fish that were

also important food sources for many people. That sugar cube in a Californian's coffee had led to the near destruction of several ecosystems and an ancient way of life on the windward side of Oʻahu—and of vast areas throughout the neighbor islands as well.

The Sovereignty Movement Takes Root

Charlie Reppun is one of six brothers who all went to the East Coast for college, then returned to the Islands to pursue their lives. Charlie, his brothers Paul and John, and his cousin Ricky still live in or near Waiāhole, raising taro, bananas, papayas, chocolate, cucumbers, and other crops, organically. The brothers' uncle, C. Eric Reppun, was head of the territorial land commission at the time Hawaiʻi became a state. Charlie's wife,

Vivian Lee, wrote a lovely essay about the struggle for Waiāhole's water, and Charlie wrote extended captions for Ann Landgraf's wonderful photographs that illustrated the essay.

Here's what Charlie wrote about the runoff to the bay and ocean, a concern he still fears is not getting anything like enough attention:

> A raindrop seeps into the ground, reemerges out of a spring, and takes hours to make its way down to the ocean, going around branches, over rocks, resting in pools, passing through a taro *lo'i.* This raindrop extracts from leaves, bacteria, fish, and rocks a huge feast which it delivers to a ravenous food web of phytoplankton, *limu, 'opae,* crabs, *nehu,* mullet, *aholehole, papio,* and, yes, baby hammerhead sharks.

Paul Reppun admires a cacao tree on property he farms with his brother Charlie. The seeds inside the orange globes on the trunk and in the branches are the source of chocolate. *Tom Turner*

And he went on to quote Dr. Robert Livingston: "Estuaries are the most productive systems on the face of the earth. Freshwater flow is the reason that estuaries are so successful in producing most of our food in the seas and coastal areas."

Indeed, the original Hawaiians devised an ingenious method of aquaculture. They would build stone walls in the estuary with holes just large enough to allow small ocean fish to enter in search of food. When the fish grew, they could no longer escape through the holes. At its peak, Kane'ohe Bay had thirty of these fish farms. At the turn of the twenty-first century it had one: the Waiāhole Ditch and other diversions had cut off half the freshwater flow into the estuary.

In 1975 there was a showdown in the Waiāhole Valley that set the stage for the events that followed. In the area where taro once flourished, tenant farmers were raising cattle and vegetables on land leased from a private owner. The owner decided to sell the land to a developer, who planned a major housing project. The farmers burned their eviction notices. They were joined by hundreds of supporters from all across O'ahu, who thronged to the site and vowed to block the evictions. A tense standoff lasted many months, until the State of Hawai'i stepped in and bought six hundred acres for an agricultural park. The land was spared the bulldozer but was still bereft of its rightful water. The passion and determination of the people who refused to be evicted from Waiāhole Valley reflected a growing sovereignty movement that would spread for the next quarter century and beyond.

The history of the United States conquest of the islands in the late nineteenth century was one of rank commercial power and shady political dealings in Washington, and after decades of docile acquiescence a new generation of Hawaiians was agitating for autonomy and retribution. The refusal to be evicted from Waiāhole was one manifestation. A

stunning milestone was reached on the centennial of the U.S. annexation of the islands, January 17, 1993, when Congress passed and President Clinton signed a bill apologizing to the Hawaiian people for the overthrow of the Hawaiian monarchy. That and two dollars will buy you a cup of coffee, but it's a symbolic start. Native Hawaiians were given special recognition under Hawaiian law and under the state's constitution, but that special treatment has been eroded by intense litigation.

Hawai'i has been a state only since 1959. The state's relative youth may have led to an unusual provision's being written into the state constitution, which was created in 1958. It requires that a statewide referendum be held every ten years with a simple question: Shall we hold a convention this year to revise or amend the constitution? If the majority says yes, a convention is held, and any amendments adopted by the convention delegates—two people represent each of fifty-one districts scattered around the state—are put to a vote of all registered voters.

After Hawai'i's first decade, a convention was duly held. Ten years later, the political establishment wasn't agitating for another convention, because there didn't seem to be much left to fix or add. But they didn't take into account the impact of the Vietnam war,

Kane'ohe Bay with the Ko'olau Mountains in the distance. The Waiāhole Valley is at the center-left of the photograph. *Douglas Peebles* struggles for civil rights, the environmental movement, even Watergate on a generation of Hawaiians. Hawai'i's citizens, it turned out, liked the idea of improving their constitution now and then. Another convention was held.

Across the island from Honolulu, some of the people who had been fighting to regain their water thought maybe they could use the convention to help their battle. One of them was Charlene Hoe, a native of Minnesota who had married Calvin Hoe, an artist, teacher, and builder of traditional Hawaiian musical instruments and implements. Calvin is known for making the best nose-flutes in the islands, and he almost single-handedly restored the making of *ipu*, or gourd drums, a practice that had nearly died out as gourds disappeared. Calvin and Charlene lived in the watershed adjacent to Waiāhole and dreamed of the day when their stream would once again flow strong enough to raise good, hard taro.

AMENDING THE CONSTITUTION

The Hoes and their friends began to draft a constitutional amendment that would require the legislature to write and adopt a water code for the state and create a commission to enforce it. The code, they said, should require the state to acknowledge its responsibilities under the "public trust doctrine" to protect its waters for the benefit of its citizens, and it should recognize the special rights Native Hawaiians have to pursue what the state constitution already referred to as their "traditional and customary" activities, such as fishing and raising taro.

The public trust doctrine, a remnant of English common law, holds generally that government has the duty to protect common resources for the benefit of the public at large. These resources include lakes, streams, estuaries, and their banks, as well as air and wildlife. Some states, notably Michigan and Pennsylvania, have explicitly defined and codified the doctrine in their laws. Hawai'i would be asked to do the same.

This modest shack, adjacent to taro *lo'i* on the Reppuns' farm, houses a water wheel that generates electricity to run lights and appliances in the houses above. *Tom Turner*

Eventually, a draft amendment was prepared and submitted to the convention. It was ratified by the delegates and enacted by the public via referendum. It states, among other things, "All public natural resources [including land, water, air, minerals, and energy sources] are held in trust by the State for the benefit of the people." Hawai'i's water politics would never be quite the same.

Coincidentally—or maybe not—another amendment adopted at the same convention called for the creation of an Office of Hawaiian Affairs to look after the long-neglected needs of the Native Hawaiian population. The office would be overseen by

Native Hawaiian trustees, elected by Native Hawaiians in statewide balloting (the provision allowing only Natives to vote was eliminated by the U.S. Supreme Court in 2000). The two amendments would cross paths many times.

Calvin Hoe and his son, Liko Hoe, are among the local activists who fought for the restoration of water to Waiāhole Stream. *Kapulani Landgraf*

The governor appointed a working group to draft language to govern the activities of the water commission. It took ten years. Until that time, water management had been concerned with supplying water for agriculture and development. The new water code, based on a model code written by three law professors in the 1970s and used by many states, said something quite different:

> Adequate provision shall be made for the protection of traditional and customary Hawaiian rights, the protection and procreation of fish and wildlife, the maintenance of proper ecological balance and scenic beauty, and the preservation and enhancement of waters of the State for municipal uses, public recreation, public water supply, agriculture, and navigation. Such objectives are declared to be in the public interest.

The governor then installed a Commission on Water Resource Management of seven members: the heads of the Department of Land and Natural Resources and the Department of Health, plus five others, informally expected to represent the major islands. The department heads are gubernatorial appointees, so the governor has complete control over the commission. It is not required that there be a representative of the Native community, the environmental community, the scientific establishment, or any other specific group.

The new water code provided for "water management areas," both for groundwater and for surface water in regions where water was in short supply. Once a management area was declared, anyone seeking to divert water from the area's streams would have to apply for and receive a permit. And to receive the permit, the applicant would have to prove that withdrawing the water would not harm the stream or the surrounding environment.

In 1988, Arnold Lum and Marjorie Ziegler, who had helped establish an Earthjustice office in Honolulu earlier that year, submitted a petition to the commission to have Windward Oʻahu declared a water management area for both surface and groundwater. They reasoned that if the Leeward users of the ditch water were forced to prove that their diversions were not harming streams and Native users on the Windward side, they'd be hard-pressed to do so. At least as urgent was the fact that Honolulu had a greedy eye on what was left of Windward's water, a development plan that envisioned forty-six new water-development projects and nineteen new reservoirs in the area to slake the city's growing thirst.

The Oahu Sugar Company promptly opposed the petition, and the battle was joined. For the next three-and-a-half years the commission held hearings, took testimony, and pondered. The contestants wrangled over whether 90 percent of the "sustainable yield" of the Windward aquifer was being utilized, as required by the water code before a management area could be designated. They argued about whether surface water and groundwater could be separated in this area where so much of the water in the streams originates in springs.

Charlie Reppun, who had worked with Marjorie Ziegler and Arnold Lum in preparing the groundwater management area petition, waxed eloquent in one of a deluge of statements:

> To argue for designation one must argue against the concept of designation. The assumption is that nondesignated areas have more than enough water to satisfy all needs: that there is excess water. From an environmental/ecological point of view that is the wrong place to start managing the resource. That assumption has led to the belief that water running into the ocean is "wasted," which is the same as saying that estuaries are not important, or worse, that water is not part of a living system … The use of the terms *surface* and *ground* to describe water is like using *leaf* and *root* to describe a plant. They are all descriptive terms of a whole entity, but to take care of one or the other separately is a sign of ignorance. It is also impossible to do.

Water Up for Grabs

On July 15, 1992, the commission designated Windward Oʻahu and its five aquifer systems a groundwater management area, the first designation made under the new water

code. Leeward users of Waiāhole Ditch water had a year to apply for permits to continue their withdrawals. The following June, the Waiahole Irrigation Company, operator of the ditch system, applied for permits for all existing Leeward users. Almost immediately, the Oahu Sugar Company announced that it was going out of the sugar business, relocating its operations to the Philippines and Southeast Asia, where labor was cheaper. The rush for Waiāhole water was on.

Calvin Hoe, maker of fine nose-flutes, is a leader of the struggle to return water to the windward side of O'ahu. *Kapulani Landgraf*

About this time, Charlie Reppun telephoned Marjorie Ziegler to ask if Earthjustice might be persuaded to represent the Windward parties in the pending battle. Ziegler said she'd talk to the head lawyer in the Honolulu office, Denise Antolini. After studying the history of the case, the law, the constitution, and other matters, Antolini agreed. It would be one of the biggest cases that office had as yet undertaken.

On November 4, 1993, the state Department of Agriculture moved to reserve all the ditch water for agriculture on the Leeward side. The Robinson Estate and other big landowners dipped their ladles in the pool, as did the huge enterprise known as Kamehameha Schools/Bishop Estate and the Department of Hawaiian Home Lands. Even the U.S. Navy asked to participate in the process. In the end, Leeward applications were submitted for nearly twice the amount of water the ditch had ever carried.

The rationale put forward by some of the applicants was, shall we say, interesting. They argued that Waiāhole water should continue to flow to the old cane fields to irrigate what they called "diversified agriculture." This appeared to mean mostly food crops that would supposedly lessen the state's dependence on expensive imported produce. In fact, these landowners had little experience in such agriculture. In addition, there was ample groundwater available beneath the 'Ewa plain if only the landowners would dig a few wells. As the proceeding progressed it became palpably evident that their applications were meant simply to secure rights to the water that would one day irrigate new golf courses and make possible other kinds of large commercial developments.

Finally, on December 7 (a date with its own notoriety in Hawai'i), Charlie and Paul Reppun, on behalf of the Waiāhole–Waikāne Community Association; Charlene and

Calvin Hoe, on behalf of the Hakipu'u 'Ohana; the Kahalu'u Neighborhood Board; and Ka Lāhui Hawai'i filed their own petition arguing that the water the sugar company would no longer use should be returned to its rightful place, where it could grow taro, support native fishes and other wildlife, and contribute to the renaissance of Native Hawaiian culture. By the time the spray settled and the protracted legal struggle began, there were twenty-five official participants in the proceedings.

A few months later, in May 1994, the Windward partisans realized that there was skullduggery afoot. Oahu Sugar had suspended its irrigation program, but there was no noticeable increase in the amount of water in Waiāhole and other Windward streams. They surmised that water was being dumped—released from a flume or penstock and allowed to flow down perennially dry gullies. They petitioned the water commission to investigate, with a strong suggestion that the practice be stopped and the water returned to Windward. It was a pivotal moment. Denise Antolini remembers Bill Paty, chairman of the commission (he would later take over as head of the Robinson Estate), saying, "Once we return the water to the streams, we'll never get it back."

And Charlie Reppun remembers that Waiahole Irrigation representatives claimed they would need to write an environmental impact statement before returning water to a stream, "like a smoker having to ask permission to quit."

The central issue of the fierce battle then brewing was that it had little to do with agriculture, almost everything to do with development. As mentioned previously, if the acres that had been growing sugar were turned to growing fruits and vegetables, they would require far less water than the sugar had consumed—and in fact there was ample groundwater available, with permits already in place, to accommodate the entire demand. The real story was that the landowners in the 'Ewa plain had long-range plans for resorts and housing developments, and they wanted to keep the water flowing so it could eventually be used for those purposes.

The black-necked stilt, or ae'o (Himantopus mexicanus knudseni), is endemic to all the main islands of Hawai'i. This wetland wader feeds in taro lo'i and, like the taro farmers, relies on a healthy supply of water to Windward O'ahu streams. *Jack Jeffrey*

(One of the more amusing interludes came during a public hearing. The subject was agriculture. Yukio Kitagawa, director of the state Department of Agriculture, was asked if he considered golf agriculture. He answered, "In a traditional sense, agriculture is the science, art, business of cultivating the soil and production of a crop and livestock. In that sense, management of turf, I consider [golf]

agriculture." The Windward partisans hooted. The water commission later declared that golf is not, after all, agriculture.)

The water commission duly held a meeting among the pretenders to the water, and the Waiahole Irrigation Company agreed to limit the amount of water it sent into the ditch to 8 mgd and restore the remainder to Windward streams.

People in Waiāhole woke up in the middle of the night, thrilled by the sound of water gushing past, a sound that hadn't been heard in the valley for nearly a hundred years. It was Christmas Eve, 1994, and the joy in Waiāhole Valley was overwhelming.

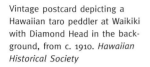

Vintage postcard depicting a Hawaiian taro peddler at Waikiki with Diamond Head in the background, from c. 1910. *Hawaiian Historical Society*

As the Hawai'i Supreme Court would itself later observe, "The interim restoration of windward stream flows had an immediate positive effect on the stream ecology. The higher flows flushed out exotic fish species that were harming native species by carrying parasites and disease, competing for food and space, and interfering with spawning rituals. Experts saw excellent potential for the repopulation of native stream life."

SHOWDOWN AT THE DITCH

The following January 25, the battle commenced in earnest at a so-called contested case hearing before the commission. But before the formal live arguments could begin, there was a bit of unfinished business. The agreement for interim stream restoration that Waiahole Irrigation had signed was to last only six months. It was, therefore, due to expire on June 24, 1995, and rumors abounded that workers were preparing to send the water back through the mountain. The people of Waiāhole and their allies were determined not to let that happen. A group vowed to form a human blockade to stop anyone from turning off their water. Someone padlocked the entrance to the tunnel where the water gate was.

Waiahole Irrigation, for its part, went to court and won an injunction ordering the protesters to leave the area. Television news cameras were stationed at the scene. At the last minute, Waiahole Irrigation blinked and called off its workers. The water was safe. For the moment.

The contested case hearing opened on November 9, 1995. Bill Tam, a deputy attorney general who would eventually draft a proposed decision for the commission and who had observed Hawaiian water battles for many years, described it as an old-fashioned morality play. The themes were colonialism and Native rights and the destruction of nature and right versus wrong. The players were the wealthiest, most powerful families and companies in the islands, a Native population that had been beaten down and stolen from for a century, and a band of upstart environmentalists and their scrappy lawyers.

Paul Achitoff, a recent addition to the Earthjustice staff, would handle the case for the Windward participants. He called upon experts in hydrology, taro farming, stream ecology, Hawaiian culture, estuarine biology, and many other fields. He cross-examined witnesses who testified on behalf of the other parties: the Campbell Estate, the Robinson Estate, the City of Honolulu, Dole–Castle and Cooke, the Department of Land and Natural Resources, and many others. A private attorney named Jim Paul represented the conservation group Hawai'i's Thousand Friends, who handled the argument that the public trust doctrine mandated stream restoration. Lawyers for the Native Hawaiian Legal Corporation assisted with constitutional arguments supporting Native Hawaiian rights.

There were, as reported, twenty-five official parties to the hearing. Eventually, the parties would put on a total of 140 witnesses and submit affidavits from twenty-one more. The hearings themselves would last for nine months, finally drawing to a close in August. The closing arguments were heard toward the end of September 1996.

Achitoff systematically dismembered the Leeward side's arguments in a written brief notable for its flair and informality. The Leeward applicants, each one, in order to secure their permits, must prove a series of points, he wrote. They must demonstrate, among other things, that their proposed use of the water is in the public interest, doesn't inter-

Once the taro is harvested—pulled—some of the stems are cut off with a little of the root or corm left attached. The stalk can be planted in a *lo'i* and will grow a new corm. *Tom Turner*

fere with other legal uses of the water, is consistent with various jurisdictions' land-use plans, and does not run afoul of Native Hawaiian rights. They must also, Achitoff argued, prove that their permit would provide water for purposes that would generate employment and lower the cost of produce to the public; demonstrate a commitment to keeping the former sugar lands in agriculture for a substantial time; and speak to a few other matters, all to the effect that *not* continuing the diversion of Windward water to central O'ahu would spell doom for the Hawaiian economy.

"During the course of the hearing," Achitoff wrote, "these claims were tested. One witness after another either assured the Commission that continued diversion would lead to fabulous benefits for the citizens of Hawai'i, or foretold catastrophe if the Windward streams were restored. One by one, each of these fundamental assertions was shown either to be plainly false, or unsupported by any credible evidence."

And he was just getting started.

Stripped of these rhetorical fig leaves, the identities of the only parties that will clearly benefit from continued diversion of this public trust resource was thrown into relief; their motive emerged clearly. Those parties are the applicants themselves. That motive is their own profit… The personal profit of a group of politically powerful landowners and developers is not an adequate basis for draining streams and depriving them of life, undermining the vitality and future of Windward communities, continuing the slow strangulation of the state's largest estuary, denying the original people of these islands their natural and constitutionally protected rights, and perpetuating a decades-old wrong.

He then set about systematically demolishing the applicants' arguments, often turning their own witnesses against them. The applicants, he demonstrated with their own words, really wanted the Waiāhole water held in reserve for future developments. Any new agriculture established in central Oʻahu would bring economic hardship to existing farms in other parts of the islands. ("Putting small farmers out of business throughout the state so that a few large landowners on Oʻahu can bank water, keep their taxes low, and maximize the return on their lands, and so that a handful of the largest farming operators can monopolize the local market, is hardly consistent with the public interest.")

Once the water began flowing again in Waiāhole Stream, this ʻauwai was filled with water in just one day. Hundreds of volunteers turned out to remove brush and rebuild ʻauwai. *Kapulani Landgraf*

And, he argued, there was ample groundwater available to accommodate all the uses of all the applicants; they wanted Waiāhole water because it was cheap.

There was more, far too much to recount here. We shall leave you with one more of Achitoff's observations, good advice in virtually any proceeding that involves politics, science, natural resources, and expert witnesses:

> All witnesses legally qualified as "experts" are not created equal. Experts vary widely in the depth, scope, and relevance to the issues of their expertise. There are also great differences in motivation among witnesses, including the pecuniary and the political. These differences are critical determinants of a witness's credibility. Where the various experts have offered contradictory or mutually incompatible opinions on the same issue, credibility becomes key.

The experts for the Leeward interests were well paid, he pointed out. Those who testified for the Windward parties were volunteers.

SPLIT DECISION

To a lay reader, Achitoff's brief seems irrefutable, unassailable, utterly compelling. But this was a political exercise as much as a legal one, and the case was far from over. Nearly a year later, on July 15, 1997, the commission produced a proposed decision. It was written by the aforementioned Bill Tam, who had been assigned the job of counsel to the commission for this proceeding. Tam's proposed decision called for dividing the baby: some water to Windward, some to Leeward. It pleased no one. Achitoff called it "fundamentally flawed." The governor of Hawai'i, Ben Cayetano, publicly criticized the proposed decision for not providing more water to the Leeward farmers. The attorney general, Margery Bronster, chimed in, in much the same vein. Bill Tam was unceremoniously sacked, a development that did not go unnoticed by the press.

On December 24, 1997, the final decision was announced: a little over half the flow of the ditch system would be provided to Leeward farmers. A little less than a quarter would be allowed to run down Windward streams. The balance would be considered a "buffer"—for which there was no provision in the water code—a reserve for future farms and golf courses. Much of the water that had been restored to Waiāhole stream and the others on the Windward side was once again thrown into jeopardy.

The Windward petitioners put their heads together and decided to take the case to the Supreme Court of Hawai'i. It was a replay of the water commission proceeding, without the witnesses but with new claims that the partisans had not had a fair hearing, given the public pressure exerted by the governor (on his own appointees), by the attorney general, and by the unceremonious firing of the author of a proposed decision for doing no more or less than his job. In sum, the petitioners' lawyers argued that the commission had not carried out its obligation to protect public trust resources, had not properly enforced the water code, and acted arbitrarily in handing over half of the Waiāhole water

Botanical drawing of taro plant, from a vintage postcard.
Hawaiian Historical Society

to Leeward interests without adequate assurance that doing so would not harm the resources it was required to protect.

The opening briefs were filed on July 1, 1998. Oral argument was held on December 15, 1999, and took up an entire day, a highly unusual, if not unique, expenditure of time on the part of the high court. The court handed down its decision on August 22, 2000. It filled 183 pages, detailed and full of insights and surprises. The court pronounced itself deeply troubled by the intervention of the governor and the attorney general and by the firing of Bill Tam, but stopped short of declaring any of this meddling illegal. It gave a ringing and gratifying endorsement of the public trust doctrine. And, in the end, it found that the final decision issued by the water commission was simply not justified by the record in the case, that it fell woefully short of providing a defensible calculation of the amount of water needed to preserve and restore Waiāhole and other Windward streams. It told the commission to try harder.

As of the autumn of 2001, the case was back before the commission, where some of the arguments would be rehashed, perhaps a few new ones offered. The Department of Land and Natural Resources dropped out, owing to its conflict of interest. Many of the commissioners were new. Two are ranchers and one an executive with Del Monte, which was not promising. Ownership of the ditch system had been assumed by the state, with uncertain consequences. The partisans were cautiously optimistic that the state supreme court's epochal ruling of August 2000 would force the commission to restore a healthy fraction of Waiāhole's water to its original streams and taro patches. A proposed ruling produced by a hearing officer in the summer of 2001 gave something to both Windward and Leeward interests. Depending on what the full commission decides to do, the case could well reach the supreme court again.

Every Wednesday, a troop of volunteers gathers at the *loʻi kalo* in Waiāhole to pull taro, plant taro, weed fallow *loʻi* in preparation for planting, and work on the elaborate but elegantly simple plumbing system of *ʻauwai* that allows Paul Reppun, Danny Bishop, Meaʻala Bishop, and others to move water from one *loʻi* to the next. Kaipo Faris ambles by with bottles in hand to continue his monitoring of the stream's temperature and chemistry. He will also check up on the hundreds of *hihiwai*—single-shelled freshwater mollusks that once grew to edible size—they had to import from Molokaʻi to restock the stream. Everyone brings food to share for lunch, and depending on the season, there will be bananas, papayas, grapefruit, and mangoes to pluck from nearby trees. Ricky Reppun brings an avocado the size of a football from a tree on his place and sets about making guacamole.

The meal begins with taro, of course, and a good-natured argument over the relative merits of one variety over another. Dozens of varieties grow in these *loʻi*. Some mature faster than others, some can be left in the ground longer without rotting. To an outsider, the difference in flavor is vanishingly subtle.

Until recently, schoolchildren regularly came to the site to learn about their heritage and get good and muddy. The state owns the land, however, and has so far not issued formal permits for the taro farming that has been under way ever since the water was restored at the end of 1994. There are insurance problems, and a neighbor has been grouchy, so the schoolkids' visits have been temporarily suspended, to everyone's regret.

The Wednesday gatherings bring people from near and far to get a hard day's exercise, a sack of taro, and to connect themselves to pre-European Hawai'i. The feel of cool water lapping at your heels as you pull taro in exactly the same way a Hawaiian might have done more than a thousand years ago is a powerful experience, a very different perspective on life in the twenty-first century.

Water flowing freely in Waiāhole Stream. *Kapulani Landgraf*

CHAPTER FIVE

MAKING THE GARCIA SAFE FOR SALMON

When California was part of Mexico, from 1821 to 1848, great tracts of land were given to prominent citizens. One was Ralph Garcia, who, on November 15, 1844, was granted nine leagues—approximately thirty miles—along the coast from Fort Ross north to the river that now bears his name. The Garcia drains a watershed of a little more than a hundred square miles between the Russian River to the south and the Eel to the north. The land grows dense with redwood, Douglas fir, tan oak, and madrone.

The region once supported thriving communities of Native Americans, whose cultures substantially depended on salmon and steelhead for food and as sources of myth and history. The forests were so vast that they seemed nearly endless, and little thought was given to using them up—or to the consequences of removing the tree cover from this dramatic up-and-down landscape. Following on the heels of the gold rush, the timber industry went after these forests in earnest. Wood was plentiful and therefore relatively cheap: the streets of San Francisco were first paved with redwood. The fish were likewise plentiful and inexpensive. In those days, salmon was poor people's food.

But by the end of the twentieth century almost all the watersheds had been at least partly logged, and the populations of fish in the rivers had crashed or disappeared altogether. In the late 1990s the fishery for coho (silver) salmon was closed, fishing for chinook (king) salmon was strictly regulated, and virtually all fishing for steelhead was confined to the catch-and-release variety.

Opposite: Restoration work taking place on the Garcia River tributary of Bluewater Hole Creek at Bewley Ranch. This shows the first year of a streamside planting project. Hardwood trees are planted next to the protective posts. *Peter Dobbins*

A long series of petitions and lawsuits in the late 1980s and '90s resulted in Endangered Species Act protection for scores of runs. Salmon are identified by the seasons in which they spawn: "spring-run," for example, or "winter-run." One river system can have as many as four distinct subspecies of the same species, patiently awaiting their turn for a trip back up the river. But listing under the ESA wasn't enough. Many runs were still in steep decline. So attention turned to the daunting task of restoration: how to undo the terrible damage inflicted on the fishes' natal streams, particularly the spawning grounds?

Legally, toward the end of the 1990s, the action moved from the Endangered Species Act to the Clean Water Act and a provision vigorously ignored for two decades and more, until private lawyers, fishermen, and other activists started making nuisances of themselves—about which more presently.

On the ground, local organizations and their seagoing allies—salmon fishermen who had watched as their livelihood dwindled—turned their attention to the cause of the problem. In the watershed of the Garcia, the problem was quite simple: logging. The reckless logging of steep slopes and, worse, the carving of poorly engineered, unmaintained roads provided a perpetual source of silt and mud that washed into the river and its feeder creeks whenever it rained, smothering spawning beds and turning the water a sickly brown.

In addition, the removal of streamside trees let more sunlight reach the stream and raised its temperature to levels that, in the low-water summer and autumn months, is lethal to baby salmon, which at that stage of life—making their magical journey to the open ocean—are known as smolts. And if all that weren't enough insult, the timber industry's practice of cutting all the big trees along the watercourses had deprived the river of another vital component, what the scientists call "large woody debris": logs that form pools in creeks and streams, which provide necessary resting places for young fish, places where they can avoid a too-early ride to the sea and where they can hide from herons and other predators. As a measure of how little was known of the fishes' requirements, until the mid-1980s the California Department of Fish and Game required loggers to clear streams of this large woody debris.

The pond and dam at the head of the flume on the Garcia River, c. 1898. On just one day early in 1893, more than 5,000 ties were sent down the seven-mile flume to Rollerville. The old Garcia Mill, built in 1869-70, produced 8 million board feet per year, all of it flumed out to Rollerville. Photographer unknown, but probably W. W. Fairbanks. *Collection Robert J. Lee/Mendocino County Historical Society*

At the beginning of the twentieth century, the lower reaches of the Garcia were active. There was a town called Garcia with a lumber mill, which processed logs felled in the upper reaches of the watershed and floated down the river. This was done in a curious fashion made necessary by the fact that the Garcia seldom has enough water in it to float logs in the summer and fall months. To conquer this problem, the loggers would build what they called splash dams to back up enough water to float the logs, then dynamite the dams to allow the water to float the logs down to the mill. But stopping the logs at the mill site was another challenge. They built a series of reinforced pylons in the river to slow the logs and divert them toward the mill. There, the logs were sawn into railroad ties and delivered via a long flume to the site of the present Highway 1 at a spot near the Point Arena lighthouse dubbed Rollerville, so called because an ingenious hydraulic device would lift the ties up a hill and roll them into train cars. From there, they were delivered to the harbor at Point Arena and loaded onto ships by means of aerial cables.

The system, taken together, was not kind to the river and its banks. The mill closed around 1905, and the buildings were destroyed by fire in about 1915. A fishing resort flourished for a time, but what few buildings remain have stood empty for thirty years or more. By the 1980s the Garcia was a pretty

Above: Looking up the Rollerville incline, c. 1882. A hydraulic device carried lumber up the steep 300-foot incline to waiting train cars. *Inset:* The water wheel that powered the lifting mechanism. *Below:* One of the trains that transported lumber from the Garcia watershed to the Point Arena harbor, 1914. *Collection Robert J. Lee/Mendocino County Historical Society*

sorry mess, the town of Garcia long gone. Louisiana-Pacific had stripped most of the drainage, then sold out to the Mendocino Redwood Company, owned by heirs to the fortune amassed by the Gap clothing empire. In the Garcia watershed at least, the Mendocino Redwood people promised to do a world-class project of restoration.

Down at the coast in Point Arena meanwhile, a band of former hippies, fishermen, farmers, and big-city refugees decided to take matters into their own hands. They declared themselves the Friends of the Garcia River (generally rendered FrOG) and set out to learn how to restore their beloved watershed. They were joined by the Coast Action Group, which had been formed by what CAG's present leader, Alan Levine, calls new settlers, to impede the subdivision and overdevelopment of the land in and near Point Arena.

AN ACT WITHOUT ACTION

The protection of the sources and purity of water for human consumption, agriculture, recreation, and other purposes has always been a prime responsibility of governments. Federal water law in the United States dates from the early days of the republic. Yet by the 1970s, a conceptual collision loomed on the horizon in Washington, D.C.

In 1948 Congress declared that the prime responsibility for water-pollution control resided with the states. In 1965 it required each state to work up plans for protecting streams and lakes that crossed state lines. These programs were to set standards of water quality rather than regulate specific pollutants, but there was no enforceable mechanism to guarantee that the standards would be achieved.

In 1966 the Supreme Court muddied the waters in a ruling that reinvigorated the Refuse Act of 1899. That law said that nearly all discharges of foreign substances and pollutants into public waterways were illegal unless blessed by the Army Corps of Engineers. Thus, Congress and the Supreme Court were at odds.

Congress saw its duty. It enacted the Federal Water Pollution Control Act Amendments of 1972, overriding President Nixon's veto (although Mr. Nixon would later claim credit for enactment of the law). The amendments marked a dramatic departure in approach. They amounted to a thorough rewrite of the law, which became familiarly known—and is now formally called—the Clean Water Act. The effort to achieve water-quality standards was given teeth: for the first time, the law required direct regulation of discharges of foreign matter and pollutants into lakes and streams from discrete sources such as pipes or ditches. These are known as "point sources."

"Large woody debris," an essential component of healthy streams, provides vital shelter for young fish journeying to the sea. Logging all the big trees along watercourses deprives rivers and fish of such resting places. *Peter Dobbins*

But point sources are not the whole problem, not even half the problem. In some watersheds, like the Garcia, virtually all pollution is carried by rainwater off farms and fields, roads and logged-over lands, parking lots and strip mines. These are known as "nonpoint sources."

The Clean Water Act set up an elaborate National Pollution Discharge Elimination System (NPDES) to control point sources, one that involves permits and self-monitoring reports and other systems and requirements. But what if cleaning up point sources doesn't render a lake or river clean enough to swim or fish in? In that case, the states are required to identify which lakes, streams, or segments of streams are "impaired," these being called "water-quality limited segments"; determine how much pollution the water body could tolerate and still support fishing and swimming; see by how much the pollution must be reduced to reach that goal; set up a ranked list of which water bodies should be cleaned up first; and then work out an allocation system among all dischargers—point and nonpoint alike—to achieve the reductions.

The resultant tolerable levels are called TMDLs, for total maximum daily loads. ("TMDL" is also often used to identify the documents that regulate discharges of various materials.) It all sounds difficult and tedious, and it probably is. We don't have enough experience to know for sure, because the states universally ignored that provision of the law for more than twenty years.

So did the Environmental Protection Agency. The Clean Water Act gives the states the task of dealing with pollution within their boundaries. The EPA is the overseer. Once the state writes a plan to regulate dischargers, it submits the plan to the EPA for approval. If the plan is not up to snuff—or if a state fails to submit any plan at all—the EPA is required to impose its own regulations.

The Clean Water Act of 1972 required that TMDLs be determined for polluted waterways by 1979, either by the states or, if the states failed to act, by the EPA. The response of the states and the EPA alike is but one of many shining reasons why there are public-interest environmental law organizations in the United States. The states were too busy with other matters. EPA tackled point sources first, and the NPDES led to dramatic improvements to waterways across the country, but nonpoint sources were ignored. Congress had bespoken itself on the matter and was busy getting rid of Richard Nixon to boot. It would fall to private groups to see that the law was enforced. Eventually.

ENTER JOE BRECHER

Joe Brecher began his public-interest work at the Native American Rights Fund in Boulder, Colorado, where he represented several Southwest tribes in the 1970s in battles over strip mines and coal-fired power plants. There, he made the acquaintance of attorneys involved with the Sierra Club, which also was a plaintiff in some of the cases. Brecher was hired by Earthjustice to work on a case involving coal-fired power plants in 1975, and later he litigated challenges to timber harvest plans—including two on the widely known Headwaters forest—and a variety of other matters.

In 1980, he built a modest vacation cabin just over the ridge from Point Arena, a mile or so directly up the hill from the Garcia River. Brecher and his family would spend long stretches of each summer there, and Joe met and befriended many of the people in the small, close-knit community. One of their chief concerns was the decline of the river; where once it teemed with steelhead and boasted healthy populations of coho and chinook, now everything was going to hell. The chinook had disappeared altogether and the coho were going fast. Logging was proceeding at a terrific pace in the steep, friable valleys upstream, and a local fellow named Billy Hay was running a major gravel-mining operation smack-dab in the middle of the river.

Steelhead trout *(Oncorhynchus mykiss)*, drawing by Dugald Stermer

Brecher and friends decided to tackle the gravel mine first.

Billy Hay had a permit for his gravel operation, issued by Mendocino County and good for ten years. When the ten years were up, he applied for a renewal. The county said fine. But on behalf of FrOG and the Coast Action Group, Brecher said, Not so fast: you need to prepare an environmental impact report; the California Environmental Quality Act says so. The county was not in the habit of preparing EIRs and told Brecher to take a hike. On February 4, 1988, he filed suit on behalf of the Garcia's partisans, and after a protracted and acrimonious struggle that involved violence and the carrying of firearms, the suit was won.

The EIR was duly prepared and, for once doing what such

Dawn on the Big River. This river flows through a watershed north of the Garcia, entering the Pacific at the town of Mendocino. Like the Garcia, it has felt the impact of waves of logging since the 1880s, though it has not been as affected by pollution from cattle grazing. *John Birchard*

documents are supposed to do, it found that continuing the gravel operation would cause major environmental harm to the river. Mr. Hay moved his operation to a safer upland location. Soon thereafter, however, he applied for permission to expand a gravel crushing and sorting operation he maintained with the city limits of Point Arena. The city said fine. Brecher and CAG again demanded an EIR and won. This time Brecher sent a bill to the Point Arena City Council, as the winning party can sometimes do in cases like this one. The councilors grumbled, but finally paid the bill.

Meanwhile, several of the attorneys in Earthjustice had been chewing over a new idea. What about trying to use the nonpoint source section of the Clean Water Act to force the cleanup of streams where the NPDES wasn't doing the job?

Kristen Boyles in Seattle had already filed a lawsuit—in July 1993—against the EPA for failing to impose TMDLs for the whole state of Idaho. Idaho had produced a list of 962 contaminated stream segments, then announced it would write cleanup plans for thirty-six of them. EPA approved the plan. Boyles, on behalf of the Idaho Sporting Congress and the Idaho Conservation League, argued in court that leaving 95 percent

of the impaired lakes and streams unattended was preposterous and illegal. The court agreed. EPA added the 926 stream segments to the cleanup roster. The judge asked EPA to come back in a year with a timetable for issuing the TMDLs.

A year later, EPA submitted a schedule that, depending how one read it, promised to get the job done in twenty-five, or maybe a hundred, years. Boyles went back to court to point out gently that the Clean Water Act expects this job to be done in considerably less than one year. Again the judge told EPA to try harder. "Nothing in the law could justify so glacial a pace," was the court's exact observation. Eventually Boyles, EPA, and the state of Idaho agreed on an eight-year schedule, with the plaintiffs getting to help determine which stream segments would be tackled first. Idaho's streams are affected by a range of assaults: sedimentation from logging and road building, runoff from old mines, damage inflicted by livestock, and more.

Tentative Steps

In the case of the Garcia, the situation was stark and clear. There were no point sources of pollution. With the gravel operation under control, the remaining problem was sediment washing off roads and logged-over lands.

The state of California actually had taken tentative first steps toward determining its TMDLs in 1990, when it began to put together a list of the state's lakes and streams that did not meet federal water-quality standards. In 1991, EPA asked to see the list. There were 239 water bodies on it. Not a single North Coast stream was on the list, even though the state of salmon populations in North Coast rivers indicated that those waterways were in serious trouble as well.

EPA asked what was up. The state said, There's no problem on those rivers. EPA disagreed, and threatened to take over the assessment process. The state still refused to list any of the North Coast waterways, so EPA listed seventeen rivers as impaired, mostly by current or historic logging operations. It was December 1994, and the state, though it had relented and listed those seventeen as impaired, said explicitly that it would not be writing any TMDLs for them.

But the Clean Water Act requires the states to determine TMDLs "promptly."

A year passed, with no evidence that either the state or the EPA was doing anything toward producing TMDLs, stretching the definition of prompt. Joe Brecher had let it be known among the North Coast organizations he had worked with for many years that a lawsuit might be necessary to get action to restore the rivers, and just in case, he had built a coalition of fourteen client groups led by FrOG, the West Coast Federation of Fishermen's Associations, the Coast Action Group, and the Sierra Club.

Brecher now decided it was time to goose the process along. He telephoned and requested a meeting with EPA brass. He was dressed, as usual, in a sweater. EPA was represented by a dozen lawyers and functionaries, natty in suits and neckties. "It took three hours for EPA to get around to saying, 'Go ask the state,' " Brecher remembers.

So he hied himself off to the North Coast Regional Water Quality Control Board, the

Opposite: Aerial view of the lower Garcia River at Oz Farm, an organic farm and retreat center. The farmer practices limited, sustainable timber harvesting, leaving trees growing close to the riverbanks, as the photo shows. *Peter Dobbins*

The Garcia would be first, and on March 16, 1998, the EPA issued a TMDL for the river. The TMDL spoke of road design and construction methods. It described how culverts should be placed. It suggested prohibitions on running heavy equipment over muddy roads, meaning either the roads should be paved or work should be avoided during the rainy season. It recommended staying away from logging or road building on very steep slopes, and other measures aimed at minimizing sedimentation.

The TMDL was forwarded to the North Coast Regional Water Quality Control Board, the first step in a fiercely complicated and convoluted journey that runs through the State Water Resources Control Board, the governor's Office of Administrative Law, and finally back to the EPA for formal certification. There were many hitches and delays along the way, with the Garcia TMDL bouncing back and forth among the agencies for nearly four years. Finally, early in 2002, all the approvals were secured, and the Garcia TMDL was enshrined in state law.

But it won't be until another awkward matter has been settled. Back in the spring of 1999 a challenge was presented on behalf of Betty and Guido Pronsolino. Years before, the couple had bought approximately eight hundred acres of cutover land in the upper Garcia watershed, hoping to regrow timber they could sell to finance their retirement. They applied to the state for a timber harvest permit. The California Department of

Peter Reimuller and other restoration workers plant trees along Bluewater Hole Creek, a tributary of the Garcia that had been severely damaged by conversion of land to grazing in the 1980s. *Peter Dobbins*

Forestry, acting as if a firm TMDL were in place, gave the Pronsolinos their permit, but with conditions. The owners would have to locate sources of sediment that would result from logging their lands and reduce the volume that reached the river by 90 percent, prevent any sedimentation from road building from entering any waterways, leave standing a modicum of mature trees to hold the hillsides in place, and harvest only between May and October, when it almost never rains. The Pronsolinos calculated that abiding by these provisions would cost them upwards of three quarters of a million dollars. On April 12, 1999, they sued.

There is some evidence that the Pronsolinos themselves might have complied with the requirements but were encouraged by the American Farm Bureau to fight. The bureau is terribly afraid that the mostly free ride farmers and ranchers have had under the water pollution laws might one day come to an end, and they would love to nip any such unpatriotic outcome in the bud. (As a sop to big agriculture, the Clean Water Act exempts farmers from the NPDES program, forbidding the administrator of the EPA from requiring permits for "discharges composed entirely of return flows from irrigated agriculture.") The Pronsolinos were joined in their lawsuit by the Mendocino County Farm Bureau, the California Farm Bureau Federation, and the American Farm Bureau Federation. They went for the kill.

The plaintiffs asked the court to find that the EPA had no authority under the Clean Water Act to issue TMDLs for water bodies, like the Garcia, that are impaired only by nonpoint sources of pollution. Had the case succeeded, it would have maimed the entire TMDL process that had been created—though left to languish—by Congress in 1972. Joe Brecher and his band of clients, expanded to include San Francisco BayKeeper, intervened in the case to defend

One-time Friends of the Garcia board member Eric Dahlhof surveys a stretch of Bluewater Hole Creek. *Peter Dobbins*

EPA's authority. The state of California chipped in with a friend of the court brief that vigorously supported EPA.

The case was assigned to William Alsup, who had served as a clerk to Supreme Court Justice William O. Douglas during the term when the court heard and decided a case involving Mineral King valley in the Sierra Nevada—a case that became a landmark in opening the courts to citizens wishing to advocate on behalf of environmental protection. Alsup was new to the bench, having wriggled through the battlements set up by Senate Republicans in the mid-1990s to block nominations submitted by President Clinton. Judge Alsup was able to beat the blockade by having his home-state senator, Trent Lott of Mississippi, go to bat for him.

Following a series of briefs and an oral argument, Judge Alsup issued his decision. It contains a masterly synopsis of the evolution of water-pollution law in the United States, harking back to the 1899 Refuse Act. And it concludes that Congress certainly did give EPA the authority and responsibility to regulate nonpoint sources of pollution, even when they're the only problem. The Pronsolinos and the Farm Bureaus lodged an appeal with the Ninth Circuit. At the end of 2001, the appeals court was still mulling over its decision.

By early 2001, the Environmental Protection Agency could count eighteen states where it was under court order or had entered into a consent decree agreeing to a timetable for producing TMDLs if the states fail to do so, and eight more where suits

Gasker Slough on Hathaway Creek, another Garcia tributary, and its seasonal wetlands as they looked before a rancher got a permit in the early 1990s to excavate the creek and drain the wetlands. Not all the damage to the Garcia River watershed is in the distant past. *Peter Dobbins*

were pending or negotiations under way. All these activities were the result of lawsuits or the threat of lawsuits filed by Earthjustice and its kindred organizations on behalf of scores of client groups large and small. Why the states and the federal government have been so reluctant to obey the clear dictates of the Clean Water Act is a question for another day.

A River Returns

It is an unusually fine day in late February 2001. There has been a break in the parade of wet winter storms, and we are touring the South Fork of the Garcia with Craig Bell, who, in addition to guiding steelhead anglers to the best pools, represents Trout Unlimited as an advisor on reclamation activities. The land is owned by the Mendocino Redwood Company, which is picking up the tab for the restoration work. Bell talks as fast as he walks.

He is quite exercised this morning about California's governor, who has recently suspended rules meant to protect young salmon and trout from lethally high water temperatures. The problem is the state's energy crisis, and Gray Davis (Bell calls him "Graywater Davis") has said, in Bell's opinion, that avoiding blackouts is more important than avoiding salmon extinction. The governor has also incurred Bell's wrath—and that of all the FrOGs and many others—by removing environmentalists from various appointed positions and replacing them with their natural adversaries. For example: Point Arena's conservation-minded mayor, Leslie Dahlhoff, served on the North Coast Regional Quality Control Board until 2000. When her term expired, Governor Graywater replaced her with a rancher. Other vacancies have gone unfilled, so at the end of 2001 the board did not have enough members to produce a quorum and thus was unable actually to do anything.

Bell proudly shows where big redwood logs have been lowered into the creek, anchored to streamside boulders with thick steel cables to form pools. He leads us quickly up a road that had been put to bed by Louisiana-Pacific, then reopened in order to provide access to a landing where thousands of cubic yards of dirt had once been dumped into a narrow declivity where two small creeks merge. A rusting culvert bears witness to the fact that the vast pile of spoils would have contributed fish-killing sediment to the river system approximately forever. The fill has now been pulled out of the streambed, which has been recontoured to more or less its original shape, the hillsides thatched and planted with tiny redwoods.

"Some people object to using heavy machinery for this work," Bell says. "I think it sometimes takes heavy equipment to undo damage caused by heavy equipment in the first place." It will take many years, but the Garcia—along with many other streams on the North Coast—is on its way back.

It may, however, take years for the salmon to make a comeback. Chinook haven't been in evidence since the 1980s. Craig Bell hasn't seen a coho in four or five years. It may be possible to release hatchery-bred smolts into the river once it has been cleaned up sufficiently and fool them into returning to spawn again like wild salmon, but that's a way down the road, and no one knows whether it will work: too much genetic diversity may already have been lost. Bell does say with pride that the day before our tour he had brought a group of schoolkids to the South Fork in time to see a female steelhead wiggle around to scoop out a redd—a shallow ditch in the stream-bottom gravel—deposit her eggs, and then watch as a male arrived to fertilize the eggs with his milt.

The next day the fair weather holds, and we canoe the bottom half-dozen miles of the Garcia in the company of Peter Dobbins, who fled the overamped world of advertising photography in Los Angeles twenty years ago and landed in Point Arena, where he spends much of his time rallying support for the Garcia and for FrOG. He points out where the gravel-mining operation used to be, and the sawmill, and the town of Garcia. He gestures hopefully at small tributaries that discharge what appears to be perfectly clear water into the main Garcia. He points to two spots near the site of the gravel mine where menacing rifle shots were once lobbed across his bow. A cackling kingfisher leads us downstream. Elegant blue herons and green herons studiously ignore us as we paddle quietly by their sandbars.

Great blue heron (Ardea herodias), drawing by Dugald Stermer

CHAPTER SIX

OF ROBBER BARONS, GATORS, AND GREED

In central Florida, there is a waterway known as Fisheating Creek, a translation of the Caloosa Indian word *Thlothlopopka*. The name works in a couple of ways: the creek is a good place to catch and eat fish, but once it was also a stream so choked with fish that it appeared to have eaten them. Either way, it is a lovely stream, lined with live oaks and cabbage palms and palmettos and bald cypresses draped with Spanish moss, and enjoyed by generations of Glades County residents, who swim, catch fish, boat, hunt deer and boar and turkey and alligators (sometimes legally), even baptize their children in its waters. They have been doing so since the 1880s. Centuries before that, the area was inhabited by the Caloosa people, who built low mounds, or hillocks, to keep their encampments safely above the floodwaters occasioned by frequent tropical storms and less frequent hurricanes. It is a tranquil place, where life moves slowly and the air is soft and comforting.

But in the spring of 1989, an event occurred that would arouse Glades County as never before. One day, people put their boats into the creek, only to find their way blocked by big cypress trees that had been chainsawed so that they fell across the water-way, blocking access. Eventually, they discovered that some forty cypresses had been felled. Later, barbed-wire and steel fences were erected, one less than ten miles from where the creek debouches into Lake Okeechobee. Nailed to the cypress trees were signs saying "Fisheating Creek Is Not a Navigable Stream—Trespassers Will Be Prosecuted [signed] Lykes Bros. Inc." The "not navigable" description may seem a bit odd and patently untrue, but on it hangs our tale, and a lively one it is.

When Juan Ponce de León first visited the land that would later be named Florida in April of 1513, the southern third of the peninsula was a vast wetland extending from Lake Okeechobee, through what is now the Big Cypress Reserve and Everglades National Park, to Florida Bay and the Keys, where the Atlantic Ocean meets the Gulf of Mexico. Modern-day Glades County, through which Fisheating Creek flows, was much like the Everglades, a wet prairie covered with water grasses and marshes that would flood and dry with the seasons but remain wet enough, long enough, to discourage the growth of trees. This would change with time as developers descended on south Florida in the 1880s. They dug drains and canals to lower the water levels in order to dry out the marshes and swamps for agriculture.

Opposite: A grand old oak stands beside Fisheating Creek, south of Picnic Lake. The photographer visited in January, when the water level in the creek was low. *James Valentine*

Alligators are common in the creek and are hunted for their skins and meat. *Joel Sartore*

In the natural scheme of things, during the six-month summer rainy season, the streams that feed Lake Okeechobee—Fisheating Creek is the second biggest, after the Kissimmee River—would fill the lake to overflowing. The water would crest the shore of the lake and spread for miles, working its way slowly south, watering the Everglades and everything between. This was the famed "river of grass" where the Seminole Indians lived until the United States waged a series of three wars against them and eventually killed many, evicted some, and chased others deep into the Everglades, where they tried to live their lives in peace. Lake Okeechobee—the second-biggest lake that is wholly within the United States—in those days was rich in aquatic life. In the 1920s it produced three boxcars-full of dressed catfish daily. That fishery crashed by 1933 and has yet to recover.

The first Europeans to explore and settle Florida were the Spanish, during the 1500s. They divided the state into east and west Florida, the latter stretching from the Suwannee River to New Orleans. During the Revolutionary War, Florida belonged—and remained loyal—to England. Spain had been active in that war, taking sides against the British, and won back control of both Floridas in 1784. Ties with the United States grew stronger as the population swelled with newcomers from the north, and Spain ceded Florida to the States in 1821.

Back then, rivers and streams were the routes of transportation—the legal term, which will play a considerable role in our story, is *artery of internal communication.* Goods were delivered on skiffs and other floating conveyances. People made journeys on boats as well. There were few roads, because the land was crisscrossed with streams and swamps. Bridges and ferries were few and far between.

In 1883, a young industrialist named Hamilton Disstan decided that he'd carve himself an artery in the form of a canal from Lake Okeechobee west to the Caloosahatchee River, the better to transport cargoes of oranges, grapefruit, alligator hides, and otter and coon skins to New Orleans and Tampa and other Gulf ports. On the return journey he would transport salt, tobacco, gunpowder, knives, axes, and other supplies to the trading posts in central Florida.

The canal worked more or less as planned, and it had at least one other profound effect, intended or otherwise. It substantially lowered the level of Lake Okeechobee.

That allowed the lake's feeder streams—Fisheating Creek et al.—to drain much faster, and that in turn caused the surrounding watersheds to dry out to the point where cypress and oak and other trees could begin to grow. It also allowed more land surrounding the lake to be used for ranching and for growing sugarcane, oranges, lemons, grapefruit, and other crops. Bonanza.

In fact, the drainage project worked well enough that it became the official policy of the state government to drain the entirety of south Florida, to do away with the mosquito- and gator-infested Everglades, turn the land to productive uses, and make lots of people very rich. They eventually dredged another five long canals to drain away the water from Lake Okeechobee and discharge it into the Atlantic Ocean, thus cutting off much of the water that sustained the Everglades and lowering the water table upstream. By the

Lake Okeechobee was once the scene of a thriving catfish fishery. Today that fishery is gone. One can still catch bass in the lake, but phosphorus-laden runoff from dairies and pastures to the north has taken its toll. *James Valentine*

1950s they had created the Everglades Agricultural Area, six hundred thousand acres, most of it devoted to sugarcane. As is so often the case with large public-works projects like this one, there were unforeseen—and catastrophic—consequences.

For one thing, the region became prone to disastrous fires, like those that ravaged the Everglades in 1999 and again the following year. For another, the early canals draining Lake Okeechobee were dramatically undersized. Even with the hurricane gates fully open, big tropical storms would drop enough water to overtop the lakeshore and produce major floods. This led to the building of a muck dike around the lake in the early 1920s.

In the summer of 1926, a mighty hurricane hit Glades County, blowing out the dike on the west side of the lake and drowning almost all the residents of Moore Haven, the county seat. The entire county and all its settlements were devastated. Two years later, another hurricane hit the region, this time breaching the dike near Clewiston and killing almost three thousand residents. There may have been a message in there somewhere, but people are notoriously slow to learn such lessons.

Lykes Brothers owned a great deal besides the land adjacent to Fisheating Creek, including Sunkist and Florigold orange juice. Vintage orange crate label, c. 1930s. *Private collection*

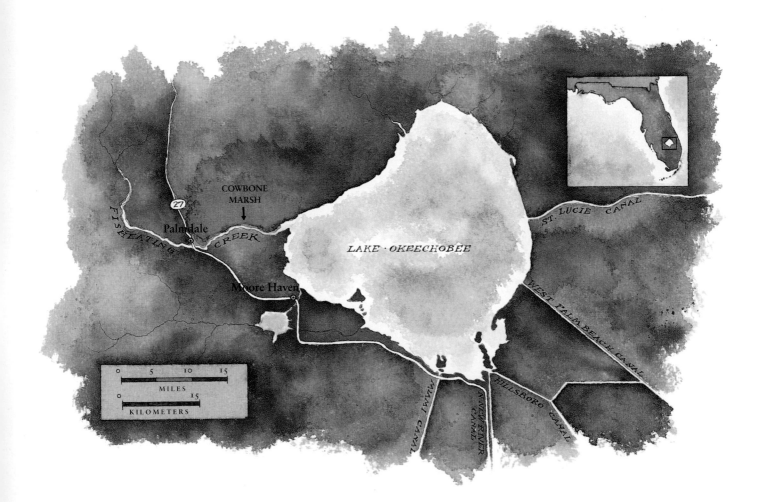

JUSTICE ON EARTH

THE LORDS OF LUNCHMEAT

Along about this time, an enter-
prising company founded by
seven brothers began to take
advantage of Glades County's
misery by buying thousands of
acres for as little as a dime an
acre. The brothers were the
sons of Dr. Howell Tyson Lykes.
They and their single sister were
born in the years between 1877
and 1888, which suggests a virile
father and a resilient mother. In
any event, in 1910 the siblings
became Lykes Brothers,
Incorporated, and by the mid-
1930s, the Great Depression having finished what the hurricanes
started, they wound up owning
two-thirds of Glades County—
nearly three hundred thousand
acres—including the land on
either side of Fisheating Creek.

Over succeeding decades,
the brothers built a mighty

At Ingram's Crossing on Fisheating Creek, cypress knees poke
up next to the tree's main trunk.
The function of the knees is
unknown. *James Valentine*

empire and made themselves fabulously wealthy. They raised cattle and sold hot dogs
and bologna. They owned and operated the First Florida Bank. They raised citrus and
produced and sold Sunkist and Florigold orange juice. They dealt in real estate. They
acquired and ran racetracks and resorts in Texas. They cut and sold timber. They produced and marketed natural gas through People's Gas. And they owned and operated a
major international shipping company to deliver their products to ports of call around the
world. They became one of the largest privately held companies in the United States.

They also essentially owned Glades County. County commissioners, judges, and the
sheriff would generally avoid doing anything that Lykes did not want them to do, and
criticism of the company was discouraged. They were, in the words of Earthjustice attorney David Guest, "classic robber barons."

"People told me the county clerk would keep a signed blank check drawn on a Lykes
account in his drawer with instructions to buy any parcel of land that came to the county
when the owner failed to pay his taxes on time," Guest remembers. The story goes that
someone asked old Tom Lykes, the patriarch of the clan through the 1950s, whether he
wanted all the land. "No. Just all the land that's next to mine" was his reported answer.

American wood storks *(Mycteria americana)* flock in a south Florida tree. *Joel Sartore*

Nevertheless, life in Glades County was more or less peaceful through most of the twentieth century, with a few exceptions. In the early '30s, there was considerable tension between the Lykes company and people who had been grazing cattle and hogs on the land before Lykes bought it. The livestock was kept unfenced on the open range back then, and residents would occasionally venture into the woods to hunt what they figured were cows and hogs descended from animals they may have owned earlier. Residents had been warned that this practice—arguably rustling—must stop. It did not, and eventually three men who were out hunting livestock were murdered at a place that became known as Dead Man's Pond on Gator Slough. No one was ever convicted of the crime.

For many decades, most of the population of Glades County was closely tied to Lykes Brothers in one way or another, and the company allowed locals to hunt wild game on its land. Lykes also opened a campground for fishermen and others on the creek at what was left of Palmdale, which had been nearly razed by the hurricane of 1928. The site had been given to the county by the brothers for a park. Subsequently the county gave it back, and Lykes did a thriving business renting canoes for use on a waterway the company would brand "not navigable" a few years later.

In the 1970s and 1980s, the chieftain of the Lykes empire was Charles Lykes, Sr., a grandson of old H. T. Lykes. Mr. Charlie was a shrewd businessman and a stern but kindly employer, liked by most people in the county. He would make occasional donations to local schools and lent a plot of land for a church. But in February of 1989, Mr. Charlie was diagnosed with leukemia. Four months later he was dead. Control over the Glades County part of the Lykes enterprise passed to Mr. Charlie's son, Charles Jr.—another manner of man altogether.

The previous year, Charlie Jr. had abruptly closed the campground at Palmdale, saying he was afraid a canoeist would get hurt and sue the company. Thirty or forty people lost their jobs on five minutes' notice, and resentment of the company began to grow. In the election the fall following Mr. Charlie's death, Lykes sympathizers were swept from the county board of commissioners and replaced by Lykes critics.

The change in attitude had started, some say, when new people began moving in to the county following World War II. Retirees moved north from Miami because prices were lower and the pace of life slower. Others began to visit from the north, as the invention of the camper shell—in these parts called "piggybacks"— and the advent of Social Security made it possible for less-than-wealthy people to vacation in Florida. Where Glades County had been the Lykes Brothers' private fiefdom, it was slowly being opened to the outside world. And the outside world was not necessarily willing to dance to the Lykes tune. David Guest dubbed the growing resistance "a peasant revolution."

One of the first acts of the new commissioners was to move to reopen an old road that ran from near Palmdale down to the creek, a road people had used steadily until Lykes put up a gate and kept it locked. A large crowd was on hand as creek liberators took a blowtorch to the metal gate. Lykes had two men stationed in trees nearby with video cameras taping the whole affair, and immediately filed suit against the county commissioners for authorizing trespassing and vandalism.

And soon, Lykes engaged in a bit of vandalism of its own. It dredged twenty-two miles of canals with none of the necessary permits, possibly to drain away water headed for

The Peace River, not far north of Fisheating Creek, was the site of another legal battle over ownership and navigability, in which Earthjustice attorney David Guest took part while working for the Florida attorney general's office. *James Valentine*

Fisheating Creek and make it appear less navigable. A company representative first produced a three-year-old permit for another project altogether, then claimed it was all a terrible mistake. Eventually the head of the state's environmental agency, Carol Browner, who would serve as head of the federal Environmental Protection Agency in the Clinton administration, extracted fines of several million dollars from Lykes and forced the company to fill in all the illegal canals.

Soon after, in early 1989, the trees came splashing down across Fisheating Creek and the battle was joined in earnest.

THE CREEK FINDS A CHAMPION

The phone jangled in David Guest's office one day in early 1989. The caller, whose identity has unfortunately been lost, was wondering whether Florida's attorney general could help him with a small problem. It seemed that someone had felled a whole bunch of trees across a popular creek in central Florida and claimed the waterway as private property.

Guest, who finished only one year of high school but did finish law school at the University of Chicago, had been working as an assistant to Florida attorney general Bob Butterworth for a few years and had achieved a considerable measure of fame when he bested Mobil Oil in another river-ownership battle, that one concerning the Peace River, not far north of Fisheating Creek. Mobil sued over mineral rights beneath the river, contending that the river was non-navigable and therefore private property. Butterworth and

David Guest relaxes on the creek in the back of a skiff piloted by Smiley Hendry Jr. *Tom Turner*

Guest joined in a ferocious legal battle to protect the river. The case was decided when Guest and a team of young upstarts found and excavated the remains of an eighty-four-foot boat sunk in the muddy bed of the river, which pretty much put the navigability question to rest.

Guest called around and concluded that what Lykes had done at Fisheating Creek looked like a rather egregious violation of state law. Butterworth and he decided to conduct a formal hearing in Moore Haven to let people present their versions of what happened.

The hearing was held on May 20, 1989, at the agricultural center auditorium in Moore Haven. "We'd been having some trouble in the legislature," Guest remembers, "so we called this hearing to remind the public that it wasn't a private-property issue but a question of traditional uses of navigable streams. And it didn't hurt having colorful villains."

The hearing was skillfully organized. Butterworth served as judge, Guest as prosecutor, and a paralegal named Monica Reimer as bailiff or clerk. Guest arranged the witness list so that people who had long used the creek for fishing and camping would testify first, figuring that the television cameras would disappear by lunchtime. It worked. By the time the Lykes employees had started arguing that the creek was nothing more than a tiny gully through a cypress swamp, the press and the TV cameras were gone.

"LYKES IT OR NOT…"

Becky Hendry, founder and president of a tiny organization called Save Our Creeks, was skeptical. Becky, her husband, Smiley, and their four children had lived much of their lives camped on the banks of Fisheating Creek, depending on its bass and wild hogs and turkeys for food. She had organized what she called a "steak out" on the creek, a rally-cum-protest that drew four hundred people for a barbecue. One was a judge from Miami who offered a slogan: "Lykes it or not, Fisheating Creek is ours."

Becky was a key figure in the growing resistance to the Lykes Brothers and their stranglehold on Glades County, and she was more than a little nervous when the big wheels from Tallahassee showed up for their circus.

"They were all dressed in suits and ties and high heels, and I asked myself, 'What are they going to do for our creek? All they want is for people to brag on their clothes,'" Becky said years later. At the end of the day she approached Guest. "All I want to know is, are you a quitter? Because Lykes will try to destroy you. They have worn out everybody that crossed them." The answer was no. Becky decided to trust the Tallahassee contingent, "and David and Monica became my best friends. They gave up birthdays, holidays,

One of the best ways to enjoy Fisheating Creek is from a canoe. Who says this creek isn't navigable? *James Valentine*

weekends. I said for David to call anytime. He did. Often at two or three in the morning. For years. He also taught me how to deal with the press."

Attorney General Bob Butterworth was nominally representing Florida's Department of Natural Resources, but the department's chief, Tom Gardner, was friendly with Lykes. Gardner studied the matter, met privately with Lykes in Glades County, and then announced that as far as his department was concerned, Fisheating Creek was a local issue that he was not going to get involved with.

Undeterred, Butterworth and Guest filed a lawsuit against the Army Corps of Engineers, seeking a declaration that indeed Fisheating Creek was federally navigable and therefore could not be blocked. Clients in the case were the citizens of the state of Florida.

At this point, Lykes began to feel a bit of heat. It reopened part of the campground, cleared the trees, and then opened one set of the gates on the creek. As for the barbed-wire fence across the creek, Lykes claimed that it had been constructed by local vandals, suggesting that Glades County has high-class vandals—they build fences rather than tear them down.

On February 1, 1990, the Army Corps of Engineers, in response to the suit filed by Guest and Butterworth, rendered its decision about the navigability of the creek in no uncertain terms:

> The physical characteristics of Fisheating Creek … taken together with its
> historic and present use in interstate commerce form a basis for a finding

of navigability…Accordingly…I find that Fisheating Creek is a navigable water of the United States for purposes of the regulatory jurisdiction of the Army Corps of Engineers from its mouth at Lake Okeechobee to the state Road 731 Bridge near Venus.

The decision was signed R. M. Bunder, Major General, USA, Commanding. Lykes wasted little time in filing suit in federal court to challenge the corps' decision.

The case was assigned to Judge Elizabeth Kovachevich, a Nixon appointee. Prospects for the lawsuit, from the perspective of the Hendrys and their allies, did not look bright. They looked even less bright when the judge refused to let the state—in the persons of Butterworth and Guest—intervene in the case. Lykes argued, and Judge Kovachevich agreed, that this was a simple matter between Lykes and the Corps of Engineers and its outcome could not possibly have any adverse effect on navigation rights under Florida law. This assurance proved a crucial strategic error that would return to haunt the company a few years later.

David Guest, Monica Reimer, and a researcher named Karen McMillan had by this time resigned from the Attorney General's Office and gone to work for Earthjustice in a brand-new office in Tallahassee. With the state barred from playing any role in the suit against the corps, Guest, Reimer, and McMillan teamed up with attorneys for the Department of Justice and the local U.S. attorney's office to fashion and argue the corps' case.

Cypress dome, prairie, and hardwoods, adjacent to Cowbone Marsh. *James Valentine*

It was clear that the outcome of the argument would turn on a short stretch of the creek about ten miles east of Palmdale known as Cowbone Marsh. Over the past sixty years, the stream channel there had become choked with water plants, and it was nearly impossible to get boats through. Proving that boats did, or could, navigate through the channel in Cowbone Marsh in 1845 would be the challenge. Lykes, for its part, argued that Fisheating Creek was really a string of "pothole" lakes that became connected only during short periods of high water after heavy rains. And it argued that the federal surveyors had classified the stream as a waterway that was not navigable, but that was instead merely a "well-defined natural artery of internal communication."

As David Guest explains it, the Lykes argument was that "navigable" waterways must cross state lines or, in the case of a lake, must have more than one state touching its banks. By this standard, the Mississippi River is federally navigable because it forms an interstate navigation route that links numerous states to one another and to the Gulf of Mexico; a river in one state that does not flow into another state or into the sea would be "an artery of internal communication," which would not qualify it as federally navigable. David Guest's argument, by contrast, was that under Florida law an "artery of internal communication"—a navigable route from one place to another—is what matters. If such an artery exists, then it proves navigability for the purposes of state law and guarantees public ownership.

The existence of a navigation channel through Cowbone Marsh became a crucial issue, because no channel meant no internal communication and no navigability. The team representing the pro-creek forces set out to find proof that there was a clearly defined channel that had made the creek navigable from Lake Okeechobee to the Glades County line in 1845.

Guest, Reimer, and McMillan interviewed all the old folks in Glades County to find out if the stream had ever been used as an artery of trade and travel. Frank Jones recalled his sixth birthday, in 1915, when his family traveled by oxcart to Fort Center on the creek. Fort Center had been erected on a huge Caloosa mound in the early 1800s as a garrison for soldiers fighting in the second Seminole War. Jones remembered trading posts and the people who came up and down the creek in homemade skiffs and canoes to trade alligator hides for supplies. And he described how the stream channel divided into a north and south channel before the two channels rejoined just upstream of Cowbone Marsh. This story was unsettling, because that channel configuration was not shown on any known map.

Guest, Reimer, and McMillan interviewed scores of witnesses and found many maps—more than forty in the end—but their lack of sufficient detail made the testimony and the maps vulnerable to attack by Lykes's lawyers. Then, in scouring archives and files all over the state, Reimer found a small piece of a previously unknown map with breathtaking detail that was clearly made from an aerial photo or survey sometime earlier than the early 1930s. (They could determine the date because the Hoover Dike, an extension of the muck dike that ran parallel to Fisheating Creek on both its banks, did not appear on the map. That dike had been built in the early 1930s.) If the complete map or photo could be found and verified, it could prove beyond question the existence of the historic navigation channel through Cowbone Marsh. They set out to ransack the state in pursuit of what they began calling the Holy Grail.

The roseate spoonbill *(Ajaia ajaja)*, a rare and wondrous creature that thrives along Fisheating Creek. *Joel Sartore*

"We went everywhere," Guest says. To the state archives, the Library of Congress, the universities, the state and county libraries. They pored over thousands upon thousands of documents, but could not turn up the evidence they needed. The last possible place was the library of the South Florida Water Management District in West Palm Beach, where the archives of the defunct Everglades Drainage District had been sent fifty years before. Reimer telephoned to ask if anyone had seen a detailed map of Fisheating Creek. The answer was no.

So they got in a car and drove to West Palm Beach to make sure. They scoured the files by subject. Nothing. Then they went through all map files no matter how they were labeled. Still nothing. They were about to leave, then said to themselves, "We've come all this way, it was a late night, maybe we overlooked it on the first search." Finally, in an unlabeled file folder inside an unlabeled file box, they found the Holy Grail. They phoned Guest and left a message: "Bring champagne. We'll get French bread and pâté and meet you at the motel."

The folder contained several documents, including a 1929 map by the Army Corps of Engineers. "It was just like a dream," Guest says. "The map was incredibly detailed and showed a river channel right through the center of the marsh, with the channel split into a north and south channel just upstream of Cowbone Marsh. It was exactly as Frank Jones had described. We figured the case was over." An 1870 survey, and another hand-drawn map from 1842, indicated a channel through Cowbone Marsh, but both would be challenged by Lykes's lawyers. The 1929 Army Corps map was airtight proof. The folder even contained a certificate by the surveyor, under oath, that the area around Cowbone Marsh had been "accurately surveyed."

THE GRAIL FAILS

Lykes managed to delay the proceedings for two years, during which the Sierra Club and the Florida Audubon Society tried to mount a boycott of their products. Then, in July 1992, the judge abruptly called a hearing on a Thursday and announced that a four-week trial, live witnesses and all, would take place starting the following Tuesday. The team that was defending the Corps of Engineers and its finding of navigability—officially the Justice Department and informally Guest and Company—had done no discovery, conducted no depositions, prepared no witnesses. They were armed with the Holy Grail, though, and, Lykes didn't know about it.

"When we presented the Holy Grail it was as if we'd tossed a sack full of live rattlesnakes on the table in front of Lykes's lawyers," Guest says. "They leaped to their feet yelling it 'wasn't anything, just an old map.'"

The scene was decidedly odd. The judge had refused to let the state participate in the case, yet here was David Guest in the audience every day, conferring with the Justice Department's lawyers and passing notes back and forth. The Lykes team was apoplectic, but there was nothing they could do. Guest was simply a spectator, albeit a very well-informed and opinionated one.

Guest and his team had figured that Lykes would challenge the authenticity of the Holy Grail, so they convinced the Corps of Engineers to attach its most formal and fancy certificate of authenticity, including a blue embossed seal, a ribbon, and a grommet. They had by this time located another copy of the map on Corps of Engineers microfilm, identified by a number printed on the map itself; but still Lykes claimed that it was a forgery. Guest et al. even found the congressional bill that had provided the money for the 1929 survey expedition, and still Lykes insisted the map was fake.

Despite all the evidence, including Frank Jones's videotaped story and testimony from old-timers who offered tales of ancestors who had used the creek as their "artery of internal communication" for generations, the judge eventually ruled for Lykes: Fisheating Creek was not, in her considered opinion, navigable. She went so far as to mention an extensive account put into evidence by the government. It was from an Indian named Billy Bowlegs and had been written down in the 1880s. Bowlegs described an extensive canoe trip up and down the creek in a dugout canoe carrying a large load of supplies from a trading post to his village. Judge Kovachevich determined that the trip had taken place but found no proof that Bowlegs had "navigated" the heavily loaded canoe over the hundred-mile voyage. The government appealed.

"We should never have had the trial at all," Guest says. "The customary procedure in a case like that would be simply to argue about whether the corps had made its determination based on a fair reading of the information it considered." The Justice Department could, probably should, have challenged Judge Kovachevich's basic approach to the matter, but chose otherwise. Guest had a bad feeling about the appeal and started drafting a complaint he would eventually file in a state court in Glades County. The federal appeals court sustained Judge Kovachevich's decision.

The complaint that Guest drafted and filed for Save Our Creeks, the Environmental Confederation of Southwest Florida, and Attorney General Bob Butterworth was unusual for Earthjustice in two ways. The most important was that it asserted not a violation of environmental law but the common law action called unlawful "ejectment." The second was that it demanded a trial by jury. No case Earthjustice had ever been involved in over its twenty-five-year history had gone before a jury. Five years later, it remains the only jury trial the organization has prosecuted.

The reason the case was appropriate for the state court, Guest argued, was that Lykes had convinced Judge Kovachevich that the case against the Corps of Engineers could do no harm to the interests of the people of Florida. Lykes predictably disagreed and held up the decision by Judge Kovachevich as having settled the matter, but Judge Thomas S. Reese of the state court said, with heavy irony, "With all due respect, this court will not recognize this order."

"Unlawful ejectment" is a fancy way of saying that the defendant—Lykes Brothers—had illegally evicted the people of Florida from their sovereign property—Fisheating Creek. A jury of six Glades County men and women would decide whether, based on all the evidence presented to it, Fisheating Creek had been navigable in 1845, when Florida became the twenty-seventh state.

Lykes responded by filing a counter-complaint claiming a "slander of title." It is illegal

Rock Lake, a wide spot in Fisheating Creek downstream from Palmdale. *Tom Turner*

taken of its attorneys, their wives, and their witnesses arrayed in front of the jury box. They then repaired to what passes for a fancy restaurant in Moore Haven for a long celebratory lunch. They should have waited.

Within an hour, the jury sent word that it had elected a foreperson, and a half-hour after that it announced that it had reached a verdict. Guest and his trial team were alone in the courtroom with the bailiff. They sent word for the judge. After a twenty-minute wait for Lykes and their lawyers, the jury delivered its verdict to the judge.

"The judge seemed to frown when he read it," Guest said, "and we didn't know how to interpret that." But the verdict was unanimous—Fisheating Creek is and was navigable and therefore the property of the people of Florida. The judge inquired if anyone wanted the jury polled. Lykes immediately said yes. And one by one, each juror took an oath that the verdict was his or her own and the verdict of the whole jury. It turned out to be one more useful turn of events, because otherwise, Lykes might have argued that one or two jurors had been coerced by the others. The winners made their way to the Anglers' Reef and celebrated until four in the morning.

Lykes immediately filed an appeal with the next higher court.

Lykes Gives In

The verdict, however, was the end of the lawsuits. After some bruising negotiations, with David Guest frequently sitting across the table from the chairman of the board of Lykes Brothers, they hammered out a settlement. Lykes agreed to drop its claim to any part Fisheating Creek and agreed to sell to the state nine thousand acres of uplands bordering the creek course from the county line to Lake Okeechobee. Included in this land acquisition are Fort Center and numerous pristine areas for the enjoyment of campers, boaters, and birdwatchers. Lykes also agreed to grant a conservation easement over an additional forty-two thousand acres of land adjacent to the creek. The state paid the appraised value of the land acquisition—$46.3 million—but paid nothing for any part of Fisheating Creek. As of late 2001, negotiations were under way to expand the easement by another ninety thousand acres, with the eventual goal of making the whole thing a state park.

It is early October, just after the searing events of September 11, 2001. Smiley, Becky, Smiley Jr., and Junior's daughter Clarissa have invited David Guest and me to camp overnight with them at a secret spot near Rock Lake, a wide spot in Fisheating Creek a half-dozen miles downstream from Palmdale.

What with airport security and side trips, we get into the boats as the light is disappearing from the sky. David and I ride in a johnboat navigated (yes!) by Smiley. This is a flat-bottomed, blunt-nosed skiff powered by a go-devil motor, an outboard with a long shaft that spins a propeller shaped exactly like a Cuisinart chopping blade. The prop rides very near the surface and makes it possible to get through places choked with hyacinth and water lettuce and fallen logs. Smiley Junior and Clarissa are in a canoe with a fifty-horse outboard on the stern. Becky is already at the camp with Ellen Peterson, another veteran of the Lykes campaign.

We push away from shore, the water so still that it's difficult to see the surface; we seem suspended halfway between sky and land. Smiley switches on a miner's lantern strapped around his

American alligator *(Alligator mississippiensis)*, drawing by Dugald Stermer head. It is powered by a car battery at his feet. He begins slowly sweeping the light back and forth along the shore on either side of the creek.

"He's looking for gators, trying to scare you," Guest says. "You can see their eyes, pairs of red dots in the water." The johnboat suddenly seems a bit flimsy. "And keep an eye out in the branches we pass under," he adds. "That's where the water moccasins like to spend the night to get away from the gators." Moccasin bites, he assures me, are seldom fatal.

We wend our way through the cypresses and oaks. The stream is clearly navigable, but if you don't know where the main channel is, you'll spend hours exploring dead ends. In an hour or so we arrive at the camp atop an old Caloosa mound, maybe four feet above the surface of the creek: a folding table, several picnic chairs, a few tents, a smoldering fire with a big iron grate above it, and a ten-foot-square roof eight feet off the ground on four posts for shelter against the frequent rains. Smiley cooks steaks, serves them with sweet iced tea in Styrofoam cups. David and Becky stay up till the wee hours reminiscing about their epic adventure against the Lykes Goliath.

Next morning, Smiley Jr. suggests we see how close to Cowbone Marsh we can get. About a mile from camp he spots a big gator, cuts the motor, and makes a gurgling, chuffing sound in the front of his mouth. The gator makes a beeline for the boat. Whether he thinks we're food or a potential lover or an enemy isn't clear. It is, however, humbling to have several hundred pounds of alligator bearing down on your canoe. The gator sinks from sight just before he reaches us. Junior laughs at his passenger's nerves.

Boy Scouts form a canoe fleet during an outing on Picnic Lake, Fisheating Creek. *James Valentine*

The technique is called "grunting" and was, maybe still is, used to lure gators close enough that they could be dispatched with a ball-peen hammer or an axe.

We resume our journey but are soon turned back by fallen branches. The Fish and Wildlife Conservation Commission is supposed to keep the channel clear, but keeping up with it remains a perennial challenge. We return to camp, and I join Becky and Smiley in the johnboat for a day on the creek admiring the scenery, searching for gators.

The big, unanswered question remains: why did Lykes abruptly try to establish ownership of the creek? Theories abound. The company claimed that it took the action to stop poaching and vandalism, but no one seems to believe it. Becky Hendry is quite sure that the company planned a big development, with hunting and fishing, and wanted to keep the public out. Others think Lykes planned to log off the valuable old cypress trees and plant the area with citrus. David Guest's private theory is that Charlie Jr. simply wanted to prove that he had the power to take possession of the creek and its banks.

No matter what the reason, the move was thwarted, and Fisheating Creek and the people of Florida are the better for it.

White ibis *(Eudocimus albus)* In a refuge on Florida's Gulf Coast. George Henry Preble reported eating—and enjoying—many ibis on his 1842 expedition to Fisheating Creek. *Joel Sartore*

CHAPTER SEVEN

THE BATTLE FOR THE LAST BIG TREES

Roseburg, Oregon, with its twenty thousand residents, lies just upstream from the confluence of the North and South Umpqua Rivers in southwestern Oregon. It is an island of sorts, in a sea of former trees—surrounded by thousands of stacks of lumber and plywood; heroic piles of sawdust; and millions of logs, endlessly bathed in sprayed water to keep them from checking and warping. The logs wait patiently to be sawn into useful sizes and shapes. The sawdust eventually will go to pulp mills to become paper and cardboard.

Playing out in the hills and mountains to the east and west of Roseburg is a desperate struggle between lumber companies, which want to cut down the biggest, oldest trees that remain—a tiny remnant of the millions of acres of ancient forest that once blanketed the region—and a band of everyday citizens, a small cadre of lawyers, and a few allies within the Forest Service and Bureau of Land Management, mostly scientists, all of whom are determined to save as much as possible of what's left and restore the rest. This struggle has been going on in earnest for well over a decade, ebbing now, flowing then, with the ground rules constantly shifting as judges from Seattle to Portland to San Francisco have found the federal government in violation of a long string of its own laws.

Such victories as the environment's defenders have been able to score have owed much to the scientists, who have risked their careers by refusing to become what some call "biostitutes": people willing to let politics overrun sound science in order to get ahead, to please their immediate bosses and the industry that has so much to gain from the final assault on these beautiful old forests. These scientists have worked in symbiosis with the attorneys: the lawsuits have clarified the law and produced court orders that have enabled the scientists to do the work they were hired and trained to do. Nevertheless, there has been retaliation, as we shall see. We will discuss the experience of a few of these scientists presently, but it is worth pointing out that they are among many fine people who enter public service for all the right reasons, then run head-on into politics and the influence wealthy industries can wield over federal agencies.

Opposite: A "nurse log" in Oregon old-growth forest. The timber industry argues that mature trees left to decay in the woods are wasted. Dozens of species of birds, animals, and plants would disagree. *Joel Sartore*

Owls and Firs

Loggers have long prized the huge, ancient Douglas firs that grow in these rainy forests. Their grain is straight, the wood is strong, and a single tree can provide enough wood to build a half-dozen small houses.

People have felled these trees for many years, but the methodical razing of the forest did not begin until the end of World War II, when thousands of returning GIs wanted to build houses and begin raising families. The forest in the drainage of the Umpqua River was one of the biggest timber producers in the entire country: in Douglas County, of which Roseburg is the county seat, there were 278 lumber mills in the late 1940s and early 1950s.

In addition to wood, the region's other great product once was fish: coho salmon, chinook salmon, steelhead trout, and a cutthroat trout endemic to the Umpqua basin. As the ancient forests disappeared under the chain saw, so too did the fisheries, their spawning beds fouled with silt, their streams warmed to dangerous levels through a dearth of shade, their rivers deprived of the fallen tree trunks that slow the water and provide vital resting areas.

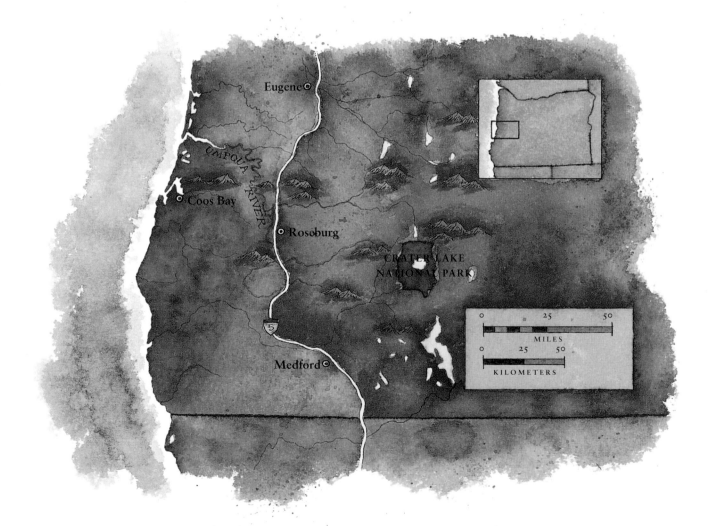

The legal campaign for the forests began in earnest in the late 1980s with a petition to the Fish and Wildlife Service seeking Endangered Species Act protection for the northern spotted owl. Little was known about the owl until a biology student, Eric Forsman—then working a summer job as a fire lookout—heard an odd sound from deep in the forest. He imitated the sound, and a pair of owls flew down to look him over. It was 1968. Surveys over the next two decades indicated that the owl was indeed rare, that its range was surprisingly large, and that it appeared to depend to a great degree on very old stands of trees for nest-

A Roseburg lumber yard. Trees that have been felled, bucked, and skinned are bathed continuously to keep them from warping and cracking. *Tom Turner*

ing sites, for shelter, and for prey. The forests the owl needed were vanishing rapidly. The Earthjustice petition asked the government to take notice and give legal protection to the species.

The government, for a variety of reasons, was not interested. It rejected the petition. Attorneys Vic Sher and Todd True, who had opened an Earthjustice office in Seattle in early 1987, filed suit. Judge Thomas Zilly ordered the Fish and Wildlife Service to come up with better reasons—any plausible reasons—for not listing the owl in the face of overwhelming scientific evidence that the species was in serious trouble, including evidence from its own expert biologist, who warned that continued logging in owl habitat would likely lead to extinction.

Meanwhile, in another lawsuit filed by Sher and True, the Ninth Circuit Court of Appeals had blocked timber sales in owl habitat on BLM lands in western Oregon, including the Umpqua River basin, under the National Environmental Policy Act. And in Seattle, Judge William Dwyer—also at the urging of Sher and True—had halted all new timber sales in owl habitat in national forests in Washington and Oregon until the Forest Service could produce a plan for protecting the owl.

The injunctions blocked nearly all logging of old-growth stands in the Northwest. The timber industry leaned on the two states' congressional delegations, who offered what was quickly becoming the ploy of choice for getting dicey matters through Congress with little scrutiny or public participation. The ploy involves attaching "riders" to must-pass legislation, frequently disaster-relief bills or bills that appropriate money for various federal agencies. In this case, a rider known variously as Section 318 or the Rider from

This beautiful meadow lay within a mining claim on U.S. Forest Service land in the North Umpqua watershed, near the headwaters of Steamboat Creek. It and other alpine meadows were destroyed when a new logging road was built into the Stewart Mine. *Francis Eatherington*

Hell was enacted and signed into law on October 23, 1989, by the first President Bush. It dissolved the injunctions and forbade further court challenges for a period of one year.

Just as the big old trees began to fall, the Fish and Wildlife Service capitulated to science and the law and pronounced the northern spotted owl "threatened" throughout its range in Washington, Oregon, and northern California.

As soon as the Rider from Hell expired, Sher and True were back in Judge Dwyer's court, this time accusing the Forest Service of ignoring the National Forest Management Act. In early May 1991, Judge Dwyer listened to a week of testimony. Biologists described how they had been pressured to produce a plan that would give the absolute minimum of protection to the owl and allow the absolute maximum logging.

Judge Dwyer issued his opinion on May 23, an indictment so sweeping that the *Washington Post* devoted most of a page to reprinting choice excerpts. "More is involved here than a simple failure by an agency to comply with its governing statute," the judge wrote. He continued:

> The most recent violation of [the National Forest Management Act] exemplifies a deliberate and systematic refusal by the Forest Service and the Fish and Wildlife Service to comply with the laws protecting wildlife. This is not the doing of the scientists, foresters, rangers, and others at the

working levels of these agencies. It reflects decisions made by higher authorities in the executive branch of the government.

The judge thereupon blocked further timber sales in owl habitat in Northwest national forests until a plan could be written that would protect not only spotted owls but also other old-growth-dependent species, including the marbled murrelet, which had recently been listed in response to yet another lawsuit, this one filed by Earthjustice attorney Adam Berger.

THE GOD SQUAD INTERVENES

Meanwhile, in western Oregon, where most of the federal timberland is managed by the BLM rather than the Forest Service, timber companies were getting restive. They had logged off their own lands and depended on a steady stream of federal trees to keep their mills humming. They leaned on the director of the Bureau of Land Management, Cy Jamison, to ask his boss, Interior Secretary Manuel Lujan, to convene a meeting of the Endangered Species Committee.

A provision for the convening of that committee was added to the Endangered Species Act in 1978 as an emergency valve for instances where strict enforcement of the act would produce a national crisis. The "God Squad," as the committee is often called because it has the power to determine life or death for vanishing species, is made up of seven cabinet-level officials. It had met only twice before, both times to consider requests that the Endangered Species Act be suspended to allow completion of dam projects. The first time, the committee refused, but Congress stepped in and ordered the dam finished. The second time, the committee allowed the dam to go forward.

Secretary Lujan agreed to convene the God Squad to consider whether to allow forty-four BLM timber sales to be logged even though the Fish and

The northern spotted owl *(Strix occidentalis)* has helped save some of the Pacific Northwest's ancient forest from the chainsaw. *Galen Rowell/Mountain Light*

Wildlife Service had warned that doing so would jeopardize the spotted owl. Thus two agencies of the Interior Department were pitted against one another, the Bureau of Land Management arguing for the logging, the Fish and Wildlife Service arguing against it. After a lengthy hearing, the squad met and approved thirteen of the sales, but they were still held up by two other injunctions in separate cases. Vic Sher and Todd True soon were leaked evidence that improper pressure had been levied on two of the squad mem-

bers by the White House. They submitted the evidence to the appeals court in San Francisco, and soon thereafter the thirteen disputed sales were taken back off the market.

The second Dwyer injunction became an issue during the following year's presidential campaign. President Bush allied himself firmly with the pro-logging forces, making a photo-op trip to Forks, Washington, a mill town hit hard by the injunctions. Bill Clinton promised to convene a summit conference within the first hundred days of his presidency to search for a solution that would save both jobs and owls, the two essentials to which the controversy had been reduced by the popular press. The election came and went, and the presidency changed hands.

The Forest Summit was held in Portland, Oregon, on April 2, 1993. President Clinton, Vice President Al Gore, Secretaries Bruce Babbitt (Interior), Mike Espy (Agriculture), Robert Reich (Labor), and Ron Brown (Commerce), EPA Administrator Carol Browner, and Alice Rivlin of the Office of Management and Budget listened carefully as scores of people weighed in. Vic Sher spoke for Earthjustice. There were also union representatives, scientists, economists, timber executives, local officials, loggers, and tribal leaders—fifty-four speakers in all, divided into panels to address separate aspects of the problem at hand. "He was extremely well briefed," remembered Diana Wales, a Roseburg lawyer and activist who sat next to Mr. Clinton. "He seemed to understand perfectly well these very complex issues and the forces pushing one way and another."

Once the long day concluded, Mr. Clinton asked a team of scientists—known as FEMAT, or the Forest Ecosystem Management Assessment Team—to come up with several alternative management strategies to provide both timber for the loggers and protection for the sensitive species. He would then choose a plan that best fit the competing demands and would satisfy Judge Dwyer. He wanted the plan in six weeks.

Frenetic study and debate ensued, all in private. The team proposed eight options. None provided enough timber to satisfy the Northwest congressional delegation. A ninth option was hastily assembled and adopted by the president. It fit one definition of a successful compromise: it pleased no one.

Opposite: The Little River, a tributary of the Umpqua River, is still beautiful, but upstream logging and the resulting runoff have deprived it of snags and gravel beds that are necessary for salmon and trout. *Tom Turner. Below:* The marbled murrelet *(Brachyramphus marmoratus)*, is a threatened seabird of the Northwest coast that depends on old-growth forest. *Dugald Stermer*

ENTER OPTION 9

Option 9, formally known as the Northwest Forest Plan, did improve protection for the spotted owl and the other species. While it reduced logging on federal lands by more than 80 percent, it still allowed some logging in old-growth reserves, to the dismay of environmentalists. They went to Judge Dwyer to argue that Option 9 did not satisfy his criteria. This time, however, the judge ruled that Option 9 did pass muster, but with no room to spare. Any deviation from the letter of the plan, the judge said, would be illegal.

A key feature of Option 9 was its Aquatic Conservation Strategy, added to meet the

requirements of the National Forest Management Act and in reaction to the notable decline in the populations of several species of fish. The strategy aimed to protect and restore streams throughout the region with the goal of sustaining and replenishing salmon, steelhead, and sea-run cutthroat trout and their landlocked counterparts.

The strategy had nine objectives, all starting with "restore and maintain": water quality, temperature, stream banks, species diversity, and so forth. The strategy also had four subparts: the identification of key watersheds, which either contain the best aquatic habitat or offer the best chance for restoration; the delineation of buffer zones to be protected along streams and rivers; watershed restoration; and watershed analysis. The analysis was the key: All the rest would flow from that. Once the analysis was complete, logging plans could permit cutting in the key watersheds and buffers only if it could be shown to improve old-growth characteristics.

Above: When the clear-cutters finish there isn't much left, and too much of that ends up in the streams below. This slide started in Unit 1 of the Right View timber sale, when the BLM logged steep, unstable slopes, and continued down into tributaries of the Wild and Scenic portion of the North Umpqua River. *Francis Eatherington. Below:* Burning a clearcut in the Paw timber sale. *Martin Stephen*

Just before the Clinton summit in Portland, environmental groups had petitioned the National Marine Fisheries Service to give legal protection to the Umpqua cutthroat trout, a once-popular game fish whose numbers had crashed nearly to the point of invisibility. These trout fall into three distinct groups. One lives its life in the small, mostly high-elevation streams in the Cascades at the headwaters of the North and South Umpqua Rivers. A second ventures down into the main stem of the Umpqua but returns to spawn higher up. The third behaves like a salmon, spending its adult life at sea and returning to spawn in fresh water. The sea-run Umpqua cutts were in the most serious trouble.

NMFS responded that the petition appeared to have merit and would be studied. The environmental groups came back with another request a few months later, seeking emergency listing in the wake of a study that indicated the fish were even worse off than previously believed. NMFS turned them down. The following spring, in May of 1994, Adam Berger filed formal notice of intent to sue NMFS if it didn't act on the petition within sixty days. Two months later the agency announced that it was proposing to list all three strains of Umpqua cutthroats as endangered, conceding that the sea-run cutts were "virtually extinct."

Congress had another sneaky trick up its sleeve, however. Following a nasty fire season in 1994, Congress, in mid-1995, approved yet another rider to an appropriations bill that would, among other things, provide relief to the survivors of the Oklahoma City bombing and the victims of recent major floods. The rider suspended all environmental laws for a year in the guise of salvaging fire- and insect-damaged trees quickly, before

Protesters carry a puppet figure of a timber boss in a parade opposing the logging of the Mt. Bailey roadless area around Diamond Lake, in 1998. Diamond Lake is the largest recreation-use area on the Umpqua, but much of it is being converted from old-growth forest to tree farm plantations. *Francis Eatherington*

natural decay and disintegration could run its course. The rider, however, was written in such a way that it allowed cutting of living trees as well, and in particular many stands of Northwest old growth that the timber industry had been denied a chance to log under the Section 318 rider. The new rider, dubbed "the salvage rider" or "Logging without Laws," was a virtual blank check, an invitation to a massive raid on the national forests—not only in the Northwest but throughout the country.

Mr. Clinton was in a box. He had hoped his summit would lay this difficult matter to rest, but here it was, back in his lap. When the bill with the rider attached first reached his desk, he vetoed it. But the heat began to rise, and when it was reenacted by Congress with only minor changes, he signed it—an act he would regret and apologize for later.

Fish Science vs. Fishy Forestry

The fisheries service, meanwhile, had proposed listing the trout in August 1994. The Endangered Species Act gave the agency a year to collect comments and make its proposal final. August 1995 came and went with no action. In December, Berger and another Earthjustice attorney, Yuki Ishizuka, went back to court seeking an order from Magistrate Judge Donald Ashmanskas that would compel the agency to act. The following May, the government told the court it needed more time. Judge Ashmanskas demanded an answer by the end of July, and in August 1996 the three strains of Umpqua cutthroat trout were officially deemed endangered.

The listing of the Umpqua cutthroat suddenly required the Forest Service and the

Bureau of Land Management to enter into formal consultation with the National Marine Fisheries Service to ensure that logging plans would neither jeopardize the survival nor hamper the recovery of the trout. Under the terms of the Aquatic Conservation Strategy of President Clinton's Northwest Forest Plan, an elaborate review system for proposed timber sales was put together, consisting of teams referred to as Level 1, Level 2, and Level 3. Level 1 teams were made up of scientists: fish biologists, wildlife biologists, botanists. Their job was to gather and review studies of various watersheds and decide whether logging could proceed without undue harm to the trout. If they agreed that logging could be tolerated, that was that. If they did not agree that logging would be tolerable, they would forward the decision to the Level 2 team, made up of administrative personnel, who were less devoted to scientific rigor and more sensitive to political pressure. Extra-difficult decisions could be passed up to Level 3, which consisted of regional managers, whose political antennae are especially sensitive.

Once the documentation was forwarded to the fisheries service, that agency would write biological opinions, giving a final and formal decision on whether the proposed logging plan would violate the Endangered Species Act. Here is where science and politics ran head-on into each other.

For one thing, semantic games enter the picture here. As clear-cutting—the removal of every tree—became more and more of a public relations problem, the foresters dreamed up what they called "regeneration harvests," which sound so much more benign. The difference between a clear-cut and a regen harvest is vanishingly small. In a regen harvest a handful of largish trees are left on each cut acre, theoretically to provide

GIRLS CAN'T DO THAT

When Francis Eatherington was nearing graduation from high school in rural Illinois she took an aptitude test to determine what sort of job she was best suited for. The answer was forest ranger. "I'd never heard of a forest ranger," she says, largely because there were no forests where she lived. So she asked her mother, "What's a forest ranger?"

"Girls can't do that," said her mother. She thought she might try anyway and lit out for the West, landing in Oregon. She found work planting trees, a backbreaking job. She did that for five years, then was hired by the Forest Service and the Bureau of Land Management to do surveys of stands of trees to decide which to offer for sale to timber companies. She couldn't help noticing that the stands of old-growth forest were rapidly disappearing.

In 1995 she started doing volunteer work for a tiny Roseburg organization called Umpqua Watersheds, which keeps an eagle eye on the two federal agencies she was working for to make sure they follow the laws and regulations that govern logging and wildlife. Eatherington resigned soon thereafter and began working full-time for Umpqua Watersheds. She has come across scores of violations over the years and has been a principal player in much of the litigation pursued by Patti Goldman and other Earthjustice attorneys in the years since 1995.

Francis Eatherington of Umpqua Watersheds stands beside one of the ancient giants she has helped protect. *Tom Turner*

seeds to restock the land with new trees. The land still looks awful, habitat is wrecked, and erosion problems remain the same.

Two of the Level 1 team members for timber sales in the Umpqua basin were fish biologists. Don Rivard worked for the Roseburg District of the Bureau of Land Management, and Jeff Dose worked for the Umpqua National Forest. They and their colleagues had surveyed scores of timber sales. Most fell within the bounds of Option 9, if only barely. About two dozen, however, were so ill-considered that they were bumped up to Level 2 and eventually to the regional managers of the Forest Service and the BLM for review.

In spring 1997, the fisheries service released a series of biological opinions on logging plans for the Umpqua basin. In an opinion that considered the management scheme as a whole, the agency found that the plan would not jeopardize the cutthroat trout. Three other opinions found that grazing and a series of timber sales would likewise comply with the Northwest Forest Plan.

Patti Goldman filed suit in federal court two months later to challenge these opinions. Her clients were led by the Pacific Coast Federation of Fishermen's Associations, a group of mostly small-boat operators who fish for salmon and other species and whose livelihoods had been becoming increasingly difficult as salmon runs declined. The case was assigned to Judge Barbara Rothstein in Seattle.

Ancient old growth and under-story species at the Paw timber sale, unit 7, in 1997. See page 144 for the fate of these trees. *Francis Eatherington*

Don Rivard and Jeff Dose read with interest and mounting indignation the biological opinions for the sales they had kicked upstairs. The documents said that their Level 1 team had found the proposed sales acceptable, when they themselves had argued the opposite. Dose decided that he could not stay quiet. He drafted a letter to two officials in the fisheries service office in Seattle, going around both his immediate supervisor and his regional director in Portland. Don Rivard reviewed the letter and decided to sign it as well.

Dose and Rivard wrote, in the measured words of careful people:

Cindy Barkhurst risked her career as a Forest Service biologist by refusing to go along with suggestions that she and her colleagues rewrite their studies in order to allow logging in especially sensitive groves of old-growth trees. *Tom Turner*

> We were professionally and ethically compelled to respond to what we consider a major inaccuracy that tends to be confusing and may even be misleading. We are specifically referring to the statements that the Level 1 Team for the upper Umpqua River basin, of which we are members, found "that the subject timber sales are consistent with the ... Aquatic Conservation Strategy objectives ..." That statement is simply untrue ... At no time were we asked to determine if the proposed actions would help achieve ACS objectives, in fact, when we started into that realm, we were expressly directed to not address that issue.

> They mailed the letter on August 4, 1997, and sent copies to their own agencies. NMFS wrote back to deny that the team had been told not to consider consistency with the aquatic strategy. Dose was treated like Typhoid Mary. Rivard was given a formal reprimand for being unfaithful to his agency and put on probation for a year.

Goldman's suit argued that the overall biological opinion was illegal because it failed to use the best scientific information in reaching its conclusion and because it assumed that the Aquatic Conservation Strategy would be followed without requiring that this be done. The suit also challenged the three site-specific biological opinions. One had to do with the impacts of grazing on the cutthroats; the other two involved logging. The complaint initially named as a defendant the National Marine Fisheries Service. The Forest Service and the Bureau of Land Management were later added to the case. The state of Oregon and three timber companies joined the suit on the side of the federal agency defendants.

The court's decision was delivered in May 1998. Judge Rothstein found that the overall biological opinion was acceptable if the Aquatic Conservation Strategy were actually implemented, but she also found that the site-specific opinions were illegal because they did not require actual implementation of the conservation strategy. Twenty-four timber sales in sensitive habitat areas or places that had already been hit hard by logging—including some of the sales that Dose, Rivard, and others on the Level 1 team had objected to—were blocked.

At this point the agencies and the Justice Department, acting as their lawyer, faced an important decision. They could appeal Judge Rothstein's ruling and try to persuade the

Ninth Circuit Court of Appeals that she had misread the law, or they could go back and rewrite their biological opinions in such a way that the court would let them proceed. They chose the latter course.

The Level 1 teams were issued new guidelines. The emphasis was on "clearer descriptions" and "clearer documentation and findings" of the conclusion of the biological opinions—to wit, that the timber sales would be consistent with the conservation strategy and would not jeopardize the fish. There was no mention of actually stopping any of the sales or scaling them back to reduce the harm they would inflict.

This approach caught the attention of the leader of the Level 1 team for the Umpqua basin, a twenty-year veteran of the Forest Service named Cindy Barkhurst. Barkhurst was the wildlife biologist for the Umpqua National Forest and coordinator of the PETS effort, a program to protect proposed endangered, threatened, and sensitive species on the forest. She had been uncomfortable with the first Level 1 team experience but had not spoken out when Dose and Rivard had. This time she did.

The Soda Springs dam and powerplant on the North Umpqua River. Environmentalists want it demolished to restore habitat for salmon and other wildlife. *Tom Turner*

She wrote a memo to members of the Level 1 and Level 2 teams, plus a member of the Level 3 team and her supervisor. She pointed out that the directive would have the scientists consider only impacts that would have a measurable effect on the entire region. In other words, even if a clear-cut would have a substantial impact on both terrestrial and aquatic habitat in a sizable watershed, that impact would not stop the project unless it reverberated throughout the entire region.

She received no direct reply, but six months later, on December, 15, 1998, she was informed by her supervisor that she was being removed from the Level 1 team.

The new Level 1 team—now missing Rivard (who had landed a job with the Fish and Wildlife

Service), Dose (who had left voluntarily in disgust), and Barkhurst—released its new biological opinion at the end of 1998. To the surprise of no one, it found that the two dozen sales (half from the earlier group, half new) were perfectly consistent with the Aquatic Conservation Strategy and could proceed. Within a few weeks, Patti Goldman was back in Judge Rothstein's court.

On September 30, Judge Rothstein ruled again. She blocked all twenty-four timber sales, saying that the justification in the biological opinion was so loose that it was hard to see how any proposed timber sale would fail to pass muster. The timber sales at issue were in the Umpqua River drainage, but the impact of the injunction would be felt throughout the region because the opinions for the Umpqua sales were being used by the Forest Service as a model for review of all other Northwest timber sales.

This time, the government decided it wasn't going to be able to write its way into the judge's good graces and filed an appeal with the Ninth Circuit in San Francisco. Barkhurst, Dose, and Rivard had been vindicated, but that didn't mean the Forest Service or the Bureau of Land Management would appreciate what they'd done.

Nearly a year later, in mid-2001, the court of appeals sustained Judge Rothstein with one heartbreaking exception. It ruled that one sale, known as Little River Demo, could proceed. The court's logic was a bit opaque, but it was the last word.

About the same time, in a remarkable about-face, the National Marine Fisheries Service stripped Endangered Species Act protection from the Umpqua cutthroat trout. The fish in the Umpqua basin were still in perilous straits, but the agency argued that these fish were indistinguishable from cutthroats in other Oregon drainages that were doing much better, relatively speaking. Nothing must get in the way of logging. Coho salmon had by this time been given legal protection, however, so consultation under the law was still required, the biological opinions the courts had rejected were still invalid, and logging was still enjoined.

A huge stump is all that remains of this 650-year-old Douglas fir, felled in 1999 as Boise Cascade began clear-cutting Paw unit 7 in the Mt. Bailey roadless area—one of the most contentious Umpqua National Forest timber sales. *Francis Eatherington*

WILD VS. TAME

In the spring of 2001, another wrench was thrown into the gears. In response to a suit filed by the Pacific Legal Foundation, a federal judge in Oregon removed

Oregon coastal coho salmon from the endangered species list on the grounds that the National Marine Fisheries Service had failed to count hatchery-bred fish along with their wild cousins—a theory Patti Goldman likened to saying that one need not protect lions on the Serengeti Plain because there are plenty of them in zoos.

Environmental groups had not intervened in that case because they figured the government—in the form of the National Marine Fisheries Service—could defend its position perfectly well by itself. Goldman had reviewed the briefs and saw that the agency was mounting a stout defense. But when the ruling came down, Goldman quickly requested permission to join the case on behalf of the Pacific Coast Federation of Fishermen's Associations and others. It was a wise move. The government, now in the hands of the second Bush administration, did not file an appeal, but said rather that it would rewrite its policies on new listing decisions to clarify the relationship between wild and hatchery salmon and comply with the court order.

A hiker rests at the base of one an old-growth fir in the Right View timber sale. *Francis Eatherington*

Goldman raced to the court of appeals and succeeded in getting protection for the coho restored, pending further proceedings. But in the period between the judge's ruling in September 2001 and the court of appeals' stay of his ruling ninety days later in December, many acres of irreplaceable old trees were felled. Even after the listing was reinstated the battle raged. Umpqua Watersheds activist (and former Forest Service and BLM employee) Francis Eatherington twice came across loggers felling trees in defiance of the court, and twice Goldman rushed to court for emergency relief.

We toured this tattered landscape in early May 2001, before the court rulings about wild and tame fish and while all parties were waiting anxiously for the appeals court to speak about Judge Rothstein's injunction. The swatches of old growth are few and scattered, which makes them even more magical and inspiring than if they were commonplace. Loaded log trucks still barrel down the roads and highways with disheartening frequency, and the hills have a decidedly moth-eaten look.

Up the North Umpqua may lie the next major tussle, an attempt by Umpqua Watersheds, the Audubon Society, and others to remove one or two of the eight dams

CHAPTER EIGHT

A TALE OF TWO RIVERS

If you amble into a bookstore, a convenience store, even the National Geographic Society store in Washington, D.C., in search of a simple map of the District, what you'll find is more than likely to omit nearly half the city. The maps include the Capitol, the White House, the Mall, the Potomac River, the business district, and Georgetown. Many do not include large portions of the southeast and northeast quadrants of the city or the District's other river, the Anacostia, which rises in Maryland and joins the Potomac near the southern tip of the city. A curious habit, to ignore nearly half the nation's capital and more than half its population, but it reflects the attitude that has prevailed for many years about the poorer sections of the city. They might as well not exist. They're more trouble than they're worth.

One thing these maps don't show, therefore, is just how many of the city's large, traffic-generating, congestion-producing facilities have been put in the forgotten parts of town. They also conceal, through omission, the fact that the Anacostia River has been woefully abused over the years, while the Potomac—with an important exception we shall come to—has received relatively better, if far from perfect, treatment.

The facilities that draw traffic and noise and pollution to the banks of the Anacostia include Robert F. Kennedy Stadium, once the home of the Washington Redskins professional football team and now the host of soccer matches and other sporting events; the D.C. Jail; the D.C. Armory, a massive, faceless, concrete half-cylinder that hosts trade shows and parties and other gatherings; D.C. General Hospital; the Benning Road incinerator; a power plant operated by the Potomac Electric Power Company; and, down the way, the Washington Navy Yard, established in 1799, a source of nasty discharges to the river and the groundwater for two centuries.

As of the early twenty-first century, the residents of these poor precincts, it almost goes without saying, are overwhelmingly African-American. But it was not always so.

In 1608 Captain John Smith, having had his life spared by the child Pocahontas, sailed up the Anacostia as far as what is now Bladensburg, Maryland, the spot where the river is no longer influenced by the Atlantic Ocean's tides. The area, particularly the part now known as Anacostia in Southeast Washington, was inhabited by the Nacotchtank (also rendered Nanotchtank) Indians, who reaped a rich bounty of fish from the river and

Opposite: Kingman Island in the Anacostia River in Washington, D.C., was slated to become the Children's Island theme park, a sort of mini-Disneyland East, until local residents got organized and signed up a few lawyers. *Tom Turner*

game from the woods. Europeans moved in, planted crops, including both food and tobacco, and the river began to collect sediment from agricultural runoff. By the middle of the nineteenth century, large ships could no longer reach Bladensburg, which dwindled from being a major port to a landlocked town. When Captain Smith sailed up the Anacostia, the river channel was about thirty feet deep. Today, at low tide, it is closer to three.

Washington, D.C., established as the federal city in 1791, always had a large African American population, both free and slave. Slave labor built the White House, the Capitol, and many of the fine old homes in the District. By the early 1800s, the black population was about half slave, half free, and the fraction of free African-Americans climbed steadily until the Emancipation Proclamation in 1862. Being free was not the same as being equal or treated well, of course, and African American residents were relegated to the forgotten precincts of the capital city. The history is too complex to go into here, but suffice it to say that at the turn of the twenty-first century, the population of the District of Columbia was about three-fourths black. The population of the city east of the Anacostia River was 97 percent African-American.

Kingman Park is the section of the District on the west bank of the Anacostia River to the north of East Capitol Street, extending a mile or so north and west of the river. It was built by the federal government in the 1930s, along with the Langston Golf Course along the river to the north, as a residential development for African-Americans, on land owned by the National Park Service. In that sense it was experimental, and the Langston Golf

The Potomac River flows serenely past the Jefferson Memorial and into the Tidal Basin before it joins its neglected sister, the Anacostia. *James P. Blair/NGS Image Collection*

Course remains the only golf course the federal government ever built expressly for African-Americans. It is now, of course, open to all.

The residents of Kingman Park were a mixture of economic classes. Doctors lived next-door to cab drivers. Families that moved in tended to stay. The neighborhood is stable and proud, and after a time, the residents felt as if they had already accommodated enough of the large facilities the city needed, and wanted to be left alone. When plans were announced in the late 1980s for a new football stadium, a new freeway complex, and a glitzy new theme park, they dug in their heels, made common cause with the environmental community, and worked wonders.

FOOTBALL FREE-FOR-ALL

Following the assassination of Robert F. Kennedy in 1968, the District of Columbia renamed its football stadium, built in 1960, for the fallen attorney general-turned-senator. RFK Stadium squats on the western bank of the Anacostia, looking, as much as anything like a pile of huge gray automobile tires. Beautiful it's not.

Beauty aside, the stadium is where the Washington Redskins of the National Football League played their home games until the late 1990s. By the mid-1980s, the franchise had been acquired by Jack Kent Cooke, who bought it from Edward Bennett Williams, a high-powered Washington attorney and confidant of presidents. Cooke had made millions in cable television; owned the Chrysler Building in New York, the *Los Angeles Times*, and the Los Angeles Kings hockey franchise; and had built and named Los Angeles's "Fabulous Forum" sports arena. He was used to getting what he wanted. In this case, Cooke wanted to change the stadium in two fundamental ways. He wanted to modernize it, adding seats and luxury boxes to increase his profits. He also wanted to have it named after himself. The former was probably impractical. The latter was patently impossible, given the mythic status of its namesake and the political hornets' nest such a move would stir up.

So Cooke set out to build himself a brand new, modern, spiffy stadium. The spot he chose was the huge parking lot just north of RFK Stadium. What other city in the land could boast two huge football stadiums right next door to one another? The neighbors over in Kingman Park, however, were less than thrilled at the prospect of even more traffic and commotion nearby. And where would everybody park if the existing lot got covered up with a new stadium? Rumor had it that Cooke had in mind paving over the front nine of the golf course to replace the parking he would cover with the new stadium.

At this point in its history, Washington was in pretty miserable straits. Having acquired a limited form of self-government in 1974—the ability to elect a city council, a mayor, and a nonvoting delegate to the House of Representatives—it had fallen on economic hard times and was looking around desperately for projects that would put money into the city's bank accounts. Congress was on the verge of appointing a control board to oversee the city's finances once it plunged into insolvency. The once and future mayor, Marion Barry (his two stints in office were separated by a stretch in prison) was cozying

Robert F. Kennedy Stadium on the western shore of the Anacostia, former home of the Washington Redskins. Jack Kent Cooke wanted to build a new, bigger, fancier stadium right next door. *Tom Turner*

up to just about anyone who would suggest a high-ticket development project in the District. Cooke filled the bill nicely. He began to woo members of the city council with visions of cash for the city's coffers.

Back then, Herb Harris was president of the Kingman Park Civic Association, which had been in existence almost as long as Kingman Park itself. He and his allies decided that their best bet to defeat the stadium plan was to go before Congress, since the city council would be so easily swayed by the prospect of money. (Frazer Walton, the current president of the association, said years later that his neighborhood was treated better before democracy came to the District.)

In the late 1980s, the mayor and the councilors were putting heat on the National Park Service to bless the stadium project, which the agency had hated. Stadium opponents managed to get Representative Bruce Vento, a Minnesota Democrat on the House Natural Resources Subcommittee on National Parks, Forests, and Public Lands, interested in the budding controversy, given that the stadium would be built on land that belonged to the federal government, as did—and does—all the land on either side of the river all the way to the District boundary. Vento seemed quite concerned that if Cooke could build his pet project on national parkland, no federal parkland anywhere would be safe.

Vento decided to air the issue at a hearing before his subcommittee. A Native American spokesperson went first and stunned everyone with an eloquent but horrifying recitation of why, before anything else was considered, the name of the football team should be changed.

Bob Dreher of Earthjustice, speaking on behalf of the Kingman Park Association and other groups, pointed out the legal problems involved with using public parkland for private, profit-making purposes and promised that, should the proposal go much further, he would be seeing Cooke in court. Herb Harris described all the sacrifices the Kingman Park neighbors had already made for the city at large and suggested that another one the size of a football stadium was asking too much. Robert Boone of the Anacostia Watershed Society outlined his organization's efforts to clean up the river and restore it as habitat for wildlife and explained that the plan under consideration would be a great leap backward for the river. It had been the formal policy of the federal, state, and District governments to restore the Anacostia since 1987; this project threatened to undo the good work just then getting under way. Jack Kent Cooke declined an invitation to testify.

The next day's *Washington Post* reported on the hearing and carried a picture of Harris, Dreher, and Boone. Cooke, clearly wanting to avoid a nasty public fight, turned his sights to Virginia and later to Maryland. He wound up building his edifice in Landover, Maryland. By this time, Cooke had altered his plan and decided to name the stadium for his sons, Ralph and John: Raljon Stadium. After the elder Cooke's death in 1997, his sons could not afford to keep the team, however, and now, in the current fashion of commercializing everything, the stadium is called FedEx Field. The team is still the Redskins.

The experience was a real shot in the arm for the Kingman Park residents and their environmental allies, and it stood them in good stead in the looming struggles over an amusement park and a freeway. "When you've beaten a billionaire," Herb Harris says, "a city councilman ain't nothin'."

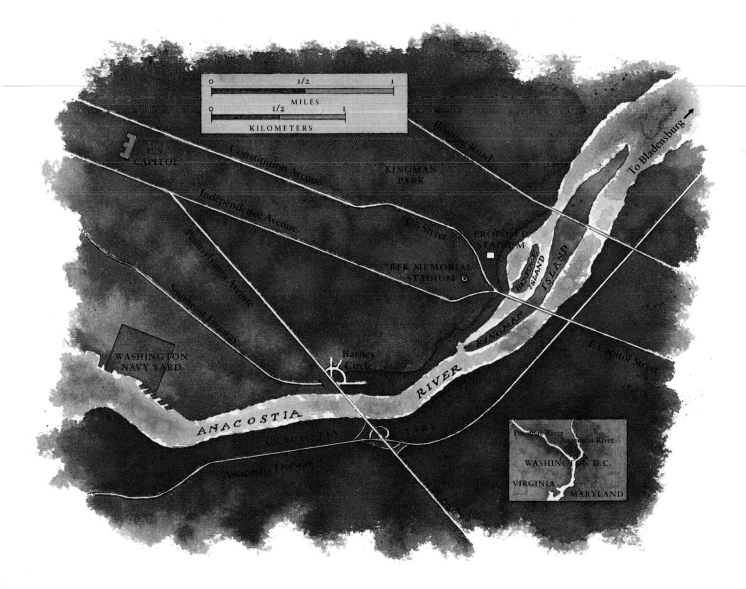

Disneyland on an Island

The new stadium wasn't the only project Mayor Barry and others had in mind for the Kingman Park neighborhood. Another was a midsize amusement park they wanted to build on two islands in the middle of the river.

Heritage and Kingman Islands had been built by the Army Corps of Engineers in 1916, with spoils dredged from the river's once abundant wetlands. The northern half of Kingman Island accommodates the first nine holes of the Langston Golf Course. Amazingly enough, the rest of the islands had never been developed, apart from victory gardens that Kingman Park residents planted during World War II. In the 1990s, the city took to using part of Kingman Island for dumping weeds and branches pruned from city parks. The islands had grown thick with brush and trees; Bob Boone and his Anacostia Watershed Society volunteers had spotted bald eagles, egrets, great blue herons, otters, muskrats, terrapins, and snakes on or near the islands.

In 1968, a developer suggested building a park akin to Tivoli Gardens on the islands, but the idea died a quiet death. Then in 1975, as part of the celebration of the nation's bicentennial, a commission had suggested building a "Children's Bicentennial Island" amusement park, a modest affair heavy with puppet shows and other low-tech amusements, a park that would fade away after three or four years. It didn't happen. No financing. In 1992, a more substantial proposal surfaced for a National Children's Island theme park, financed by a mysterious, Indian-born investor, Contessa Bina Sella de Monteluce, who was married to an Italian nobleman.

Great egret *(Casmerodius albus)*, drawing by Dugald Stermer

The contessa's dream included nine pavilions (the Doug Henning Pavilion of Wonder, Communications and Computers, Miracles of Medicine, the Infinite Crystal and Enchanted Crystal Forest Pavilion, the Hall of Sports, the American Music Center, Dynamic Motion Theater, the Underwater World, and the Elements) and two covered bridges jammed with shops, restaurants, and cafés. It would cover all of Heritage Island, the southern half of Kingman Island, and a few acres on the riverbank. Patrons would park next to the football stadium (or stadiums), and pay their parking fees to Jack Kent Cooke.

The theme park's admission fee would average around eleven dollars, which, compared to Disneyland or Epcot Center, is not shocking. But as critics pointed out repeatedly, the other attractions that draw people to Washington—the Smithsonian Institution, the Washington Monument, the Lincoln Memorial, and the rest—are all free. Who would trek to an out-of-the-way part of town to spend eleven dollars a head for a bush-league amusement park? The contessa argued that Disney's America, a Civil War theme park then being considered in northern Virginia, would lure plenty of spillover business to Children's Island. The theme park experts Herb Harris consulted all disagreed (and Disney's America was never built, anyway).

The National Park Service declared its reluctant support for Children's Island when the project was announced. Earthjustice attorney Fern Shepard says the agency had no real love for the project but steadfastly believed that it was uneconomic and would therefore never be built, and the agency was tired of being harassed by the city council. The Park Service decreed that there was no need to do any environmental analysis of the project, since all the agency proposed was to hand control over the islands to the District of Columbia. A simple "paper transaction," it called the maneuver. The transfer was accomplished in the waning days of the first Bush administration, much the way many environmental initiatives were announced at the end of the Clinton administration. Mr. Clinton's initiatives were largely to preserve tracts of land, however, not hand them over to private developers.

At the end of 1992, then, the Interior Department handed Heritage Island and half of Kingman Island to the District of Columbia. The District immediately signed a thirty-year renewable lease with the theme park developer, Island Development Corporation.

At this point, Fern Shepard filed suit on behalf of the Anacostia Watershed Society, the Kingman Park Civic Association, and Friends of the Earth to require that the Park Service perform environmental studies on the transfer of ownership. The court agreed, and the project was put on hold.

The developers, not wanting to wait for such time-consuming trivialities, decided to turn to Congress, and there they found a champion in their nonvoting delegate, Eleanor Holmes Norton. She leaned on her colleagues, argued that the District desperately needed an influx of investment capital, and won their support. Efforts were made to persuade by-then President Clinton to veto the bill, but he had his hands full with Newt Gingrich and

Above: Herb Harris was president of the Kingman Park Civic Association, which teamed with many other organizations to fight off the stadium, the theme park, and the freeway. *Below:* A wooden bridge conveys visitors from the mainland to Heritage Island. *Both, Tom Turner*

the Contract with America, and he signed the bill, formally transferring title to the land to the District.

This effectively ended the lawsuit, so Shepard and her colleagues in the new D.C. Environmental Network turned their efforts to lobbying for provisions that would ensure at least a modicum of environmental-impact review before

the project went irrevocably forward. This network had been created through the efforts of Friends of the Earth's Brent Blackwelder and others, who thought it was well past time that the city's large environmental lobby paid some attention to their immediate surroundings and their neighbors. The network, made up now of close to eighty organizations, has had considerable success in fighting for environmental quality within the District, including the battles outlined here.

Now that the District of Columbia controlled the islands, it was up to the city council to approve or disapprove the project. Pressure was intense. The D.C. Environmental Network turned up the heat every way they could think of. Damon Whitehead, a brand-new Earthjustice lawyer, was sent to testify before the city council, only to discover that the city's lawyer on the case was the dean of Georgetown Law School, from which Whitehead had just graduated. "I was afraid he'd take away my law degree," Whitehead joked later. Eventually the project was approved by a single vote.

But that wasn't the last of it. Congress eventually had appointed a control board to oversee the District's financial affairs, and that body would have to approve the project as well. The project's opponents sent a delegation to meet with the board, including Friends of the Earth's Blackwelder and Howard Fox and Damon Whitehead of Earthjustice.

They presented a detailed memo Fox and Whitehead had prepared for the city council, showing that both federal and District law required that an environmental impact statement be prepared before the long-term lease could be approved. In their oral argu-

Kingman and Heritage Islands, once slated to become an upscale theme park, will now be lightly developed as an environmental education center and nature park. *Tom Turner*

JUSTICE ON EARTH

ment before the control board, Fox and Whitehead pointed out that the theme park would never draw enough visitors to produce the amount of revenue the developer was promising. Worse, it might actually turn out to be a financial drain on the strapped city. The city council had cavalierly brushed aside their views. They hoped the control board would react differently.

It did. "These were a tough-minded bunch of fiscal types," Blackwelder remembers. "They got it right away." The project was promptly vetoed and died a quiet death.

Building Freeways to Reduce Traffic

A motorist who wants to drive from Arlington or Alexandria, Virginia, to Baltimore or points north has a choice. He or she can take the Beltway, Interstate 95, and waste many miles and minutes going the long way round, or she or he can take Interstate 395, the Southeast Freeway, to the point where it abruptly ends at Barney Circle, exit the freeway, cross the Anacostia on the John Philip Sousa Bridge, then hop on Interstate 295, also known as the Anacostia Freeway.

The Frederick Douglass Bridge, which carries South Capitol Street across the Anacostia River, looking northward towards the Capitol Hill side of the river. On the piling is a large osprey nest.
Tom Turner

In the early 1980s, there was a plan to build an inner beltway, but protest and litigation prevailed and much of the money was used instead to improve and expand the District's splendid public transit system, known as the Metro. There remained in the Department of Transportation coffers, however, two hundred million dollars that was to have paid for the southeast leg of the inner beltway. In 1994, the department decided to build a multilane freeway across the Anacostia to connect I-395 to I-295 and, for good measure, to build an accompanying road along the west side of the river, right through Anacostia Park, from Barney Circle north to the Benning Bridge.

The rationale offered for this project, known as the Barney Circle Freeway, was not to speed traffic from Alexandria to Baltimore, however. It was to ease congestion on the streets of Capitol Hill, a dubious proposition at best. Kingman Park residents saw through it immediately, and opposition to the freeway project joined the football stadium and Children's Island as a *cause célèbre*. The Anacostia Watershed Society, Friends of the Earth, and eight other organizations joined in opposing the scheme, arguing that it would just bring more noise, air pollution, and traffic into a neighborhood that didn't need any more.

Howard Fox and Fern Shepard took a careful look at the project and determined that it would be in violation of five federal laws. For one thing, a special act of Congress was needed before permission could be granted to build "any structure" on federal parkland

the messenger hadn't been so formal and high-ranking," Whitehead says.

He, Shepard, and Lynn Sferrazza sent more requests, citing the Freedom of Information Act. The navy responded by asking for meetings. Eventually, the lawyers were able to confirm that navy studies had uncovered evidence of contamination by PCBs, arsenic, mercury, and lead, all fiercely dangerous substances. The contaminants were washing straight into storm drains and from there into the river. In other places, they were melting slowly into the soil. The pollution, which had been going on to one degree or another for two centuries, did not have the benefit of a permit from the Environmental Protection Agency and was therefore illegal. Very illegal. Such a permit would presumably force the navy to curb its discharges.

News of the navy's pollution problem began to spread. Greenpeace hung a banner from the USS *Barry,* moored outside the Navy Yard, that read "Dishonorable Discharges." Stories ran in the forty biggest media markets in the country.

Shepard, Whitehead, and Sferrazza sent a letter to the navy to announce that it had sixty days to stop the pollution or face Earthjustice in court. Lois Schiffer, assistant attorney general in the environmental section of the Department of Justice, telephoned Shepard to request more time, claiming an investigation was under way that might result in criminal charges, and that a civil suit would just get in the way. Shepard considered the request carefully but decided that the chance of a conflict between a civil suit and such an investigation was so small as to be trivial. She went ahead and filed the suit, alleging that the navy's pollution violated the Clean Water Act and the Resource Conservation and Recovery Act. Plaintiffs were the Barry Farm Resident Council and the other organizations that had battled the Barney Circle Freeway, Children's Island, and the stadium.

The navy immediately asked the court to defer the suit until the criminal investigation was complete. The judge refused, finding the government's argument "disingenuous and far-fetched," and sternly ordered the navy to answer the complaint within thirty days. This brought the navy to the table to seek a settlement, promising fervently to take swift, aggressive steps to clean up its mess.

As this was being written, cleanup of the yard was well under way, though much remains to be accomplished. Once again, a well-placed lawsuit, like the two-by-four with the mule, got the government's attention.

SEWAGE, THE GREAT LEVELER

Much has been made of the fact that the two main waterways coursing through our nation's capital have received dramatically unequal treatment. This is true, but there's an exception. When it comes to human waste, no stream in Washington is treated particularly well.

It is embarrassing to report that when a member of Congress uses the toilet closest to his or her office during a heavy rain, the contents of the toilet may be flushed directly into the Anacostia River. Toilets over a large area of the District discharge untreated sewage into the Anacostia, Rock Creek, and the Potomac—the city's three main waterways—whenever a storm drops more than a half-inch of rain. That happens eighty or more times a year. The total annual pollution can exceed a staggering one billion gallons. There are, in all, fifty-nine combined sewer outfalls in the District, an amazing and appalling situation that is unknown to most of the country and even to many in the District—so unknown that it has taken a great deal of public agitation to get the mayor's attention.

The problem, simply stated, is that the city operates a combined sewer system. That is, storm water from streets and gutters and wastewater from homes, businesses, offices, and other sources travel in the same pipes to sewage treatment facilities. When there's too great a volume for the system to handle, the mixture of storm water and raw sewage goes straight into the Potomac, the Anacostia, and Rock Creek. Given that both the Potomac and the Anacostia are influenced by Atlantic tides, it can take some considerable time for the material to wash out to sea or otherwise dissipate. People use these waterways quite heavily for canoeing, kayaking, fishing, even swimming. It is quite a scandal.

The sewer system is operated by a semi-independent agency known as WASA, the Water and Sewer Authority. Although the dumping has gone on for decades, it was not until 2001 that WASA proposed a plan to deal with the problem—and clean-water advocates say it doesn't go nearly far enough. The WASA plan would still allow large quantities of raw sewage to flow into D.C. waters.

Riverbank signs warn of Washington's dirty little secret: when heavy rains come, raw sewage flows into the Potomac and the Anacostia. *Tom Turner*

In another wrinkle, the District had been required by the Clean Water Act since 1979 to adopt limits on overall pollution. In theory, such limits would take care of the sewage problem if they had been adopted—which they hadn't. Howard Fox filed and won a suit requiring the determination of TMDLs, or total maximum daily loads, for a host of pollutants, but such things take time.

To greet the new century, clean-water activists mounted a two-pronged effort, one in the courts, one very much in the public, to force WASA and the mayor to take the problem as seriously as it deserves, and to do something about it. They call it the Cut-the-Crap campaign. The results have yet to be seen.

PRESERVING POSSIBILITIES

It is December 5, 2001, and seventy degrees on the Anacostia. A harbinger, perhaps, of globally warmed winters to come. A dozen people have gathered for a reunion of sorts on a pontoon boat owned and operated by the Anacostia Watershed Society. Bob Boone and Jim Connolly of the society are there, as are Herb Harris, former president of the Kingman Park Civic Association; Dorn McGrath, a George Washington University professor and former chairman of the Committee of 100 on the Capital City; and John Capozzi, a consultant and anti-freeway rabble-rouser, and his daughter Camille. Fern Shepard is here too, as are Howard Fox, Joan Mulhern, and Todd Hutchins of Earthjustice, and John Moyers of the Florence Fund and TomPaine.com, an Internet journal of opinion. The battle for the Anacostia, like so many others, has brought together people from wildly different backgrounds and differing but agreeable interests. The lawyers, in many cases, were the lubricants.

Above: An osprey built its nest on top of an old pipe stuck in the bed of the Anacostia. Despite all the challenges, a surprising diversity of wildlife survives along the river. *Tom Turner*

The boat's engine is a four-stroke rather than two-stroke model, a bit more expensive but much less polluting. We push off from James Creek Marina. Boone points out a couple of sites where the Army Corps of Engineers has restored wetlands and a spot where he hopes to see a boat launch installed. Dorn McGrath points out a great mansion across the river where Frederick Douglass once lived, the first African-American to take up residence in that part of town.

Great blue herons rise slowly and with great dignity from the mudflats. A kingfisher takes off upstream, scolding us for disturbing its peace. Herb Harris reports that he saw a bald eagle along here just last week. We're right in the middle of Washington, D.C.

We happen upon a small boat from which two scientists—one from the Fish and Wildlife Service, the other a graduate student from the University of Maryland—are listening to electronic beeps from gadgets planted in the stomachs of bottom-feeding catfish and picked up by hydrophones dangling in the water. Their study—which aims to track the fishes' movements and determine how far they range, therefore whence may hail the pollution that causes tumors to form on their lips—is almost finished, and the warm weather has crossed them up. The water is supposed to be cold by now, but it isn't. They're hoping for a good cold storm before the end of the year.

It has hardly rained in several months and the river is sluggish, with lots of plastic bottles and other flotsam, some tossed into the river deliberately, some washed in when the treatment plant was overburdened. It would be much, much worse if not for the efforts of Bob Boone, Jim Connolly, and the legions of volunteers who have hauled tons of trash out of the river. Boone keeps careful track. Over the decade or so from 1989 to 2001, the Anacostia Watershed Society has removed 327 tons of debris and 7,218 tires, with the help of 25,666 volunteers. In addition, they have planted 10,603 trees with the help of 7,800 inner-city kids.

A basketball floats forlornly past. As Fern Shepard says, "We preserved possibilities. The possibilities are still there, but there's a great deal to do."

One of those possibilities has drawn closer with the recent announcement that the former theme park site will finally be turned into an environmental education center and park in honor of three city students, three teachers, and two National Geographic Society staff members who were killed when a hijacked passenger jet slammed into the Pentagon on September 11, 2001.

Opposite bottom: Bob Boone of the Anacostia Watershed Society has ambitious plans for restoring the river. His organization has already removed many tons of tires and other trash from the waterway. *Tom Turner. Below:* Fishing from the banks of the Potomac. D.C. residents living near the Anacostia look forward to the day when their neighborhoods will enjoy similar recreation opportunities. *Joel Sartore*

TIMBER REFORM IN THE TONGASS

If you go to the lumber yard in Juneau, Sitka, or Ketchikan to get a two-by-four, chances are that what you buy will be Douglas fir from Oregon, Washington, or British Columbia, possibly pine or redwood from California.

Although these towns sit in the densely forested Tongass National Forest of Southeast Alaska, the wood taken from there—and vast amounts have been taken over the past fifty-plus years—has seldom gone to meet the needs of the people who live closest to it. Much of it, including majestic old Sitka spruce and western hemlock hundreds of feet tall, has been turned into "dissolving sulfite pulp"—nearly pure, long-fiber cellulose—and much has been sold into the Asian market, where it has been made into rayon, disposable diapers, film and photographic paper, cellophane, carbon fibers used in the nose cones of rockets, smokeless gunpowder, fireworks, even filler for ice cream. Red and yellow cedars, along with some of the finest spruce logs, have been trimmed of their branches and shipped to Japan. What wood has gone through the sawmills in Southeast has mostly been cut to metric dimensions and shipped to markets in the Far East.

This rather odd circumstance came about courtesy of the Forest Service and was getting going in earnest just as Alaska joined the Union in 1959. In order to build a vibrant market-style economy in the Southeast region, the Forest Service set out to liquidate what it characterized as a moribund, overmature, decadent forest, which had evolved in the thousands of years since the last ice age ended, and turn it into fast-growing, profit-producing, job-creating tree farms.

The folly of that approach from any of many points of view should have been obvious at the time, but it wasn't, and so it has led to tragic destruction and one of the longest, most fiercely fought and widest-ranging environmental confrontations in American history. Let us back up a century or two and get a running start.

Southeast Alaska, sometimes referred to as the panhandle or simply Southeast, is a marvel of topography. Islands large and small sit off the coast. Both the mainland and the islands are mountainous, heavily forested at the lower elevations and crowned by snow and ice at the summits. Immense glaciers have carved deep, dramatic valleys throughout the region, and many remain, hard at work. One of the towns that figures

Opposite: Lower Checats Creek, Tongass National Forest, Alaska. The dense forests and rushing streams of Southeast Alaska have provided habitat for animals—and subsistence for people—for millennia. *Carr Clifton*

prominently in our story is on the mainland—Juneau, the state capital. Ketchikan is on Revillagigedo Island, and Sitka lies on Baranof Island.

THE GREAT LAND AS COMMODITY

The first Europeans to settle in Southeast were Russian trappers and fur traders, living uneasily with the native Tlingit, Haida, and Tsimshin people, who had occupied the area for thousands of years. The Russians had pretty well exhausted the supply of fur-bearing animals by the middle of the nineteenth century, and they sold all of Alaska to the United States in 1867, for $6.5 million. This purchase was widely derided in the United States as economic insanity—"Seward's Folly," for Secretary of State William Seward, who engineered it.

Folly or genius, the sale perplexed the Native Alaskans. They had never claimed to own the land in the way Europeans did, and the concept of Russia's having sold it out from under them was simply incomprehensible. The United States, for its part, did not try to confine the Alaska Natives on reservations and did acknowledge that they had a legitimate claim to at least some of their traditional lands, but deferred a decision on that score into the distant future. Indeed, it would be a century before the nation came to

Burroughs Bay, Misty Fiords National Monument. In Southeast Alaska, the biggest trees typically grow on the coast, where they provide vital habitat for deer and other creatures. They are also the most valuable and easiest to transport to mills, so have been in great demand by timber companies. *Carr Clifton*

JUSTICE ON EARTH

SETTLING NATIVE CLAIMS

In the late 1960s, geologists discovered oil beneath the tundra adjacent to Prudhoe Bay on Alaska's arctic coast. After a protracted court battle and a legislative skirmish in which former vice president Spiro Agnew cast the deciding vote, the government authorized the building of a seven-hundred-mile-long oil pipeline from Prudhoe Bay to Valdez, on Prince William Sound, where the crude oil would be stored in large tanks and then shipped to refineries on the west coast of the Lower Forty-eight, and, later, exported to Asian markets.

Among the several obstacles to that plan were the pending claims that various Native groups had to land along the proposed pipeline route. So Congress got busy and enacted the Alaska Native Claims Settlement Act in 1971. That law awarded forty-four million unspecified acres of land and nearly a billion dollars to a series of Native corporations, with Natives born in or before 1971 as shareholders. Each village had its own corporation, as did the cities. Over these were imposed thirteen regional corporations to create region-wide cultural and economic enterprises. Each corporation was given the right to select several tens of thousands of acres, the amount depending on the population of the village or city and its location.

The corporations were given a daunting order: start making money. This led to a rapid liquidation of natural resources, including the clear-cutting of large swaths of Southeast. The Native lands were not subject to the environmental protection laws that nominally controlled logging on federal lands, so the destruction there was even worse than it was in the national forests. It was—and remains—an experiment that enriched some people, impoverished others, and led to considerable cultural and environmental destruction.

As one Inuit witness testified to an Interior Department hearing, "They set us down and said, 'You're a corporation, now act like one.' It would be like setting a bunch of Wall Street people down in the Arctic and saying, 'Now go catch a whale.' "

grips with Native land claims in Alaska. The way they were settled would create as many problems as were resolved.

At the beginning of the twentieth century, the federal government began setting aside large tracts of public forestland, having seen the eastern forests fall rapidly, cleared for their timber and to create farmland and pasture. Much of Southeast Alaska was designated the Alexander Archipelago Reserve in 1902. In 1908 this was renamed the Tongass National Forest, after a group of Tlingits, and expanded to a total of seventeen million acres, the country's largest national forest by a long stretch.

The land was sparsely settled, with Native villages sprinkled here and there and a handful of small towns housing European Americans, who lived by fishing, mining, and hunting. In 1947 Congress enacted the Tongass Timber Act, which encouraged the nascent logging industry, but it wasn't until the 1950s that the razing of the Tongass began in earnest.

In 1954, a large pulp mill opened in Ketchikan, followed in 1959 by a similar plant in Sitka. The Ketchikan mill, owned and operated by the Ketchikan Pulp Corporation, was to devour the trees in the southern part of the forest. The Sitka mill, run by Alaska Lumber and Pulp, later renamed the Alaska Pulp Corporation (a subsidiary of a Japanese consortium headed by Mitsubishi, later acquired by the Industrial Bank of Japan), would

Totem at Totem Bight State Park, north of Ketchikan. The Tlingit Indians of Southeast are master totem carvers. *Carr Clifton* be fed trees from the northwestern part of the forest. A third mill was planned for the mainland near Juneau, but a fierce campaign by people inside and outside Alaska stopped that one before it was built and saved most of Admiralty Island, where much of that mill's feedstock would have come from. (This story is related in considerable detail in *Wild by Law*.)

FIVE-HUNDRED-YEAR-OLD CHEESEBURGERS

To provide a measure of stability and attract the investment necessary to construct the big mills, the Forest Service offered fifty-year contracts that would supply ample volumes of timber—13.5 billion board feet to the two mills combined over the life of the contracts, inflicting clear-cuts on several hundred square miles. The price for timber would be

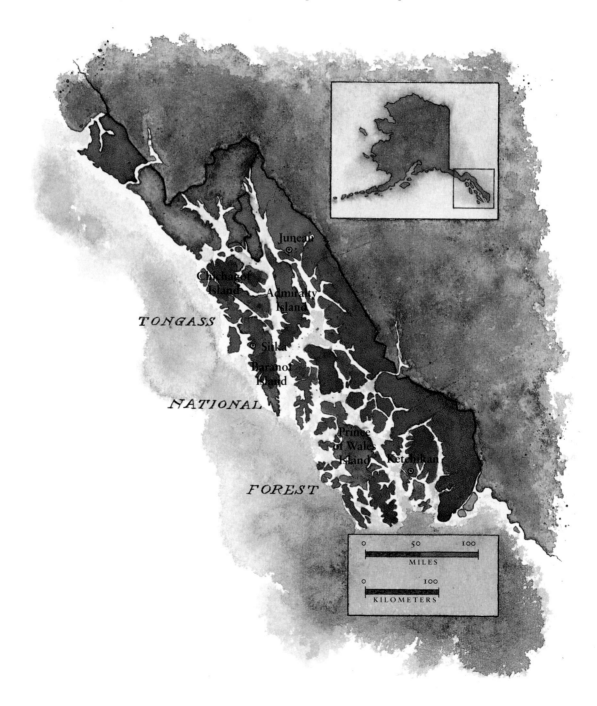

heavily subsidized by the government. If the price of pulp on the world market dropped, the government would lower the price it charged the mills for trees. At the lowest points, the Forest Service was charging the mills less than two dollars for a thousand board feet of timber. At those rates, you could theoretically buy enough unmilled wood to build a single-family house for twenty dollars, a figure that led some lawmakers to observe that

a several-hundred-year-old spruce or hemlock, in the twisted economics of the Forest Service, was worth about as much as a cheeseburger.

The Forest Service not only encouraged the destruction of the nation's largest national forest, it also squandered millions upon millions of taxpayer dollars to accomplish the feat. In other words, in order to build an unstable boom-and-bust timber economy in Southeast, the Forest Service planned to eliminate the best of the ancient forest and feed it to the two huge pulp mills, notorious for air and water pollution, as anyone who

Heavy rain supports a lush and complex understory in the forest of Southeast Alaska and makes fires rare. *Carr Clifton*

has spent time near similar facilities will readily attest. The impact on wildlife habitat, subsistence resources, and recreation caused by this headlong rush to clear-cut the forest would galvanize a wave of resistance that would eventually wash over the entire country.

DEATH CLOUD

Florian Sever grew up in Pittsburgh, surrounded by steel mills and coal mines, and became an airplane mechanic. He took a hunting trip to Southeast in the mid-1970s and was bowled over. He brought his wife and children to see what he had seen, and they collectively fell in love with the place. They moved to Sitka in 1976.

There were no aircraft jobs available, but the Alaska Pulp Corporation mill was hiring, largely because many workers had left for better-paid jobs on the North Slope, where the oilfield was just going into production. Sever started a new profession as a millwright.

Every day, as he would recount later, a "death cloud" would creep from the mill site, on the shore of Silver Bay, and cover Sitka, a few miles to the north. The cloud stank of vinegar and rotten eggs. The water under the bridge that connects Sitka to its airport would frequently turn black as ink. The shellfish and herring that were once plentiful in Silver Bay had all but disappeared. Yet the company and many of the people in Sitka refused to

Above: The Louisiana-Pacific mill at Ketchikan at the height of its operation in 1986. *Robert Glenn Ketchum. Below:* Flo Sever and his plane on the beach at Sea Lion Cove on the north side of Kruzof Island. Sever blew many whistles in an attempt to bring the Sitka pulp mill's environmental violations to the attention of the public and appropriate officials. *Tom Turner*

admit what the mill was doing. It paid many salaries, after all. On rare occasions, when the mill was closed for repairs or maintenance, the cloud would disappear. This was laid to coincidence.

Into this scene walked Irene Alexakos, an employee of the federal Environmental Protection Agency responsible for monitoring compliance with several federal laws controlling toxic substances. She visited Sitka in the mid-1980s to check out the mill. Flo Sever and Larry Edwards, who also worked at the mill, suggested that she ask to look at the company's paperwork concerning the fly ash that was left at the end of the pulping process.

She did. Mill officials refused the request. Alexakos telephoned an EPA lawyer, and much wrangling ensued. Finally the company produced the documents. They revealed that the fly ash contained high concentrations of two poisonous chemicals: dioxins and furans. They also indicated that large volumes of the ash were being dumped directly into Silver Bay. APC's Clean Water Act permit had no provision for dioxins and furans. EPA suggested that criminal prosecution of mill higher-ups might be possible.

The APC officials promised to stop dumping the ash into the bay and, according to Sever, began loading it onto open trucks for the trip to the city dump. "But by the time the trucks got there, all the ash would have blown away. The trucks were empty." A stop was put to that practice, and the mill operators began mixing the ash with concrete and depositing it in Sitka's unlined landfill.

Even the discharge permits the mill did receive from the EPA were something of a joke, Sever says. The company would routinely discharge volumes of "red liquor," another leftover of the pulping process, into Silver Bay far in excess of its permit. It would then notify EPA that there had been an "accident." EPA would levy a tiny fine, and business as usual would continue.

But Irene Alexakos's cracking open of the fly-ash fiasco was a turning point in the spreading campaign to bring the mills under tighter controls and force them to abide by appropriate laws and regulations. "That was a very courageous act on her part," Flo Sever says. As the government moved to require the mill to comply with the various pollution laws, APC's mounting costs began to threaten the economics of its operation, to expose it

for the marginal operation it really was, dependent on skirting the law in order to stay in business, despite the taxpayer subsidy.

There were other contamination problems as well. The state was responsible for enforcing the Clean Air Act, and it mounted an enforcement action against the mill in the late 1980s . Earthjustice attorneys Lauri Adams and Fern Shepard intervened in the case, and that eventually led to the installation of better pollution-control equipment and improved monitoring.

The federal government was responsible for enforcing water pollution laws and regulations. It also was lackadaisical. As Sever remembers, "That mill used eight hundred metric tons of chlorine every two weeks. It came in on ships and none of it ever left the island. Every drop went into the air or the water. The water used in the pulp process had to be filtered.

"APC cared more about the cleanliness of its pulp than Sitka cared about the cleanliness of its drinking water. APC took sawlogs, cellulose, and money. It left behind poison, heartache, blame, and shame." At one point the mill site was nominated as a Superfund site, which might have spurred cleanup efforts, but Alaska governor Tony Knowles objected, fearing that such a move would tarnish the state's reputation. Some people in Sitka felt decidedly betrayed.

Sitka Harbor. Until the Alaska Pulp Corporation mill in Sitka was closed, large volumes of fly ash left over from the pulping process were routinely dumped into adjacent Silver Bay. *Carr Clifton*

Things were the same, possibly even worse, down the marine highway in Ketchikan. Tim Bristol had been hired by the Southeast Alaska Conservation Coalition to visit the far-flung communities in Southeast and build alliances with fishermen, hunters—anyone who could be enlisted in the growing movement to stop the rapid destruction of this vast and magnificent temperate rain forest. The campaign was two-pronged: save the most beautiful places and the most important wildlife habitat, and mount a political attack on the contracts themselves, which, if they were carried out to the letter, would destroy the ecological integrity of the forest.

"Our slogan was 'Enough is enough. The trees are running out,'" Bristol says. But it wasn't easy. Loggers and mill workers were hostile. Still, he was able to find people who understood what was going on, and slowly the ranks of self-confessed environmentalists swelled.

Buck Lindekugel, also of SEACC, was another member of the team. He ran a series of workshops all over Southeast that he called "Taking Charge." These would introduce people to the basics of several laws and how citizens could use them: the National Environmental Policy Act, the Freedom of Information Act, the Clean Water Act, and others. "We trained people as paralegals," Lindekugel says. By the 1990s, SEACC consisted of fifteen or sixteen groups, small local outfits like the Sitka Conservation Society and the Tongass Conservation Society of Ketchikan, and large nationals like the Sierra Club and The Wilderness Society. They knew that it would take national pressure to save the Tongass, and to build that would take a long, concerted effort on many fronts.

Alaskan brown bear in deep understory. *Galen Rowell/ Mountain Light*

TIME FOR REFORM

The plight of the Tongass and the clear-cutting of national forest and Native lands alike had begun to catch the attention of the public outside Alaska by the late 1980s, thanks largely to the work of SEACC and other groups, including The Wilderness Society.

Representatives George Miller of California and Robert Mrazek of New York proposed a Tongass Timber Reform Act. A long string of witnesses debated the matter before the House Interior Subcommittee on Energy and the Environment in May 1987. The Alaska congressional delegation opposed the bill, as did representatives of the timber industry. A long string of environmentalists spoke for it. Flo Sever, who had put his job in jeopardy by agreeing to testify, summed up his view as follows:

> I ask you now, is it right that the Congress of the United States of America should subsidize the Industrial Bank of Japan…? How many times must we pay these people to come in and take our timber? How long must the taxpayers of this country endure the hardship of keeping afloat a sinking ship?

Another witness was Matt Kirchhoff, a biologist and member of the Alaska chapter of The Wildlife Society, a group of professional scientists. Kirchhoff outlined to the committee one of the fundamental flaws with the way the conversion of the Tongass had been planned and was being executed. The theory was that the forest could be cut every hundred years and provide a steady stream of lumber and pulp. It was assumed that wildlife species, including the fish and deer so fundamental to the Native peoples' culture and to the western economy as well, would adapt to life in second-growth forests. Science and simple observation were by this time indicating that the theory was fatally flawed.

Kirchhoff's principal concern was "high-grading." This was the practice of cutting the biggest, oldest, and therefore most valuable trees that grew mostly close to sea level, which made them even more attractive for the pulp companies because transportation costs were minimized. They could be felled, trucked or skidded to the ocean, tied together into rafts, and towed to the mills. Kirchhoff's concern, which had been analyzed in studies conducted on Admiralty Island a decade earlier, was that those same stands of big, old trees appeared to be vital to the survival of Sitka black-tailed deer in the dead of winter, when the higher elevations were buried under a deep mantle of snow. Kirchhoff and a partner had undertaken a careful study of the deer's habits

Above: Sitka blacktail deer *(Odocoileus hemionus sitkensis),* a species endemic to Southeast Alaska. *F. Stuart Westmorland/ Photo Researchers.* Below: Wolf pup, Chilkat Valley, *Galen Rowell/ Mountain Light*

and found that they would spend seventeen times as much time in old-growth forests as in the far denser second-growth stands that would grow after logging. So the immediate effect of clear-cutting was drastic damage to habitat for deer, at least, and possibly other species as well.

A second flaw in the picture had to do with the rate at which the forest would return. The contracts assumed that merchantable trees would regrow in fifty or a hundred years, but examination of stands cut by the Russians in the 1800s and earlier showed a far slower rate of growth, especially if the goal was to regain old-growth characteristics.

The complex ecosystem of Southeast Alaska's old-growth forest evolved over millennia and would take hundreds of years to regrow, once the big trees are cut. *Carr Clifton*

Something one must remember about Southeast Alaska is that it is extremely wet. You think Seattle is wet? Try Sitka, or Ketchikan, or Juneau, where it rains on average between fifty and two hundred inches a year. The abundance of moisture has many effects, a principal one being the near complete absence of forest fires. With no fires to provide openings for new trees to get started, that task falls to the wind, which is also prodigious in these parts. The great storms that blow in off the Pacific, and the extreme up-and-down geography of Southeast, provide powerful gales that frequently whistle up valleys and topple small patches of grand old trees, spurring the cycle of renewal.

An old-growth forest in Southeast, seen from a distance, is a raggedy affair: trees of various heights, many with broken tops, with frequent gaps in the canopy. Close at hand, the forest is a damp, spongy, verdant concatenation of a hundred shades of green: mosses, lichens, vines, berries, snags, and living trees of many sizes. Nowhere do you see bare earth. Every square inch is buried to a depth of many inches with living and dying organic material. To regrow such a complicated ecosystem would take at least 250 years. What would happen to wildlife and the people dependent on it in the meantime?

One target of the reformers was a provision inserted in the Alaska National Interest Lands Conservation Act of 1980 that provided the Forest Service with forty million dollars a year to prepare for timber sales in the Tongass National Forest: money to build roads, survey timber, and build log dumps. Another provision of that act ordered the agency to sell no less than 450 million board feet, a staggering amount, each year.

Back in Washington, the hearings ground to an end, and the legislators withdrew to digest the information and arguments. It took a while longer, but in 1990 the Tongass Timber Reform Act became law. It eliminated the supply fund. It protected a number of

places most prized by environmentalists, hunters, fishermen, and Natives. It modified but did not eliminate the contracts, and it was silent on the subject of clear-cutting. It was a big step forward, but the journey had just begun. A few years later a new traveler joined in. The Alaska Rainforest Campaign—composed of national groups including The Wilderness Society, the Sierra Club, Earthjustice, Natural Resources Defense Council, Defenders of Wildlife, and regional organizations such as the Alaska Center for the Environment and SEACC—would help take the crusade national.

Above: Paintbrush and bluebells on Storm Island, Tongass National Forest. *Carr Clifton*
Below: River otters *(Lutra canadensis)*, drawing by Dugald Stermer

THE SCIENCE OF WILDLIFE .

At that time, the Tongass National Forest was being managed under terms of a forest-wide Tongass Land Management Plan referred to jocularly as "T-Lump." It was the first such plan adopted after Congress in 1976 rewrote the Forest Service's governing law, the National Forest Management Act. This first T-Lump, adopted in 1979, was woefully out of date by 1990, especially considering the provisions of the Timber Reform Act. The Forest Service was hard at work on a new T-Lump as the election campaign of 1992 played out. The members of the first Bush administration tried mightily to produce a revised T-Lump before the election, and they did

BROWN BEARS OF THE TONGASS

Richard Nelson is an anthropologist and natural-history writer in Sitka, one of the forest's most eloquent defenders and publicists. One of his principal concerns is for the brown bears—grizzlies—that inhabit the ABC islands: Admiralty, Baranof, and Chichagof of Southeast.

"The ABC bears are different from all other brown bears," he says as we sit on the shore of an island where Nelson has a tiny cabin, waiting in vain for a young bear to return to a whale carcass. "Recent studies of DNA have shown profound differences from other browns. They've been isolated for a very long time. They have more in common with the Asian brown bear and with the polar bear than with the brown bears of the mainland."

As he describes it, the ABC bears are a relic population of brown bears from Asia. They're smaller, darker, and more compact than their cousins on the mainland. They may soon be designated a distinct subspecies, he thinks. They seem to be more susceptible to human disturbance than other brown bears. They move through but do not use clear-cut and second-growth areas.

"Near Hoonah [on Chichagof Island] they found that building roads led to killing by hunters, which depleted the bear population so fast that they closed the hunt. Hoonah is a warning signal. These bears are very vulnerable.

"They're healthy now," Nelson points out, "twelve hundred on Baranof alone, more than in the entire Lower Forty-

eight. In pre-Columbian times there were fifty thousand to a hundred thousand grizzlies in the Lower Forty-eight. The fact that we can bring our children to a place where we can see a pre-Columbian landscape is startling, and it's even more startling that we'd do anything to jeopardize it.

"The ABC bears have a very low reproductive rate. The young stay with their mothers for up to four years. This was not known ten years ago. There are still many secrets in the natural world. We must preserve the chance to have these revelations."

Scientists have determined that every species present in Southeast at the time the Russians came is still there. In addition, because of the climate, the forest is not plagued with exotic species the way many other places are.

"I have no quarrel with loggers," Nelson says. "I use paper. I use wood. I have no problem with a stump in the forest, but a forest of stumps breaks my heart.

"This landscape supports a vanishing way of life. Subsistence is wholly dependent on wide expanses of wild lands. This is not just scenery. The land sustains our culture. We want to keep it a place to live in."

Brown bears, bald eagle, and gulls on the McNeil River, Alaska.
Galen Rowell/Mountain Light

produce a draft, but they could not take it to final form before Bill Clinton swept George Bush, senior, from office.

Before the election, the Forest Service had appointed a team of biologists from the Forest Service, the Fish and Wildlife Service, and the Alaska Department of Fish and Game to assess whether the management plan then in use was threatening wildlife and what might be done to avoid losing species over large areas. Matt Kirchhoff was a member.

The committee made a list of the vertebrate species known to occupy the Tongass. It numbered 356. They winnowed the list to nine species that appeared to be vulnerable to logging and road building—some in evident danger of disappearing from the Tongass—and that used a variety of habitat types. If massive clear-cut logging was bad for these species, they reasoned, then it was bad for the forest as a whole. The species they decided to investigate in detail were the great blue heron, northern goshawk, boreal owl, gray wolf, brown bear, marten, river otter, mountain goat, and northern flying squirrel.

They surveyed all the studies they could find on these species and their habitat requirements. On brown bears, for example, they determined that the species reproduces slowly, roams widely, and therefore needs large contiguous blocks of foraging territory, and that road building inexorably leads to bears getting killed by hunters. For bears and the other species, they proposed the establishment of "habitat conservation areas" of up to forty thousand acres, no more than twenty miles apart, where logging and road building would be forbidden.

They submitted the report to the Forest Service, which was not at all ready to hear this news, much less disseminate it publicly. As Kirchhoff wrote later, in the Spring 1994 issue of *Defenders* magazine,

> Some in the Forest Service as well as the timber industry were displeased
> with the committee's preliminary recommendations. Skeptics challenged
> the adequacy of the supporting science. Pressure was applied to individ-
> ual committee members to alter or suppress their report and recommen-
> dations.

The committee countered by threatening to give the report to the Fish and Wildlife Service for publication, and somehow a copy made its way into the hands of Bridget Shulte of the *Washington Post*. Her story ran in the *Post* and the *Anchorage Daily News*.

The Forest Service relented and published the scientists' report and recommendations in 1993. It also asked its Pacific Northwest Experiment Station to arrange for a review of the recommendations by a team of independent scientists, plus one lawyer and one economist. Those worthies studied the report and pronounced it sound, with one criticism: it didn't go far enough. The habitat conservation areas should, if anything, be even bigger than the first team had recommended. The Forest Service thanked the peer reviewers and put both reports on the shelf. A new T-Lump would have to wait a little longer.

A month later, however, APC threw in the towel. It announced that it would shut its Sitka mill immediately. But it also said it would like to hang on to its contract. Tongass defenders appealed immediately to the Forest Service, arguing that APC had breached the contract by shutting down the mill, and the contract was therefore null and void. The officials said they'd think it over. The following spring the contract was canceled.

KELP BAY

Despite the improvements put into place by the reform act, the Forest Service in 1992 offered for sale trees surrounding Kelp Bay on Prince of Wales Island. The agency said that of the approximately seventeen hundred acres to be logged, only thirty-four were "high-volume" and therefore prime deer habitat. Matt Kirchhoff and his colleagues did

Totem at the entrance to a ceremonial lodge, Totem Bight State Park. *Carr Clifton*

their own measurements and found that the entire seventeen hundred acres had high-volume stands on them. The Wildlife Society appealed the sale and asked the Forest Service to withdraw it. They heard nothing for weeks; then Kirchhoff got a phone call from the office of the chief of the Forest Service, commending the society on an "excellent appeal."

Excellent or otherwise, the agency itself remained mum. "We figured the Forest Service was stonewalling us," Kirchhoff remembers. "It was time to go to court. I phoned Eric Jorgensen of Earthjustice, who agreed to listen to our story. We explained the situation, and a week later Eric called to say they'd take the case. We rounded up The Wilderness Society and the Sierra Club to join as plaintiffs."

Attorney Tom Waldo took the lead. "Tom eventually knew the technical issues—all the statistics—as well as anyone in the Forest Service, and better than most," Kirchhoff says. "Tom skewered the government on every point. We won every claim. The judge sent the matter back to the Forest Service." Waldo and the Forest Service negotiated some important changes in agency policy. The service was forced to disclose and ultimately reduce its practice of high-grading and to reform the way it conducted forest inventories.

The Forest Service, meanwhile, announced that it would still offer a number of valuable and beautiful roadless areas for logging, areas that had been slated to be cut by APC.

"The people were up in arms," Tom Waldo remembers. This was a major change in circumstances. One of the two gigantic pulp mills that had been devouring the forest had hung up its chain saws and gone home, and one of the long-term contracts had been canceled, yet the Forest Service was pushing ahead as if nothing had happened. At the very least, a new set of environmental documents should be prepared. A new lawsuit was readied to block the timber sales. The lead plaintiff was the Alaska Wilderness Recreation and Tourism Association, joined by the Organized Village of Kake, a Native community, and several environmental groups.

They lost in the first round and appealed the decision. The Ninth Circuit thereupon issued an injunction so the trees wouldn't be slaughtered during the appeal, a rather unusual tactical victory. The appeals court moved quickly and overturned the district judge, ordering the Forest Service to write a new environmental impact statement. It sent the case back to the judge in Juneau to determine whether some of the timber could be cut in the meantime. This was in July 1995. Scant days later, the infamous salvage rider was passed by Congress, as discussed in chapter 7. A little-noted companion rider passed at the same time, a creation of Alaska's senior senator, Ted Stevens, an environmental nemesis of the first order. It was intended to override the Ninth Circuit in the AWRTA suit and release the timber the Forest Service wanted to sell.

As soon as the bill containing the rider was signed by President Clinton, the Justice Department raced to the appeals court to ask that the injunction be dissolved in the face of the Stevens rider. Tom Waldo and Eric Jorgensen argued, in part, that the rider was unconstitutional and should be ignored. The three-judge panel of the Ninth Circuit that had decided the case rejected the government's motion and refused to modify its injunction. It said, in effect, that Senator Stevens had not written his rider carefully enough. No one could argue that the decision was politically motivated: two of the judges had been appointed by Republican presidents, one by Richard Nixon, the other by the first George Bush.

"This period marked a turning point in the Clinton presidency," Jorgensen observes. "Until that time Clinton had been indifferent to the environment. But the impact of, and the public reaction to, the salvage rider made him see that he could gain public favor and political advantage by doing good things environmentally."

The case returned to the district court, where the judge who had rejected it initially was to determine the scope of the injunction. Jorgensen and Waldo decided the time was ripe to seek a settlement, and the government agreed. The parties gathered in Seattle for

The Tlingit village of Angoon on Admiralty Island. Native residents joined with environmentalists and their lawyers to stop a plan to clear-cut virtually the entire island. Admiralty is now a wilderness national monument.
Carr Clifton

Clearcuts on land owned by the Klawock-Heenya Indians on Prince of Wales Island. Native corporations, encouraged by timber companies, cut most of their lands on the island destructively, trading their natural heritage for short-term profits. *Robert Glenn Ketchum*

three long days of negotiations. Jorgensen and Waldo were joined by Bart Koehler and Buck Lindekugel of SEACC and Niel Lawrence of the Natural Resources Defense Council. The administration sent Jim Lyons, undersecretary of agriculture in charge of the Forest Service, and Lois Schiffer of the Department of Justice.

It was rough going but eventually they struck a deal. All but one of the key roadless watersheds was taken off the chopping block. Part of Saook Bay, an indentation near Kelp Bay, was left to the loggers' mercy. "This was a huge victory for the Tongass," Jorgensen says. "We had managed to put together all the volume the Forest Service wanted without invading any of the pristine areas. But losing part of Saook Bay was a bitter pill." In fact, as of early 2002, it appeared that the Saook Bay sale may be too expensive to log. It, too, may survive intact.

The timber industry had been left out of the negotiations and was furious. It demanded a hearing. The district judge listened, then approved the settlement with minor modifications. A fair piece of the Tongass seemed safe, at least for the time being. If the Forest Service wanted to go after the areas again, it would have to start the EIS process over.

T-Lumping Along

The revised T-Lump finally was issued in 1997. At the same time, Louisiana-Pacific closed the Ketchikan pulp mill (the Ketchikan Pulp Corporation is a subsidiary of Louisiana-Pacific). The new management plan was a major improvement over the status quo, but still far from satisfactory. Comments poured in from activists and scientists alike. The scientists pointed out that the new plan was based on the wildlife protection strategy first proposed in 1993 and found to be lacking back then; they also pointed out that they knew a lot more four years later, and what they knew was that for wildlife to survive, logging and road building would have to be curtailed further. Much further.

Jorgensen, his colleague Janis Searles, and Niel Lawrence filed a formal appeal on behalf of the Sitka Conservation Society and NRDC, arguing among other things that the

T-Lump failed to protect subsistence resources, failed to address the high-grading problem adequately, failed to consider wilderness protection for unprotected roadless areas, and continued a heavy reliance on clear-cutting to the detriment of wildlife—in short, that it failed to protect old-growth-dependent wildlife. Tom Waldo filed a separate appeal on behalf of two Native organizations. The industry appealed what it didn't like. In the end, a total of thirty-three appeals were lodged with the chief of the Forest Service.

In 1999, Undersecretary Jim Lyons issued decisions on the individual appeals and a new and final version of the management plan. He rejected arguments that the '97 plan violated the Wilderness Act and the National Environmental Policy Act and other laws but set aside an additional half-million acres, putting them off-limits to logging. The areas included many fought over in the AWRTA litigation, plus Poison Cove and Ushk Bay, prized areas north of Sitka on Chichagof Island, which had been the subjects of a separate and successful Earthjustice legal battle. The agency also lengthened the timetable for logging—the so-called rotation—from a hundred to two hundred years in some of the most sensitive areas of the Tongass.

It was a huge improvement, but still it fell short. It protected many priceless areas and reduced the volume of timber to be cut each year. But it failed to protect hunting and fishing grounds adequately. It still ignored the high-grading problem, allowed clear-cutting to continue, and left two million roadless acres unprotected. There were no suggestions of areas to be added to the wilderness system. Tom Waldo and Eric Jorgensen went to court to ask for an order that would stop timber sales in potential wilderness areas—the vast majority of the wild Tongass—until further review was conducted. The timber industry, for its part, challenged the final T-Lump on the grounds that it was so fundamentally different from the initial plan that it required a whole new round of environmental analysis.

Aerial view of clearcuts and logging roads on Prince of Wales Island. One of the largest islands in Tongass National Forest, just across the channel from Ketchikan, "POW" Island (as locals ironically call it) has been almost 60 percent cut over. Not much is left. *Robert Glenn Ketchum*

THE ROADLESS RULE

A couple of years earlier, the chief of the Forest Service, Michael Dombeck, had imposed an eighteen-month moratorium on road construction in areas of the national forests that were then without roads. The reason was that the Forest Service was responsible for far more roads than it could maintain—nearly four hundred thousand miles of mostly rutted dirt tracks, ten times the length of the interstate highway system, enough to circle the globe eight times. Those

Back in Alaska, in the spring of 2001 and against the backdrop of the roadless-area debate, Judge James Singleton was ready to rule in the lawsuits brought to challenge the 1999 T-Lump.

First, he vindicated the environmentalists by agreeing with them: the failure to consider new wilderness areas was illegal, the judge ruled, and he told the Forest Service it could take no action affecting the wilderness eligibility of roadless areas until it carried out a new wilderness review. In the case brought by the timber industry, the judge issued an injunction blocking the implementation of the 1999 T-Lump and told the Forest Service to take its guidance from the '97 plan until it prepared a new environmental impact study to explain the changes.

At this point the timber industry formally moved to oppose the environmentalists' case. It asked the judge to reopen the proceedings and call a hearing with witnesses who could testify about the hardships they would endure if logging were suspended in roadless areas. The Justice Department asked the judge to vacate the injunction, claiming he hadn't offered an adequate rationale for it. Waldo argued that the industry was much too late to join the case and that the judge's order was final. Any appeals should properly go to the court of appeals.

In May, the judge spoke again. He suspended his injunction until the requested hearing could be held. Waldo sprinted for the court of appeals. But in the summer of 2001, that court declined to step in, and Waldo began preparing for a hearing aimed at reinstating the injunction. Meanwhile, the Forest Service started the new wilderness review of Tongass roadless areas, and activists geared up to voice their support for protection.

On the T-Lump front, the Bush Forest Service decided it was quite content with the 1997 plan and refused to appeal the judge's action stopping the final 1999 decision. So conservation groups intervened, again represented by Waldo and colleagues, to go it alone in the court of appeals defending the 1999 Lyons decision.

At the time of this writing, the fate of roadless areas on the Tongass and all other national forests was very much up in the air. The Alaska Rainforest Campaign and other groups were pushing legislation to proclaim a number of new wilderness areas on the Tongass, but its fate was uncertain, and at best it would be several years before there would be any likelihood of its enactment.

Nevertheless, it seemed clear that the long campaign had galvanized public opinion and would make destruction of roadless areas more difficult, no matter what the official policy eventually said. As Eric Jorgensen says, "Even if we lose the roadless rule, the public attitude has firmed up. Millions of people are now paying attention thanks to all the commotion. Any time the Forest Service tries to sell timber in a roadless area it will be a big deal."

"We've changed the terms of the roadless debate," Tom Waldo chimes in, "and that's forever."

CHAPTER TEN

THE TROUBLE WITH TRADE

Ever since a cave dweller first hit on the idea of trading an extra piece of meat for a skin to keep warm, or a chip of obsidian to turn into a knife or an arrow point, people have been exchanging items they have in excess for things they need and don't have. Barter, it's called, and it has probably been practiced since human antecedents began walking upright.

At first, it was strictly a matter of trading one good for another. Eventually, however, beginning sometime around 9000 B.C. there slowly began to develop the abstract idea of money, first in the form of livestock, later shells, precious metals, and eventually coins and paper money that have little intrinsic value but instead operate on trust. At the dawn of the twenty-first century, money was becoming even more abstract, with more and more economic transactions being conducted electronically, and vast sums of money being traded instantaneously with the click of a computer key.

Trade, in other words, has always been with us, and it has largely been considered a boon to both participants and the intermediaries—shipping companies, customs officials, marketers, advertising agencies, and all the rest—who make their livings facilitating the exchange of goods.

But somewhere along the way, adjustments had to be made. If, for example, labor was substantially cheaper—that is, wages were substantially lower—in one country than another, then goods manufactured in the low-wage country could be sold for less than the same goods manufactured in the higher-wage country. This would threaten the economy of the importing country, since workers engaged in the manufacture of the goods in question would lose their jobs as people bought the cheaper imported items.

That led to the imposition of duties, or tariffs, or taxes—call them what you will—generally enacted to protect a country's domestic economy, workers, and industries. Sometimes the tariffs made sense; sometimes they were arbitrary and illogical. Frequently they were supported by labor unions and opposed by industrialists, for obvious reasons. The unions wanted to protect jobs while the businesspeople wanted to expand their markets. Debates about duties and tariffs have been vigorous and frothy for many years.

Following the end of World War II, a meeting was held at Bretton Woods in New Hampshire with the aim of creating a postwar international economic system that would lead to prosperity for all and guarantee the extinction of great wars. Out of Bretton Woods

Opposite: Green sea turtle in lagoon, Hawai'i. Supporters of sea turtles made common cause with Teamsters at the World Trade Organization meeting in Seattle in late 1990. *Frans Lanting/Minden Pictures*

sprang two new institutions—the World Bank and the International Monetary Fund—and a treaty called the General Agreement on Tariffs and Trade. The latter, whose aim would be to reduce or eliminate tariffs and other barriers to international trade, was known colloquially as GATT, which coincidentally, is similar to old slang (gat) for an early version of the machine gun. The coincidence, in the view of many, is more than apt.

GATT was in effect until the mid-1990s, when it was incorporated into a charter for a wildly powerful new institution, the World Trade Organization. The WTO, which includes nearly all the countries of the world, represented a remarkable ceding of authority by sovereign governments to a supranational organization, headquartered in Geneva. The WTO's mission is to lower trade barriers and settle disputes between member nations. The dispute resolution process involves secret deliberations by anonymous panels of functionaries. The public is not permitted to participate in the process, a fact we shall discuss in more detail presently. Even before the WTO was born, the United States, Canada,

Demonstrators protesting the WTO meeting in Seattle focused strongly on environmental issues. *Loren Callahan/Reuters/Landov*

and Mexico had fashioned their own regional version of GATT known as NAFTA, the North American Free Trade Agreement. At the beginning of the twenty-first century, many other trade agreements were under construction, the most visible and controversial in the Western Hemisphere being the proposed Free Trade Area of the Americas.

Environmental organizations, having their hands full with chain saws and bulldozers, had not historically paid a great deal of attention to international trade, apart from trying to eliminate the commerce in elephant ivory, exotic birds, and other rare and wondrous items that some people simply must have even if it means eliminating the creature involved from the face of the earth.

But when NAFTA was hatched in the early 1990s, some prescient observers began to make warning noises. What would the loosening of restrictions on trade mean for natural resources domestically and abroad? How would "illegal barriers to trade," which the WTO has the power to abolish, be defined? Would a country be permitted to refuse to buy certain goods based on the way they were manufactured—if they were made by slaves or children, for example, or if they might harbor exotic pests? And what about the sanctions placed on countries that kill porpoises in the process of fishing for tuna? These sanctions had finally begun to reduce the slaughter of porpoises from the peak of several hundred thousand annually it had reached in the 1970s. Would they be permitted under NAFTA?

These and other concerns drove a deep wedge into the environmental community. Many organizations lobbied against adoption of NAFTA, but a few prominent groups supported it, arguing that safeguards would be built in to "environmental side agreements" and that the agreement as a whole would in fact help to clean up badly contaminated sites in Mexico. NAFTA was adopted.

It soon became clear that the concerns voiced during debates over whether the United States should join NAFTA and the WTO were real, and that not only were resources in jeopardy, but also domestic laws and institutions. What follows is a string of examples of where the headlong rush toward completely unfettered international trade has gone badly awry, and of efforts mounted by individuals and organizations in several corners of the world to set matters right.

CLEAR THE AIR, FOUL THE WATER

Automobiles, trucks, buses, and other vehicles are, as everyone knows, responsible for a large fraction of the pollution that hovers above many cities and rural areas, impairing health, damaging crops and forests, and obscuring views. One way to lessen the severity of this pollution is to manufacture gasoline that burns as thoroughly as possible, and one way to approach that goal is to add oxygen to the fuel. This is known as oxygenating the gas, or reformulating it.

There are two chemicals now used to add oxygen to gasoline in the United States. One is known as methyl tertiary butyl ether, or MTBE; the other is ethanol, or grain alcohol, the kind much admired by some tipplers. MTBE is made from methanol and isobutylene, both derived from natural gas. Ethanol is currently made from corn kernels but could be made from nearly any plant.

Amendments to the Clean Air Act adopted in 1990 require eighteen states to supply oxygenated gasoline in their most polluted places: Arizona, California, Connecticut, Delaware, Indiana, Kentucky, Illinois, New Hampshire, Massachusetts, Maryland, Missouri, New Jersey, New York, Pennsylvania, Rhode Island, Texas, Virginia, and Wisconsin. (A few states that were not required to oxygenate their gasoline did so voluntarily.) Of those

Traffic in downtown Gatlinburg, Tennessee, in the Smoky Mountains. Cars pollute the air and the gasoline additive MBTE can pollute the water. *Michael K. Nichols/NGS Image Collection*

only the big corn states, Wisconsin and Illinois, use ethanol. The rest use MTBE. California, being the biggest and most car-addicted, accounted for nearly half the MTBE used in the country in the late 1990s.

The oil companies are very fond of MTBE, or at least they were before the bad publicity came washing up on their doorsteps. The chemical, which Elisa Lynch of the Bluewater Network refers to as "hamburger helper," is a cheap filler that inflates the volume of gas and therefore lowers the cost of a gallon—to the oil companies, at least.

The midwestern states, meanwhile, and some environmental organizations favor ethanol, which is not a scarce fossil fuel and could easily be made from farm wastes that are now discarded or burned. A switch to ethanol, they argue, would result in a sharp reduction in greenhouse gases as an added fillip.

Jetskis on Lake Tahoe, California. The two-stroke engines used in Jetskis are a major source of MTBE—methyl tertiary butyl ether—a chemical that makes gasoline burn cleaner but has fouled hundreds of reservoirs and underground sources of drinking water. *George F. Mobley/NGS Image Collection*

MTBE was developed to replace lead as an octane enhancer at low concentrations in high-test gasoline, lead having been found to cause horrible damage to young human brains. In the early 1990s, the concentration of MTBE—which, as previously mentioned, also increases the fraction of oxygen in the fuel—was substantially boosted in gasoline bound for the most polluted places in the country: Los Angeles, Houston, Denver, New York, and elsewhere.

By most accounts, the MTBE worked well in its appointed task of reducing smog, but, as is so often the case with evidently miraculous cures, it had unwelcome and unanticipated side effects. (Side effects, in the words of the biologist Garrett Hardin, are "surprise results, the existence of which we will deny as long as we possibly can.") MTBE developed an unpleasant habit of leaking from underground storage tanks, being spilled onto the ground at gas stations and elsewhere, or invading groundwater supplies, where, even at extremely low concentrations, it renders the water foul-smelling and undrinkable.

It also migrates in soil and groundwater very quickly and can travel long distances. In addition, the two-stroke engines that power small recreational vehicles—including the Jetskis that zip around many lakes and reservoirs used for drinking water—are notoriously inefficient, expelling as much as 30 percent of their fuel unburned into the water. Russell Long of the Bluewater Network has calculated that a single Jetski, operating for two hours, will discharge enough MTBE to contaminate the amount of water consumed daily by ninety thousand people.

Worse yet, the stuff causes cancer in laboratory animals and is suspected of doing the same in humans. A Bluewater Network report based on unsealed court documents and released in August 2001 estimated that at least fifty thousand public and private wells nationwide, along with countless lakes and reservoirs, were contaminated with MTBE. The bill for cleaning up the mess was expected to reach a hundred billion dollars.

In 1996, residents of Santa Monica, California, began to complain about their water. It tasted bad and smelled worse. The cause was eventually identified as MTBE in gasoline leaking from underground storage tanks. In one well field, concentrations were measured at more than 600 parts per billion. Most people can detect the chemical when concentrations reach 15 ppb. Two well fields, from which Santa Monica pumped half its water, had to be closed. Replacement water was brought in by tanker trucks.

Soon reports came in that the stuff was cropping up all over the place, and people began agitating for a ban on the use of MTBE and a cleanup of existing contamination. Communities for a Better Environment filed suit against Chevron, Exxon, Unocal, Texaco, and a joint venture of Shell and Texaco called Equilon, demanding that they clean up the MTBE mess they'd made in California. On March 25, 1999, California governor Gray Davis ordered that MTBE be phased out of gasoline sold in his state by the end of 2002. (On March 17, 2002, having endured a politically explosive energy crisis, he delayed the ban until the end of 2003.) Sooner would be better. As of mid-2001, Arizona, California, Colorado, Connecticut, Illinois, Iowa, Kansas, Michigan, Minnesota, Nebraska, New York, South Dakota, and Washington had taken action against MTBE in gasoline, and legislation was pending in Congress for a nationwide ban.

Ethanol, or grain alcohol, is made from corn and used in some corn-growing states as an alternative to MBTE for oxygenating gasoline. *Medford Taylor/NGS Image Collection*

Then the hammer fell. A Canadian company called Methanex, which manufactures methanol and sells most of it to producers of MTBE, filed a challenge under chapter 11 of the NAFTA rules and regulations alleging that its sovereign right to earn profits from its enterprise was being illegally impeded by California. Methanex demanded a levy of a billion dollars if the state's MTBE ban should go into effect as scheduled. The claim came under provisions in the agreement aimed at protecting investments. (Methanex owns two plants in the United States.) Similar provisions exist in many international free-trade agreements and treaties.

In other words, it was a none-too-subtle exercise in what Martin Wagner, the director of the international program for Earthjustice, calls extortion: "If Californians want to drink clean water, Methanex must get a billion dollars." Something is dangerously wrong with this picture. Critics had long warned

A bias toward commerce and away from concern about public health and the environment has long been built into our government's structures for conducting international trade negotiations, but Earthjustice and other NGOs have begun to make some inroads at the federal level.

The United States has on its books a simple and commonsensical law called FACA, the Federal Advisory Committee Act. This law guides the formation and conduct of dozens of committees that advise federal agencies on a wide range of matters of public concern. Among many other features, the law requires that representation on the committees be "balanced."

The office of the U.S. Trade Representative, the agency that represents the United States at the World Trade Organization, has some thirty committees that provide advice on matters such as trade in wood and wood products, paper and paper products, chemicals, and many others. As environmental groups became more closely involved with trade matters, they noticed a curious thing: the committees that advise on environmental matters contained not a single representative of an environmental organization. Indeed, they included almost exclusively CEOs and other high officials from the industries involved: timber, paper, chemicals, et cetera. No environmentalists, no scientists, no labor representatives.

Appeals were made to the trade representative, who explained that sensitive matters were involved, privacy was a large concern, and the pesky environmentalists should go bother someone else. Earthjustice attorney Patti Goldman filed a lawsuit in 1999 against the trade representative, seeking to force the appointment of at least one public representative to the committee that advises on trade in wood and wood products. She represented the Northwest Ecosystem Alliance, Pacific Environment, Defenders of Wildlife, Buckeye Forest Council, and the International Forum on Globalization. It was a reasonably straightforward case; a federal judge in Seattle granted the request and ordered the trade representative to add an environmental representative to the panel.

The Clinton administration, which had been saying democratic-sounding things about openness—transparency, it's often called in these circles—announced that it would appeal the decision, then changed its mind. So Goldman went after the chemicals panel, and while the federal government seemed resigned to the inevitable, the industry fought hard to keep the committee its private domain, filing its own suit against the trade representative to block any appointment of an environmental representative to the panel. Goldman and Martin Wagner intervened in this case, fearing that the new Bush administration would not provide a vigorous defense, given its antipathy to public participation in environmental decision making, and they won.

As of 2001, there are environmental representatives on the committees, and the attorneys were consulting various organizations to see if there were other advisory committees in need of opening up.

that NAFTA would jeopardize environmental cleanup and protection efforts by giving trade precedence over domestic sovereignty. The MTBE suit promised to test that thesis.

The suit was filed June 15, 1999, against the United States. A three-judge tribunal was appointed, one nominated by Methanex, one by the U.S. State Department, and one agreeable to both. In this case, the panel was composed of one Canadian and one British arbitrator and Warren Christopher, the former U.S. secretary of state.

The NAFTA dispute resolution panels, like those of the World Trade Organization and other bodies, are set up to protect the privacy of the parties to the dispute. Their paperwork is secret; their hearings, if any, are secret; and their deliberations are secret. This may be appropriate when the dispute is small and involves only matters of commerce, but the MTBE matter, and several others that have been taken before NAFTA tribunals, are of great public concern. As Martin Wagner pointed out in the *New York Times*, "The fact that the drafters of NAFTA chose this secretive process to resolve these disputes is further evidence that they weren't foreseeing matters of broad social concern coming before these panels."

And with that, Wagner and his colleague Scott Pasternack, on behalf of Bluewater Network, Communities for a Better Environment, and the Center for International Environmental Law, politely asked the tribunal if they could please join the case as a friend of the court—an amicus curiae—to make sure that the public interest was vigorously represented in the arguments, something that had never before been allowed in such a proceeding.

Methanex, to no one's surprise, objected strenuously, arguing that the NAFTA panels were set up the way they were to protect privacy and that letting outsiders participate would be messy and expensive. The United States said it had no objection to letting the environmental groups file an amicus brief. The governments of Canada and Mexico, not parties to the specific dispute but making up two-thirds of NAFTA, weighed in with their own arguments, Canada supporting the aspiring amici, Mexico opposing them. In the spring the tribunal members spoke. They found that they could accept an amicus brief if they wanted to but they'd leave a final, formal decision for later. The door sealing off NAFTA from public scrutiny may have been nudged open a hair's breadth.

Meanwhile, in the real world, MTBE and Methanex were suffering one public relations disaster after another. On August 11, 2001, Exxon agreed to pay twelve million dollars to help clean up a mess at South Lake Tahoe, where MTBE in its gasoline had contaminated groundwater. Exxon itself owns no facilities there but acknowledged that its gasoline is a "defective product," which must have made its stockholders happy. That case was litigated by Vic Sher, a former attorney for and president of Earthjustice.

A week later, Communities for a Better Environment settled its suit against the oil companies, which agreed to clean up various contaminated sites around California. And Gray Davis, governor of California, filed his own suit against the Environmental Protection Agency, seeking to establish that California could stop using any oxygenate, MTBE and ethanol alike. This, in turn, provoked a split in the environmental community, with the Natural Resources Defense Council siding with the governor and Bluewater Network and others insisting that ethanol was in all respects something that should be added to gasoline for a spate of reasons.

In the background, the Environmental Protection Agency was slogging through the process of writing a new rule under provisions of the Toxic Substances Control Act to ban or severely limit the use of MTBE, and Congress was considering a ban as well. If the investment tribunal should award Methanex a billion dollars for California's ban, the company would surely come back for more if the substance were banned nationally. And if Methanex can extort that kind of money from governments simply trying to protect their citizens from environmental contaminants and disease, other companies are sure to notice. An earlier precedent was not comforting: U.S.-based Ethyl Corporation had sued Canada in a NAFTA tribunal for banning one of its gasoline additives. Canada had settled the case by paying Ethyl some thirteen million dollars, apologizing, and rescinding the ban.

A Transatlantic Food Fight

The exquisite torture that nations have willingly inflicted on themselves and one another in the blind pursuit of free trade is nowhere more starkly apparent than in the monumental battle over beef growth hormones. These chemicals can be natural or synthetic and are routinely given to beef cattle in the United States to make them grow bigger and faster than they otherwise would. This has been going on for several decades. As of 1995, 63 percent of all U.S. cattle and 90 percent of those raised in feed lots were being treated with growth hormones.

A growing body of scientific research, meanwhile, suggests that the hormones may be worth worrying about. They can cause cancer in lab animals and, in some cases, in humans. In 1980, in response to these studies, the European Union instituted a series of bans on the use of the hormones within its member countries. Soon after, it announced that it would no longer permit the import of beef that had been treated with the hormones. This new prohibition had the greatest impact on beef producers in the United States and Canada.

Beef cattle in the United States are fed a hormone to make them grow big, fast. Europeans are suspicious of such a chemical. Should the Europeans have the right to decide what they eat? The U.S. government thinks not.
Chris Johns/NGS Image Collection

Sixteen years later, soon after the birth of the World Trade Organization, Canada and the United States filed a formal complaint with the WTO alleging that the European ban on hormone-treated cattle was an unfair barrier to free trade. The Europeans argued back that they had every right to protect their citizens against what looked to be a serious threat to public health. The WTO, via one of its shadowy tribunals, sided with the beef industry. The Europeans appealed, and the Appellate Body of the WTO—established to review such complaints—acknowledged that studies "do indeed show the existence of a general risk of cancer," but affirmed the first ruling.

Environmental groups in the United States, meanwhile, represented by Martin Wagner and Patti Goldman of Earthjustice, had tried to insinuate themselves into the process to help the E.U. make its case. They wrote a lengthy submission summarizing the scientific research that had been conducted on growth hormones. And they provided a ringing defense of the so-called precautionary principle, which is fancy lingo for "better safe than sorry," or "look before you leap." The principle suggests that in the face of uncertainty concerning the possible deleterious effects of, in this case, a family of chemicals, it is legitimate for a government to ban the chemicals until their safety is assured.

The WTO, however, is less than interested in what the public thinks. There is no mechanism, as there is in many other international institutions, for participation by what are known as nongovernmental organizations. The WTO informed the submitters that their offering would be ignored.

So the lawyers tried the back door. They provided copies of their submission to member nations of the E.U., several of which included the arguments and data in their own submissions to the WTO. They also provided copies of the brief directly to the panelists and were informed by an employee of the U.S. Trade Representative that the panelists had the brief at each hearing. Public Citizen, one of the authors of the brief, had a panelist come into its D.C. office while he was on vacation and ask for another copy because he had forgotten to bring his along.

In the end, or at least as of mid-2001, it was all for naught. The WTO, while acknowledging the cancer risk as mentioned, ruled that the burden of proof was on the Europeans: they must prove conclusively that the hormones do pose a tangible risk of cancer before they would be permitted to refuse to import the treated beef, a bizarre twist on innocent until proven guilty.

The Europeans, for their part, held firm and continue to refuse to import hormone-treated beef from anywhere. In retaliation, the WTO authorized the United States to impose more than a hundred million dollars in trade sanctions each year the ban remains in force. If you wonder why truffles are so expensive, this is part of the reason. The sanctions, in turn, have led to colorful demonstrations in France and elsewhere against McDonalds restaurants and other symbols of American carnivorousness. And remember, no one forced the European countries—or any others—to join the World Trade Organization.

GETTING THE LEAD OUT OF LA OROYA

While lead has been removed from gasoline and paint to protect public health, the metal is still used in other applications—the lion's share for batteries in cars, trucks, and buses—and it's still the same old lead, posing the same old hazards. One particularly ugly example is high in the mountains of Peru, in a town called La Oroya. Earthjustice staff scientist and chemist Anna Cederstav calls it "one of the western hemisphere's greatest environmental and public health disasters."

Cederstav works in the small International Program of Earthjustice, which in turn works closely with a coalition of environmental-law organizations in the hemisphere known as AIDA, the Asociación Interamericana para la Defensa del Ambiente, or the International Association for Environmental Defense. AIDA includes law groups from Canada, Chile, Colombia, Costa Rica, Mexico, Peru, and the United States. They collaborate to devise and implement international legal strategies for solving environmental problems. La Oroya is a pressing priority.

Peru's Urubamba Valley is a classic Andean agricultural landscape, similar to the one devastated by the Doe Run mining operation in La Oroya. *Galen Rowell/Mountain Light*

A multi-metal smelter in La Oroya that dates from around 1918—originally built and owned by an American company—has been poisoning the thirty thousand townspeople for the better part of a century with toxic contaminants such as lead, arsenic, and cadmium. In 1974, Peru nationalized much of its industry. The smelter at La Oroya was one of the facilities seized by the government. Then, in the latter part of the century, the political tide shifted and in 1997, the government sold the facility in La Oroya for $246 million to a subsidiary of the Doe Run Company. Doe Run, a U.S. corporation, is the world's largest primary lead producer and the owner of mines and plants that caused tremendous environmental damage in states such as Missouri, though its performance is much improved in recent years. Here we must digress just a little; the temptation is irresistible.

Doe Run is one of many enterprises owned by a shadowy, Brooklyn-bred, self-made man named Ira Leon Rennert. Rennert's holdings include a Utah magnesium plant ranked first on the Environmental Protection Agency's list of most prolific air polluters in the land (123 pounds of toxic air pollutants released every *minute*). The Doe Run lead operation in Missouri ranks thirty-seventh on the EPA's 1998 list of the fifty top polluting facilities when water, air, and land are considered jointly. His companies make the army's fabulously inefficient all-terrain vehicle known as the Humvee and its civilian counterpart, the Hummer. He owns steel plants, energy companies, and a lumber company. As of this writing, Rennert was in the process of building on Long Island, N.Y., what may be the largest private, single-family residence in the country: bigger than the White House, bigger than Grand Central Station, more than twice as big as Bill Gates's mansion near Seattle—approximately a hundred thousand square feet including outbuildings, with more than thirty bedrooms, a similar number of bathrooms, and parking for a hundred vehicles. Some family. He is, in short, a one-man environmental wrecking crew. Now he owns the lead smelter in La Oroya, Peru.

The statistics for La Oroya are nothing short of shocking. A recent health survey of five hundred La Oroya children conducted by the Peruvian government found that fewer that 1 percent of them have blood levels of lead considered healthy, and that nearly 20 percent should be taken straight to the hospital. But there are no local medical facilities with the expertise to handle this kind of epidemic, no money to create them, and no money to send the children away for the care they so desperately need. Even if treatment were available, the problem would reappear once the children returned to the contaminated environment of La Oroya. The company insists it is doing all it can, and Cederstav concedes that there has been some improvement—but she notes that progress to date is minimal compared to what is needed.

The contract under which Doe Run took over La Oroya shelters the company from liability and exempts it from environmental regulation until 2006. The company tackled water pollution problems first, likely because they're cheapest to fix and because Peru had no air-quality standards. At the same time, the company increased production quickly to recoup its cash investment. This caused a dramatic increase in air pollution with severe consequences for public health.

Meanwhile, in late 2000, back home in Missouri, Doe Run settled a lawsuit brought against it by the Environmental Protection Agency, agreeing to replace contaminated soils in residential neighborhoods around the smelter, conduct blood screening and education about lead poisoning in the community, implement technologies to reduce emissions to meet strict U.S. air-quality laws, and reduce production if air-quality goals are not met, among other things. Interestingly, a few months thereafter, "to enable Doe Run to effectively compete in the present global market" and because of "poor global markets for refined lead," as

The La Oroya smelter and, inset, boys posing for Anna Cederstav's camera in front of it. The twin smokestacks emit lead in such concentration that fewer than one percent of local children have what is considered a healthy level of lead in their blood. *Both, Anna Cederstav*

explained by Doe Run CEO Jeffrey Zelms, the company began to reduce production and lay off workers in the United States.

According to Cederstav, "With new trade agreements like the FTAA likely to further undercut the already weak environmental protections afforded by NAFTA, and with ever-expanding international commerce, there is little to stop companies like Doe Run from shifting operations to places like La Oroya or to prevent individuals without scruples from amassing fortunes at the expense of the environment and populations beyond our borders." In other words, though there is no trade agreement between Peru and the United States at present, adoption of a NAFTA-like agreement would make a bad situation worse.

AIDA has taken on the cause of the people of La Oroya with its Peruvian member organization SPDA, Sociedad Peruana de Derecho Ambiental, which, with Cederstav, analyzed air-quality data to demonstrate the continued impact of the Doe Run facility. Together they are pressing the company, the government, and international institutions to take action. Peru is in the process of establishing pollution-control laws, and AIDA seeks strong standards for toxic substances such as lead. Not surprisingly, the metallurgical industry has vehemently opposed such laws. It remains uncertain when or whether Doe Run will be forced to cut air emissions.

Long-term salvation for the people of La Oroya probably means moving the town. Doe Run says paying for that is not the company's responsibility, since it was so late to come on the scene. The Peruvian government says it doesn't have the money. There does not appear to be any simple solution. Mr. Rennert could probably finance the move out of petty cash, but he has made no such offer.

RESOURCE EXTRACTION ON THE MOVE

"People say free trade hasn't caused polluting industries to move," Anna Cederstav says, and then draws a line down the middle of the industrial map. High-skill industries with very expensive equipment—semiconductor manufacturers, for example—tend to stay put. They may move assembly operations overseas, but the manufacturing plants generally remain where they are. "But resource-extracting industries are skipping town to countries with scant environmental regulations and deficient enforcement," she says.

"Some trade agreements, like NAFTA, require that countries not lower their environmental standards to attract foreign investors, but none oblige those with poor or nonexistent standards to create or strengthen them. When economically destitute nations like Peru compete for foreign investment, the companies have the upper hand in negotiations. With deals based on favorable tax arrangements and limited regulation, foreign investors reap abundant profits while nations sell resources at discount rates and under conditions that compromise the environment and human health."

"TEAMSTERS LOVE TURTLES"

One of the more arresting sights during the rowdy meeting held by the World Trade Organization in Seattle at the end of 1999 was a bunch of burly truck drivers parading arm-in-arm with young activists dressed up as sea turtles. "Turtles love teamsters," one group would chant, with "Teamsters love turtles" chanted warmly back. The odd alliance stemmed from the fact that the WTO is no more friendly to labor than it is to wildlife. And it spoke specifically to another instance where obeisance to unfettered trade threatened to trample attempts by one country—the United States—to put pressure on other

The olive ridley sea turtle nests mostly In Costa Rica and Mexico; this one was photographed in the Galapagos. *Tul de Roy/ Minden Pictures*

countries—India, Malaysia, and others—with the aim of saving vanishing creatures that roam the open ocean and belong to no one.

In this case, the United States, under intense pressure from the Sea Turtle Restoration Project and other groups, had decided to refuse to allow the importation of shrimp from countries that did not force their shrimpers to use so-called turtle excluder devices, or TEDs: simple, inexpensive grates that shunt turtles to safety as the shrimp pass through into the nets. Many countries have required their shrimp fleets to use the devices, but there have been some holdouts, resisting as much as anything else for reasons of pride and reluctance to give in to what they see as bullying by the United States. No matter what the reason, far too many turtles continued to die each year, and drastic measures, it seemed, were in order.

The shrimpers took their case to the World Trade Organization, arguing that the United States had no right to refuse their shrimp under WTO rules, which generally forbid countries to block trade on the basis of how the merchandise to be traded is produced or, as in this case, harvested.

There are seven recognized species of sea turtle. All are scarce and getting scarcer. At this moment, four of the species are classified as endangered, that is, in imminent peril of going extinct, and three as threatened, that is, in peril of becoming endangered. The smallest, the Kemp's ridley—twenty-four to twenty-eight inches long and weighing at most a hundred pounds—is also the most severely endangered. Its only major nesting

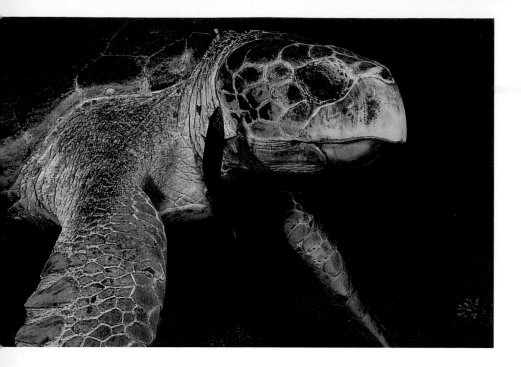

Loggerhead turtle, off Lizard Island, Great Barrier Reef, Australia. *Fred Bavendam/ Minden Pictures*

site is a single beach in Mexico, at Rancho Nuevo. The next most imperiled is the hawksbill—the source of tortoise-shell glasses, combs, and other such items. Hawksbill turtles nest on beaches throughout the Caribbean, rarely on American sand. The leatherback—the only sea turtle without a hard shell but with a leathery skin instead— is also endangered and is the largest of the sea turtles, growing up to eight feet long and weighing well over a thousand pounds. A few nest in Florida. Leatherbacks feed almost exclusively on jellyfish and have been known to perish after mistaking plastic bags for their normal fare.

Green turtles are endangered as well, but substantial numbers of them still return to nest on the Atlantic coast of Florida. The olive ridley, threatened and on the small side as sea turtles go (generally less than a hundred pounds), nests mainly in Costa Rica and Mexico. The loggerhead, the most common of a vanishing group, runs to three-plus feet in length and up to 350 pounds. Loggerheads nest in Oman on the Persian Gulf and on the Atlantic coast of Florida, between Cape Canaveral and Sebastian Inlet, many of them in the Archie Carr National Wildlife Refuge, which was set aside precisely to protect nesting sites for the turtles. The seventh species is the flatback, a medium-size turtle that confines itself to nesting sites in Australia and Papua, New Guinea.

All the species have traits in common. They are mysterious, spending months and years at sea (no one knows precisely where), returning to land only to lay their eggs. They are ancient, having occupied the earth since before the dinosaurs appeared. They prefer warm equatorial waters. And, as explained, they are all in danger of being driven to extinction.

Several factors are responsible for the disappearance of so many turtles. People kill the turtles for meat. Indeed, when wooden sailing ships plied the high seas exploring uncharted waters, turtles were a staple food. People gather eggs, also for food. People kill turtles for their shells. And most recently and lethally, turtles are accidentally drowned (they all need to breathe air now and then) in shrimp and fish nets and through being snagged by hooks meant to catch swordfish and other finfish.

A panel of the World Trade Organization pondered the evidence presented to it, including a letter signed by 265 scientists from thirty-one nations urging that the decision be based on science, not trade. On April 6, 1997, the WTO ruled that the U.S. ban on importing shrimp from nations that did not require excluder devices on shrimpers was illegal, an improper infringement of free trade. So sweeping was the ruling that it more or less eliminated such exceptions as had been included—though rarely invoked—in the General Agreement on Tariffs and Trade that allow for trade restrictions aimed at protecting human health and the environment, rules by which the WTO was nominally bound.

The United States appealed the ruling, this time bolstered by a lengthy document prepared by Martin Wagner of Earthjustice on behalf of the Sea Turtle Restoration Project. A year and a half later, in October of 1998, the Appellate Body repudiated the reasoning in the earlier ruling but found the procedures used by the United States to implement its shrimp ban also illegal. The water, in other words, remained extremely murky. India, Malaysia, and others remained defiant. The United States, meanwhile, suggested it could abide by the WTO ruling and still retain strong protection for vanishing turtles. And environmental groups pledged to keep the heat on. With this ruling the WTO kept its perfect record intact: Whenever a regulation aimed at protecting the environment or human health ran up against a WTO-approved free-trade rule, trade had won. Every time.

To be fair, that was true when the decision came down, but the situation has changed. The Appellate Body has since decided that France could ban asbestos. It has also upheld (against continued challenge by Malaysia) the United States' modified implementation of the shrimp-turtle ban as not violating the WTO rules. The WTO and the United States tout the latter decision as vindicating the WTO's claims to being environmentally friendly, but the United States made several changes to address the WTO's concerns—most significantly altering its ban from a prohibition on shrimp coming from a country that does not require *all* its shrimpers to use TEDs (which uses the U.S. import market as a carrot for nationwide protections) to a ban only on individual *shipments* of shrimp not caught with TEDs (meaning that

The ulmo, or roble de Chile *(Eucryphia cordifolia)*, is a flowering evergreen tree native to the forests of central and southern Chile. It was threatened by a proposed wood-processing plant near the resort town of Puerto Montt. *Geoff Bryant/Photo Researchers*

turtle-deadly shrimp could still be caught in that country but just sold somewhere other than the United States). The change makes it nearly impossible, however, to guarantee that the shrimp imported into the United States is really turtle-safe.

WHERE THE TREES ARE

Much is made of American companies' proclivity for moving their operations abroad, where labor is cheap and labor laws lax. A companion habit is moving resource extraction activities overseas as domestic supplies shrink and environmental protection laws and

Above: The slender-billed conure, or choroy *(Enicognathus leptorhynchus),* is native to the Chilean forests of the Lake District. *Stephen Cooper/Photo Researchers.* Likewise the South American puma *(Felis concolor).* *Heinz Plenge/Peter Arnold, Inc.*

regulations impede the freedom of companies to operate as they please. In the timber industry, there has been a well-documented migration of logging activities from the Pacific Northwest, now largely cut over, to the Southeast, where logged-over lands have regrown enough timber to provide an economically significant supply, at least for pulp mills.

Boise Cascade, the giant company headquartered in Idaho (and coincidentally, a leader in the battle to undo the Clinton administration initiative to put remaining roadless areas in the national forests off limits to road builders; see chapter 9), decided to go its peers one better and proposed a major wood panel and chip plant in Chile, having closed its Idaho mills and laid off 253 workers. It would be a joint venture with a Chilean company known as Maderas Cóndor.

The plant, to be built near Puerto Montt, about five hundred miles south of Santiago and a thousand miles north of Cape Horn, would accelerate the destruction of the surrounding forest, which has already lost approximately 80 percent of its native forest to logging. This is the celebrated Lake District of southern Chile, a spectacular archipelago whose numerous national parks draw hordes of tourists each year. Chilean environmental groups were aghast at the plan to log the forests surrounding Puerto Montt, land that is not only beautiful but also habitat for a variety of wild creatures. This particular operation, whose production would be entirely for export, would consume around six million trees annually, denuding more than twelve thousand acres—nearly twenty square miles. A half-dozen Chilean organizations turned for help to that country's leading public-interest environmental law organization, Fiscalia del Medio Ambiente. FIMA in turn appealed to AIDA for assistance.

The Chilean government had approved the project with no assessment of its environ-

mental impact. Indeed, Boise Cascade argued that the only impact that need be examined was the one on the plant site itself, since it would buy raw timber from small landowners who are exempt from environmental impact regulations. Chilean law requires environmental studies of large-scale forest exploitation, but the government decided to ignore its own laws, as so frequently happens in the United States.

But lawyers for Earthjustice, its Canadian counterpart, Sierra Legal Defence Fund, and FIMA knew that Chile was party to a bilateral trade agreement with Canada known as the Canada–Chile Free Trade Agreement. That pact includes an Agreement on Environmental Cooperation between Chile and Canada, which is nearly identical with the so-called environmental side agreements attached to NAFTA: it provides a mechanism whereby private groups and individuals can challenge a government's failure to enforce its own environmental laws effectively. The panel accepted the submission from AIDA and FIMA and ordered Chile to explain its alleged failure to enforce its laws. The story was covered extensively in the Chilean press, and Boise Cascade, claiming changed economic circumstances, canceled the project.

The best single word to sum up the tension between free trade and environmental protection is probably *unsettled*. It is very early in the day for these and many other concerns: patenting seeds and other life forms and the fast-growing controversy over genetically modified food, to name just two. These are matters that will not go away, and the public will continue to insist that it has every right to participate in the debates and have an influence on their outcome. Many, without doubt, will end up in court or courtlike forums. Groups including AIDA, CIEL (the Center for International Environmental Law), Sierra Legal Defence Fund, and Earthjustice will be kept busy for many years to come.

Another denizen of the Chilean forest, the coypu, or nutria *(Myocastor coypus)*, depends on wetlands. *John Cancalosi/Peter Arnold, Inc.*

Closing the Courthouse Doors

Justice on Earth tells quintessentially American stories—stories of citizens who go to court to protect the public good, and of judges who hold powerful interests to the law in order to save people's communities and health and the wild places and creatures they love. The stories are true. There are many more of them than could be told in this book or in an earlier book, *Wild by Law*, also written by Tom Turner and published by Earthjustice in 1990.

Although both *Wild by Law* and *Justice on Earth* celebrate the ability of Americans to enforce laws when the government won't, and even to enforce them against the government itself, the two books must end on different notes. Twelve years ago, when Tom Turner wrote his afterword to *Wild by Law*, he could still anticipate that, with the help of Earthjustice and others, the courts would continue to vindicate our rights to clean air, clean water, and at least some working parts of a natural world. But, as Bill McKibben warns in his foreword here, that can no longer be assumed.

What has happened? The concerned citizens are still there, and so are the lawyers of Earthjustice and others who represent these citizens. The problem is that a growing number of judges are effectively closing the courthouse doors to the public. Over the last two decades, a patchwork of antigovernment zealots, politicized religious groups, "new economy" free-marketeers, and "old economy" resource industries have joined forces to pack the federal judiciary with a new breed of judges. Merely conservative judges do not satisfy them. They have sought, and are getting, judges whose views range well outside the mainstream of legal and constitutional scholarship, who are willing to reinterpret laws and regulations without regard to precedent or to narrow them according to their personal dogmas. Indeed, by invoking novel constitutional theories, they often seek to eliminate not only the particular provision of law before them but the very power of government to act for the common good.

The Constitution requires that the president and senate together determine the composition of our third branch of government, the judiciary. Candidate by candidate, the president and senate must agree on those who are best qualified to serve as judges—men and women who will try to stand a step removed from the immediate political fray, maintaining the balance between the executive and legislative branches and between private citizens and government. While every judge brings to bear his or her own convictions, the framers of the Constitution knew that the rule of law requires judges who will carry out their duties as free from partisanship as possible and in accordance with precedents and canons of interpretation developed over centuries of experience. In the long run, the rule of law and the health of our democratic system require judges who are at or near the center of American constitutional and political thinking, not at the fringes.

We are losing that center, judicial appointment by judicial appointment. Too many presidents and too many senators have come to view the nomination and confirmation of judges as an electoral spoil, not a constitutional responsibility, and regard judicial appointments as cheap treats to satisfy the cravings of the far right. Unless the American people challenge this view, and insist that presidents and senators look more to the ideological or political middle when nominating and confirming judges, the sequel to *Justice on Earth* will be a slimmer and sadder volume.

Vawter Parker
Executive Director, Earthjustice

Citations to Cases Mentioned

CHAPTER 1

Standing cases

STORM KING
Scenic Hudson Preservation Conference v. FPC, 354 F2d
608 (2d Cir. 1965).

MINERAL KING
Sierra Club v. Morton, 405 US 727 (1972).

LUJAN V. DEFENDERS
Lujan v. Defenders of Wildlife, 504 US 555 (1992).

FOE V. LAIDLAW
Friends of the Earth v. Laidlaw Environmental Services,
528 US 167 (2000).

ONBOARD VAPOR RECOVERY
Natural Resources Defense Council v. Reilly, 788 F. Supp.
268 (E.D. Va. 1992); *Natural Resources Defense Council v.
Reilly,* 983 F2d 259 (D.C. Cir. 1993).

CHAPTER 2

Beartooth Alliance v. Crown Butte Mines, 904 F. Supp. 1168
(D. Mont. 1995).

CHAPTER 3

In the Matter of Louisiana Energy Services, L.P., 44 NRC
331, LBP-96-25 (Dec. 3, 1996) (licensing board ruling on
need for the facility; no action alternative; financial qualifi-
cations).

In the Matter of Louisiana Energy Services, L.P., 45 NRC
367, 391, LBP-97-8 (May 1, 1997) (licensing board ruling
on environmental justice).

In the Matter of Louisiana Energy Services, L.P., 57 NRC 77
CLI-98-3 (April 3, 1998) (commission ruling on environmental justice).

CHAPTER 4

In re Water Use Permit Applications, 94 Hawai'i 97, 9 P3d
409 (2000).

CHAPTER 5

*Pacific Coast Federation of Fishermen's Associations v.
Marcus,* Northern Dist. of Cal. No. 95-4474 MHP, filed
March 6, 1997.

Pronsolino v. Marcus, 91 F. Supp.2d 1337 (N.D. Cal. 2000).

CHAPTER 6

*People of the State of Florida, ex rel Robert A. Butterworth
v. Lykes Bros., Inc.,* 903 F2d 828 (11th Cir. 1990).

*Lykes Bros., Inc. v. United States Army Corps of Engineers
and Trustees of the Internal Improvement Trust Fund,* 959
F2d 973 (11th Cir. 1992).

Lykes Bros., Inc. v. United States Army Corps of Engineers,
821 F. Supp. 1457 (M.D. Fla. 1993).

United States Army Corps of Engineers v. Lykes Bros. Inc.,
64 F3d 630 (11th Cir. 1995).

CHAPTER 7

Portland Audubon Soc'y v. Lujan, 784 F. Supp. 786 (D. Ore.
1992) (order and opinion granting motion for preliminary
injunction); *Portland Audubon Soc'y v. Lujan,* 795 F. Supp.
1489 (D. Ore. 1992), *modified in part,* No. 87-1160-FR,
1992 WL 176353 (D. Ore. July 16, 1992).

Seattle Audubon Society v. Robertson, No. C89-160-WD
(W.D. Wash. March 24, 1989) (order on motion for preliminary injunction).

Seattle Audubon Soc'y v. Evans, 771 F. Supp. 1081 (W.D.
Wash.), *aff'd,* 952 F2d 297 (9th Cir. 1991).

Marbled Murrelet v. Lujan, No. 91-522 (W.D. Wash. 1991).

Portland Audubon Soc'y v. Endangered Species Comm., 984
F2d 1534 (9th Cir. 1993).

Seattle Audubon Soc'y v. Lyons, 871 F. Supp. 1291 (W.D.
Wash. 1994), *aff'd,* 80 F3d 1401 (9th Cir. 1996).

*Oregon Council of the Federation of Fly Fishers v. Ron
Brown & Roland Schmitten,* No. 95-1969-AS (D. Ore.
1995).

*Pacific Coast Federation of Fishermen's Associations v.
NMFS,* No. C97-775-R (W.D. Wash. May 29, 1998).

*Pacific Coast Federation of Fishermen's Associations v.
NMFS,* 71 F. Supp.2d 1063 (W.D. Wash 1999); *Pacific
Coast Federation of Fishermen's Associations v. NMFS,* No.
COO-1757-R (W.D. Wash. 2000).

*Pacific Coast Federation of Fishermen's Associations v.
NMFS,* 253 F3d 1153 (9th Cir 2001), as amended on denial
of reh'g, 2001 U.S. App. LEXIS 19742 (Sept. 5, 2001).

Alsea Valley Alliance v. Evans, No. 99-6265-HO (D. Ore.
1999) (appeal pending).

CHAPTER 8

CHILDREN'S ISLAND
Anacostia Watershed Society v. Babbitt, 871 F. Supp. 475 (D.D.C. 1994), *motion for clarification denied,* 875 F. Supp. 1 (D.D.C. 1995).

BARNEY CIRCLE
Anacostia Watershed Society v. Peña, D.D.C. 94-1051 PLF.

NAVY YARD
Barry Farm Resident Council v. United States Dept. of the Navy, 45 ERC 1599, 1997 U.S. Dist. LEXIS 2754 (D.D.C. 1997).

D.C. TMDLS
Kingman Park Civic Assn. v. EPA, 84 F.Supp.2d 1 (D.D.C. 1999).

CHAPTER 9

USHK BAY
Friends of Southeast's Future v. Morrison, 153 F3d 1059, (C.A.9 Alaska 1998).

AWRTA
Alaska Wilderness Recreation & Tourism Ass'n v. Morrison, 67 F3d 723, 732 (9th Cir. 1995).

CHAPTER 10

United States – Import Prohibition of Certain Shrimp and Shrimp Products, Report of the Panel, WT/DS58/R (15 May 1998).

United States – Import Prohibition of Certain Shrimp and Shrimp Products, Report of the Appellate Body, AB-1998-4 (12 Oct. 1998).

European Communities – Measures Affecting Asbestos and Asbestos-Containing Products, AB-2000-11, Report of the Appellate Body, WT/DS135/AB/R (12 March 2001).

United States – Import Prohibition of Certain Shrimp and Shrimp Products, Recourse to Article 21.5 of the DSU by Malaysia, AB-2001-4, Report of the Appellate Body, WT/DS58/AB/RW (22 Oct. 2001).

EC Measures Concerning Meat and Meat Products (Hormones), Report of the Panel, WT/DS26/R (18 Aug. 1997).

EC Measures Concerning Meat and Meat Products (Hormones), AB-1997-4, Report of the Appellate Body, WT/DS48/AB/R (16 Jan. 1998).

Northwest Ecosystem Alliance v. Office of the US Trade Representative, No. C99-1165R, 1999 U.S. Dist. LEXIS 21689 (W.D. Wa. Nov. 8, 1999).

Gamble v. Zoellick, Memorandum Opinion, Civ. No. 01-0018, May 8, 2001.

Earthjustice Clients

1,000 Friends of Kauai, Hawai'i

Action for the Environment, South Dakota

Adirondack Council, New York

AFL-CIO

African-Americans for Environmental Justice, Mississippi

Alabama Coastal Alliance

Alabama Conservancy

Alameda County Recycling Initiative Committee, California

Alaska Center for the Environment

Alaska Clean Water Alliance

Alaska Marine Conservation Council

Alaska Sportfishing Association

Alaska Wilderness League

Alaska Wilderness Recreation and Tourism Association

Alaska Wildlife Alliance

Alaskans for Juneau

Alliance for the Wild Rockies, Montana

Alpine County, California

Alpine Lakes Protection Society, Washington

Amazonian Quichua Indians, Ecuador

American Buffalo Foundation, Montana

American Canoe Association

American Federation of State, County, and Municipal Employees

American Fisheries Society

American Lands Alliance

American Littoral Society

American Lung Association

American Lung Association of Hawai'i

American Lung Association of Northern Virginia

American Oceans Campaign

American Rivers

American Society for the Prevention of Cruelty to Animals

American Wilderness Alliance

American Wildlands

Americans for the Environment, Florida

Anacostia Watershed Society, District of Columbia

Anchorage Audubon Society, Alaska

Ancient Forest Defense Fund, California

Ancient Forest Rescue, Washington

Animal Protection Institute of America

Animal Protection of New Mexico

Animal Welfare Institute

Apalachee Audubon Society, Florida

Arc Ecology, California

Arctic Audubon Society, Alaska

Arizona Toxics Information

Arizona Wildlife

Arizona Wildlife Federation

Arizonans for a Quality Environment

Arkansas Wildlife Federation

The Armuchee Alliance, Georgia

Asia Pacific Environmental Exchange

Asian-Pacific Environmental Network, California

Aspen Wilderness Workshop, Colorado

Association of Community Organizations for Reform Now, California

Association of Superior Councils of the U'wa People, Colombia

Atlantic Salmon Federation, Maine

Atlantic States Legal Foundation

Audubon Society of the Everglades, Florida

Back Country Horsemen of Montana

Barney Circle Neighborhood Watch, District of Columbia

Barry Farm Residents Council, District of Columbia

Bay Area Trails Preservation Council, California

The Bay Institute, California

Bayview Hunters Point Community Advocates, California

BC Wild

Beartooth Alliance, Montana

Beaverhead Forest Concerned Citizens, Montana

Big Island Rainforest Action Group, Hawai'i

Big Pine Key Civic Association, Florida

Bighorn Forest Users, Wyoming

Bighorn River Watershed Coalition, Montana

Biodiversity Associates, Wyoming

Biodiversity Legal Foundation, Colorado

Biscayne Bay Foundation, Florida

Black Hills Audubon Society, South Dakota

Blue Mountain Audubon Society, Washington

Blue Mountain Native Forest Alliance, Oregon

Blue Mountains Biodiversity Project, Oregon

Blue Ocean Preservation Society, Hawai'i

Bluewater Network, California

Bob Marshall Alliance, Montana

Boise Forest Watch, Idaho

Boot 'n Blister Club, California

Border Power Plant Working Group, California-Mexico

Boulder County Nature Association, Colorado

Boulder–White Clouds Council, Idaho

Buckeye Forest Council, Pacific Northwest

Buena Vista Audubon Society, California

Butte Environmental Council, California

Cabinet Resource Group, Montana

California Association of Professional Scientists

California Coalition for Alternatives to Pesticides

California Council for Survival Resources

California Council for Trout Unlimited

California Native Plant Society

California Natural Resources Federation

California Public Interest Research Group

California Sportfishing Protective Alliance

California Striped Bass Association

California Trout

California Waterfowl Association

California Wilderness Coalition

Californians Against Waste

Cape Arago Audubon Society, Oregon

Cape Cod Commercial Hook Fishermen's Association, Massachusetts

Capitol Hill Restoration Society, District of Columbia

Caples Lake Homeowners Association, California

Caples Lake Resort, California

Caribbean Conservation Corporation, Florida

Carmel Mountain Conservancy, California

Carmel River Steelhead Association, California

Carson Forest Watch, New Mexico

Cascadia Fire Ecology Education Project, Oregon

Cenaliulriit Coastal Management District, Alaska

Center for Auto Safety, District of Columbia

Center for Biological Diversity, Arizona

Center for Environmental Law and Policy, Washington

Center for International Environmental Law

Center for Marine Resources, District of Columbia

Center for Native Ecosystems

Center for Sierra Nevada Conservation, California

Center on Race, Poverty, and the Environment, California

Central Coast Conservation Center, California

Central Oregon Audubon Society

Centro Mexicano de Derecho Ambiental

Chassahowitzka River Restoration Committee, Florida

Chemehuevi Tribe of Indians, Arizona

Chesapeake Bay Foundation, Maryland

Chester Residents Concerned for Quality Living, Pennsylvania

Citizens Against Noise, Hawai'i

Citizens Against Nuclear Trash, Louisiana

Citizens Against Refinery Effects, Virginia

Citizens Against Rocky Flats Contamination, Colorado

Citizens' Alert Regarding the Environment, Pennsylvania

Citizens Association of Bonita Beach, Florida

Citizens Coal Council, District of Columbia

Citizens Coalition for Responsible Power, Florida

Citizens Committee to Complete the Refuge, California

Citizens Committee to Stop It Again, District of Columbia

Citizens Council on Conservation and Environmental Control, Ohio

Citizens for a Healthful and Safe Environment, California

Citizens for a Healthy Environment, Mississippi

Citizens for a Mojave National Park, California

Citizens for Balanced Transportation, Colorado

Citizens for Responsible Energy Development, Hawai'i

Citizens for Teton Valley, Idaho-Wyoming

Citizens for the Protection of Logan Canyon, Utah

Citizens for Water, Florida

Citizens' Preservation Council, Florida

Citizens United for Responsibility to the Environment, Colorado

Citizens with Space Concerns, Hawai'i

City of Angoon, Alaska

City of Aurora, Colorado

City of Colorado Springs, Colorado

City of Moss Point, Mississippi

Clark County Natural Resources Council, Washington

Clark-Skamania Fly Fishers, Washington

Clavey River Preservation Coalition, California

Clean Air Council, Pennsylvania

Clean Up Rincon Effluent, California

Clean Water Action, Colorado

Clearwater Biodiversity Project, Idaho

Clearwater Flycasters, Idaho

Clearwater Outfitters, Idaho

Coalition for Amazon Peoples and Their Environment

Coalition for Clean Air, California

Coalition to Restore Coastal Louisiana

Coast Action Group, California

Coast Range Association, Oregon

Coastal Conservation Association, Florida

Cochise Conservation Council, Arizona

Cofan Indians, Ecuador

Collier Audubon Society, Florida

Colorado Environmental Coalition

Colorado Mountain Club

Colorado Open Space Council

Colorado Public Interest Research Group

Colorado Wild

Colorado Wildlife Federation

Columbia River Crab Fishermen's Association, Oregon

Columbia River United, Washington

Columbia RiverKeeper

Committee of 100 on the Federal City, District of Columbia

Committee for Green Foothills, California

Committee for the Permanent Repair of Highway One, California

Committee to Save the Mokelumne River, California

Common Cause

Common Cause Hawai'i

Communities for a Better Environment, California

Communities Organized to Improve Life, Maryland

Concerned Citizens for Nuclear Safety, New Mexico

Concerned Citizens for Responsible Mining, Idaho

Concerned Citizens of East Columbus, Georgia

Concerned Citizens of Highland Beach, Florida

Concerned Citizens of Putnam County, Florida

Concerned Parents of Leland, Mississippi

Confederation of Indian Nationalities of the Ecuadorian Amazon

CONFENIAE

The Conservancy of Southwest Florida

Conservation Action Project, Maine-New Hampshire

Conservation Council of Hawai'i

Conservation Council of North Carolina

Conservation Foundation

Conservation Law Foundation

Coosa River Basin Initiative, Georgia

Coral Reef Coalition, Florida

Coral Reef Society

Crow Indian Tribe, Montana

Dakota Rural Action, South Dakota

Danube Circle

D.C. Federation of Civic Associations

Defenders of the Ouchita Forest, Arkansas

Defenders of Wildlife

Delaware Valley Citizens' Council for Clean Air, Pennsylvania

DeltaKeeper, California

Denali Citizens Council, Alaska

Denver Action for a Better Community, Colorado

Desert Citizens Against Pollution, California

Desert Protection Society, California

Desert Protective Council, California

Desert Survivors, California

Desert Tortoise Council, California

Desert Tortoise Preserve Committee, California

DeSoto Citizens Against Pollution, Florida

Dinee CARE, Southwest

Dioxin/Organochlorine Center, Washington

Dubois Wildlife Association, Wyoming

Eagle Mountain Landfill Opposition Coalition, California

Earth Island Institute

Earth Media

Earthtrust

East Diamond Head Community Association, Hawai'i

East Oahu County Farm Bureau, Hawai'i

East of Huajatollas Citizens' Alliance, Colorado

East Silver Lake Improvement Association, California

Eastern Kenai Peninsula Environmental Action Association, Alaska

The Ecology Center, Idaho

The Ecology Center, Montana

El Dorado County Taxpayers for Quality Growth, California

Electric Vehicle Association of America

Endangered Habitats League, California

Endangered Species Committee of California

Environment Hawai'i

Environmental Confederation of Southwest Florida

Environmental Council of Sacramento, California

Environmental Defense

Environmental Defense Center, California

Environmental Planning and Information Council of Western El Dorado, California

Environmental Policy Institute

Environmental Protection Information Center, California

Environmental Resource Centre of Alberta

Everglades Audubon Society, Florida

Farm Labor Organizing Committee, Ohio

Federation of Fly Fishers, Washington

Federation of Western Outdoor Clubs

Five Valleys Audubon Society, Montana

Florida Audubon Society

Florida Biodiversity Project

Florida Canoeing and Kayaking Association

Florida Coalition of Fishing Clubs

Florida Conservation Association

Florida Defenders of the Environment

Florida Keys Citizen Coalition

Florida Keys Coalition

Florida League of Anglers

Florida Marine Life Association

Florida Public Interest Research Group

Florida Wildlife Federation

Florida Wildlife Society

Forest Concerns of the Upper Skagit, Washington

Forest Conservation Council, Oregon

Forest Guardians, New Mexico

Forest Service Employees for Environmental Ethics

Forest Watch, Indiana

Forty-niner Council of the Boy Scouts of America, California

Four Corners Action Coalition, Colorado

Four Rivers Audubon Society, Florida

Friends Aware of Wildlife Needs, California

Friends of Berner's Bay, Alaska

Friends of Castle Rock State Park, California

Friends of Falls River, Idaho

Friends of Georgia

Friends of Glacier Point, Alaska

Friends of Hope Valley, California

Friends of Lake Okeechobee, Florida

Friends of Mount Aventine, Virginia

Friends of Neary Lagoon, California

Friends of Northern San Jacinto Valley, California

Friends of Santa Clara County Creeks, California

Friends of Santa Paula Creek, California

Friends of Sierra Valley, California

Friends of Southeast's Future, Georgia

Friends of the Abajos, Utah

Friends of the Bitterroot, Montana

Friends of the Columbia River Gorge, Oregon

Friends of the Crystal River, Michigan

Friends of the Earth

Friends of the Elk River, Oregon

Friends of the Everglades, Florida

Friends of the Garcia River, California

Friends of the Horsepasture, North Carolina

Friends of the Navarro River, California

Friends of the Owls, Arizona

Friends of the River

Friends of the Santa Clara River, California

Friends of the Sea Otter, California
Friends of the Seashore, Mississippi
Friends of the Swainson's Hawk,
  California
Friends of the Ventura River,
  California
Friends of the Westwater, Utah
Friends of the Wild Swan, Montana
Frontera Audubon Society, Texas
Fund for Animals
Gallatin Wildlife Association, Montana
Georgia Environmental Organization
Georgia ForestWatch
Get Oil Out, California
Gifford Pinchot Alliance, Washington
Gifford Pinchot Task Force,
  Washington
Gila Watch, New Mexico
Girl Scout Council of Southeast
  Louisiana
Golden Eagle Audubon Society, Idaho
Golden Gate Audubon Society,
  California
Golden Gate Fishermen's Association,
  California
Grand Canyon Trust, District of
  Columbia
Grand Council of the Crees, Quebec
Gray Wolf Committee, Idaho
Great Bear Foundation, Idaho
Great Burn Study Group, Idaho
Great Old Broads for Wilderness,
  Utah
Greater Ecosystem Alliance,
  Washington
Greater Gila Biodiversity Project,
  Arizona
Greater Yellowstone Coalition
Green Sand Community Association,
  Hawai'i
Greenbelt Alliance, California
Greenpeace Foundation, Hawai'i
Greenpeace International
Greenpeace USA
The Grizzly Project
Group Against Smog and Pollution,
  Pennsylvania
Grupo de los Cien, Pacific Northwest
Gulf Island Conservancy, Mississippi
Gulfport Concerned Citizens
  Coalition, Mississippi

GVEA Ratepayers Alliance, Alaska
Hakipuu Ohana, Hawai'i
Hana Community Association, Hawai'i
Hawai'i Audubon Society
Hawai'i Green Party
Hawaiian Botanical Society
Hawai'i's Thousand Friends
Hayward Area Planning Association,
  California
Headwaters, Oregon
Heal the Bay, California
Heartwood, Kentucky
Hells Canyon Preservation Council,
  Idaho
Help Save the Apalachicola River
  Group, Florida
Henry's Fork Foundation, Idaho
High Country Citizens Alliance,
  Colorado
High Peaks Audubon Society, New
  York
Hihiwai Stream Restoration Coalition,
  Hawai'i
Hillsborough County, Florida
Holy Cross Wilderness Defense
  Fund, Colorado
Ho'olehua Homesteaders Association,
  Hawai'i
Hoonah Indian Association, Alaska
Hoosier Environmental Council,
  Indiana
Horned Lizard Conservation Society,
  Arizona-California
Houston Audubon Society, Texas
Huachuaca Audubon Society, Arizona
Huaorani Indians, Ecuador
Hughes River Watershed
  Conservancy, West Virginia
Hui Alanui O Makena, Hawai'i
Hui Ho'opakele 'Aina, Hawai'i
Hui Malama 'Aina O Laie, Hawai'i
Human Rights Advocates
Humane Society International
Humane Society of the United States
Humboldt Watershed Council,
  California
A Hunter's Voice, Wyoming
Idaho Conservation League
Idaho Environmental Council
Idaho Rivers United

Idaho Salmon and Steelhead
  Unlimited
Idaho Sporting Congress
Idaho Sportsmen's Coalition
Idaho Steelhead and Salmon United
Idaho Watersheds Project
Idaho Whitewater Association
Idaho Wildlife Federation
Indiana League of Women Voters
Informational Network for the
  Spaceport, Hawai'i
Inland Empire Public Lands Council,
  Idaho
Inland Empire Public Lands Council,
  Washington
Inland Northwest Wildlife Council,
  Idaho
Institute for Fisheries Resources,
  Oregon
Institute for the Advancement of
  Hawaiian Affairs
Institute for Transportation and the
  Environment, Washington
International Forum on Globalization
International Fund for Animal Welfare
International Indian Treaty Council
International Rivers Network
International Wildlife Coalition
Inter-Tribal Bison Cooperative,
  Montana
Investigative Network
The Izaak Walton League of America
Jackson County Citizens for a Healthy
  Environment, Mississippi
Jackson Hole Conservation Alliance,
  Wyoming
Jefferson Valley Sportsmen, Montana
Jumping Frog Research Institute,
  California
Juneau Audubon Society, Alaska
Ka Lāhui, Hawai'i
Ka 'Ohana O Ka Lae, Hawai'i
Kahalu'u Neighborhood Board
Kapoho Community Association,
  Hawai'i
Kaua'i Friends for the Environment
Keep the Sespe Wild Committee,
  California
Kentucky Conservation Committee
Kentucky Resources Council

Kettle Range Conservation Group, Washington

Kingman Park Civic Association, District of Columbia

Kirkwood Associates, California

Kirkwood Meadows Public Utilities District, California

Kissimmee River Valley Sportsmen's Association, Florida

Kit Carson Lodge, California

Kitsap Audubon Society, Washington

Klamath Basin Audubon Society, Oregon

Klamath Forest Alliance, Oregon-California

Klamath-Siskiyou Wildlands Center, Oregon-California

Klamath Tribes, Oregon

Koa Mana, Hawai'i

Kona Hawaiian Civic Club, Hawai'i

Koolau Agricultural Company, Hawai'i

Lake Kirkwood Association, California

Lake Michigan Federation

Lake Pend Oreille Club, Idaho

Lanaians for Sensible Growth, Hawai'i

The Lands Council, Idaho-Washington

Lane County Audubon Society, Oregon

Lassen County Air Pollution Control District, California

Last Stand, Florida

Latino Issues Forum, California

Leaf Adopt-a-Forest, Washington

League for Coastal Protection, California

League to Save Lake Tahoe, California

League to Save Sierra Lakes, California

Life of the Land, Hawai'i

Lighthawk: The Environmental Air Force

Logan Canyon Coalition, Utah

Los Angeles Audubon Society, California

Louisiana Audubon Council

Louisiana Environmental Action Network

Louisiana Wildlife Federation

Lower Elwha S'Klallam Tribe, Washington

Lower Umpqua Fly Fishers, Oregon

Lynn Canal Conservation, Alaska

Madrone Audubon Society, California

Maine Audubon Society

Maine Council of Atlantic Salmon Federation

Maine Lobstermen's Association

Makawai Stream Restoration Alliance, Hawai'i

Malama Makua, Hawai'i

ManaSota-88, Florida

Manor Area Neighbors Organization, Texas

Marble Mountain Audubon, California

Marianas Audubon Society, Guam

Maricopa Audubon Society, Arizona

Marin Audubon Society, California

Marin Horse Council, California

Marine Environmental Consortium, Washington

Marsh Canyon Citizens, California

Maryland Conservation Council

Maryland Environmental Interest Group

Maui Air Traffic Association, Hawai'i

Maui Meadows Homeowners Association, Hawai'i

Maui Tomorrow, Hawai'i

The Mazamas, Oregon

Medical Alliance for Healthy Air, California

Mendocino Environmental Center, California

Mendocino Unified School District, California

Methow Forest Watch, Washington

Michigan United Conservation Clubs

Mineral Policy Center, District of Columbia

Mississippi River Basin Alliance, Missouri

Mississippi Wildlife Federation

Mobile Audubon Society, Alabama

Molokai Chamber of Commerce, Hawai'i

Mono Lake Committee, California

Monroe County Humane Society, Indiana

Montana Audubon

Montana Council of Trout Unlimited

Montana Ecosystems Defense Council

Montana Environmental Information Center

Montana River Action Network

Montana State Parks Foundation

Montana Wilderness Association

Montana Wildlife Federation

Monterey Parkway

Monterey Peninsula Audubon Society

Mount Diablo Audubon Society, California

Mount Shasta Area Audubon Society, California

Mount Shasta Bioregional Ecology Center, California

Mountain Lion Foundation, California

The Mountaineers, Washington

Na 'Apio Aloha 'Aina, Hawai'i

Na Mamo O 'Aha'ino, Hawai'i

Na Opio Aloha 'Aina, Hawai'i

Nanakuli Surf Club, Hawai'i

Napa-Solano Audubon Society, California

Narrows Conservation Coalition, Alaska

National Audubon Society

National Coalition Against the Misuse of Pesticides

National Coalition for Marine Conservation

National Council of Negro Women

The National Indigenous Organization of Colombia

National Outdoor Leadership School

National Parks Conservation Association

National Trust for Historic Preservation

National Wildlife Federation

Native Coalition for Medicine Lake Highlands Defense, California

Native Ecosystems Council, Wyoming

Native Ecosystems Defense Council, Montana

Native Fish Society, Oregon

Native Forest Council, Oregon

Native Forest Network, Montana

Native Plant Society of Oregon

Native Village of Minto, Alaska

Natural Resources Council of Maine

Natural Resources Defense Council

The Nature Conservancy

The Nature School

Nebraska Wildlife Federation

Nevada Outdoor Recreation Association

New England Coalition for Energy Efficiency and Environment

New England Fishery Management Council

New Mexico Audubon Society

New Mexico Energy, Minerals, and Natural Resources Department

New Mexico Wilderness Association

New York Public Interest Research Group

New York Zoological Society

Newton County Wildlife Association, Arkansas

No Way L.A. Coalition, California

North Carolina Wildlife Federation

North Cascades Audubon Society, Washington

North Cascades Conservation Council, Washington

North Central Washington Audubon Society

North Gulf Oceanic Society, Alaska

Northcoast Environmental Center, California

Northern Alaska Environmental Center

Northern Arizona Audubon Society

Northern California Council, Federation of Fly Fishers

Northern California Guides Associations

Northern Plains Resource Council, Montana

The Northern Rockies Preservation Project

Northern Sierra Summer Homeowners' Association, California

Northwest Coalition for Alternatives to Pesticides, Oregon

Northwest Conservation Act Coalition

Northwest Ecosystem Alliance, Washington

Northwest Energy Coalition

Northwest Environmental Advocates, Oregon

Northwest Environmental Defense Center, Oregon

Northwest Resource Information Center, Oregon

Northwest Rivers Alliance

Northwest Sport Fishing Industry Association

Northwest Wyoming Resource Council

Nunam Kitlutsisti, Alaska

Oahu Rainforest Action Group, Hawai'i

Ocean Advocates

Ocean Conservancy

Ocean Mammal Institute, Hawai'i

Ocotillo Community Council, California

Ogeechee River Valley Association, Georgia

Ohlone Audubon Society, California

Oil and Gas Accountability Project, Colorado

Okanogan Highlands Alliance, Washington

Okanogan Wilderness League, Washington

Olijato Chapter of the Navajo Tribe, Arizona

Olympic National Park Associates, Washington

Orange County CoastKeeper, California

Oregon Council of the Federation of Fly Fishers

Oregon Environmental Council

Oregon Natural Desert Association

Oregon Natural Resources Council

Oregon Nordic Club

Oregon Rivers Council

Oregon Student Public Interest Research Group

Oregon Trout

Oregon WaterWatch

Oregon Wildlife Federation

Organized Village of Kake, Alaska

Orleans Audubon Society, Louisiana

Ouachita Watch League, Arkansas

Our Children's Earth, California

Pacific Coast Federation of Fishermen's Associations

Pacific Crest Biodiversity Project, Washington

Pacific Environment and Resources Center, California

Pacific Marine Conservation Council, Pacific Northwest

Pacific Rivers Council, Oregon

Pahoa Business Association, Hawai'i

Palm Beach Garden Club, Florida

Palouse Audubon Society, Idaho

Park County Environmental Council, Montana

Park County Resource Council, Wyoming

Park Hill for Safe Neighborhoods, Colorado

The Pegasus Foundation, Florida

Pele Defense Fund, Hawai'i

Penasquitos Lagoon Foundation, California

Pennsylvania Public Interest Research Group

Penobscot Indian Nation, Maine

People Against Chlordane, New York

People for Puget Sound, Washington

Pilchuck Audubon Society, Washington

Pineros y Campesinos Unidos de Noroeste, Oregon

Pit River Tribe, California

Planning and Conservation League, California

Plasse Homestead Homeowners' Association, California

Plasse's Resort, California

Point Reyes Bird Observatory, California

Portland Audubon Society, Oregon

Powder River Basin Resource Council, Wyoming

Predator Conservation Alliance, Montana

Predator Project, Montana

Prescott Audubon Society, Arizona

Preserve Area Ridgelands Committee, California

Preserve South Bay, California

Preserve Wild Santee, California

Prince of Wales Conservation League, Alaska

Professional Wilderness Outfitters Association, Montana

Project Jonah
Project Land Use, California
Protect Maalaea Coalition, Hawai'i
Protect Our Waters and
  Environmental Resources,
  Washington
Puako Community Association,
  Hawai'i
Public Access Shoreline Hawai'i
Public Citizen
Public Employees for Environmental
  Responsibility
Puget Sound Alliance, Washington
Puget Sound Gillnetters Association,
  Washington
Puget SoundKeeper Alliance,
  Washington
Pukalani Hula Halau, Hawai'i
Puna Outdoor Circle, Hawai'i
Punaluu Community Association,
  Hawai'i
Rabun County Coalition, California
Rainforest Action Network
Ramonans for Sensible Growth,
  California
Recycle Now!, Florida
Red Mesa Chapter of the Navajo
  Tribe, Arizona
Red Mexicana de Accion Frente al
  Libre Comercio
Redwood Region Audubon Society,
  California
ReefKeeper International
REFLEX, Hungary
Resources Center, California
Resources Limited, Montana
Responsible Growth Management
  Coalition, Florida
Rest the West, Oregon
Rivers Council of Washington
Rock Creek Alliance, Idaho-Montana
Rogue Valley Audubon Society,
  Oregon
Royal Society for the Prevention of
  Cruelty to Animals
Sacramento River Council, California
Sacramento River Preservation Trust,
  California
Safegrow, California
Salem Audubon Society, Oregon
Salmon for All

Salmon Trollers Marketing
  Association
Salmonid Restoration Federation,
  California-Oregon
Salt River Valley Farms, Arizona
San Bernardino Audubon Society,
  California
San Bruno Mountain Watch,
  California
San Diego Audubon Society,
  California
San Diego BayKeeper, California
San Diego Biodiversity Project,
  California
San Diego Herpetological Society,
  California
San Francisco BayKeeper, California
San Joaquin Audubon Society,
  California
San Juan Citizens Alliance, Colorado
San Pedro 100, California
Sanibel-Captiva Audubon Society,
  Florida
Santa Barbara ChannelKeeper,
  California
Santa Barbara Urban Creeks Council,
  California
Santa Clara Valley Audubon Society,
  California
Santa Clarita Organization for
  Planning and Environment,
  California
Santa Monica BayKeeper, California
Sassafras Audubon, Indiana
Save Chelan Alliance, Washington
Save 'Ewa Beach 'Ohana, Hawai'i
Save Our Aquatic Resources and
  Environment, Florida
Save Our Bays and Beaches, Hawai'i
Save Our Butte Save Our Basin
  Society, Washington
Save Our Creeks, Florida
Save Our Forests and Ranchlands,
  California
Save Our Sealife, Florida
Save Our Surf, Hawai'i
Save San Francisco Bay Association,
  California
Save the Dunes, Alabama
Save the Manatee Club, Florida
Save the St. Johns River, Florida
Save the West, Pacific Northwest

Scenic Hudson Preservation
  Conference, New York
Scenic Shoreline Preservation
  Conference, California
Sea Turtle Restoration Project,
  California
Sea Turtle Survival League, Florida
Seattle Audubon Society, Washington
Secoya Indians, Ecuador
Selkirk-Priest Basin Association,
  Montana
Sequoia Audubon Society, California
Service Employees International
  Union
Shuar Indians, Ecuador
Sierra Club
Sierra Nevada Forest Protection
  Campaign, California
Silver Lake Water Company,
  California
Sinapu, Colorado
Siona Indians, Ecuador
Siskiyou Audubon Society, Oregon
Siskiyou Regional Education Project,
  California-Oregon
Sitka Conservation Society, Alaska
Siuslaw Task Force, Oregon
Slovak Rivers Network, Slovakia
Society Advocating Natural
  Ecosystems, Oregon
Society for American Archaeology
Soda Mountain Wilderness Council,
  Oregon
Sonomans for Gentle Growth,
  California
Sorensen's Resort, California
South Dakota Resources Coalition
South Fork Mountain Defense
  Committee, California
South Silver Lake Homeowners'
  Association, California
Southeast Alaska Conservation
  Council
Southeast Neighborhood Associates,
  District of Columbia
Southern Appalachian Biodiversity
  Project
Southern California Alliance for
  Survival
Southern Rockies Ecosystem Project
Southern Utah Resource Council

Southern Utah Wilderness Alliance

Southwest Environmental Center

Southwest Research and Information Center, New Mexico

Southwest Trout

Spearfish Canyon Preservation Trust, South Dakota

Sportsmen Conservationists of Texas

Stanislaus Audubon Society, California

The Steamboaters, Oregon

Stewart Park and Reserve Coalition, New York

Stichting Greenpeace Council, Hawai'i

Sugarloaf Citizens Association, Maryland

Surfrider Foundation

Susitna Valley Association, Alaska

Swan View Coalition, Montana

T & E Inc., Arizona-New Mexico

Taku Conservation Society, Alaska

Tamalpais Conservation Club, California

Taxpayers for the Animas River, Colorado

Tenmile Creek Association, Oregon

Texas Natural Resources Committee

Thane Neighborhood Association, Alaska

To Save the Forest, Georgia

Tongass Conservation Society, Alaska

Torres-Martinez Desert Cahuilla Indians, California

Tour Aircraft Control Coalition, Hawai'i

Transportation Solutions Defense and Education Fund, California

Treasure Coast Environmental Coalition, Florida

Trial Lawyers for Public Justice

Tri-Valley CAREs, California

Tropical Audubon Society, Florida

Trout Unlimited

Trust for Public Land

Trustees for Alaska

Tucson Audubon Society, Arizona

Tucson Herpetological Society, Arizona

Tulare Audubon Society, California

Tule River Conservancy, California

Turnagain Arm Conservation League, Alaska

Turtle Island Restoration Network, California

Umpqua Valley Audubon Society, Oregon

Umpqua Watersheds, Oregon

Union of Concerned Scientists

United Anglers of California

United Farmworkers of Washington State

University of California, Riverside

University of Oregon Survival Center

Upper Snake River Fly Fishers, Idaho

Urban Habitat Program, California

Urban Protectors, District of Columbia

U.S. Public Interest Research Group

Utah Council of Trout Unlimited

Utah Mountain Bike Association

Utah Wilderness Association

Vermont Natural Resources Council

Village of Birch Creek, Alaska

Virgin Islands Conservation Society

Voices of the Wetlands, California

Waiāhole-Waikāne Community Association, Hawai'i

Waiālae Iki Ridge Parks Beautification Association, Hawai'i

Waipi'o Valley Community Association, Hawai'i

Wasatch Clean Air Coalition

Washington Environmental Center

Washington Environmental Council

Washington Native Plant Society

Washington PEER

Washington Toxics Coalition

Washington Trollers Association

Washington Trout

Washington Wilderness Coalition

Washington Wildlife Federation

WaterKeeper Alliance

WaterKeepers Northern California

WaterWatch of Oregon

We Care Austin, Texas

West Virginia Citizen Action Group

West Virginia Highlands Conservancy

West Virginia Rivers Coalition

Western Ancient Forest Campaign

Western Colorado Congress

Western Land Exchange Project, Washington

Western Nebraska Resources Council

Western Sanders County Involved Citizens, Montana

Wetlands Action Network, California

Whale and Dolphin Conservation Society

Whale Center, California

Whidbey Environmental Action Network, Washington

White Mountain Conservation League, Arizona

Wild Alabama

The Wilderness Society

The Wildlands Center for Preventing Roads

Wildlands CPR, Montana

Wildlife Damage Review, Arizona

The Wildlife Society

WildSouth, Alabama

Willits Environmental Center, California

Willow Creek Ecology, Utah

Wolf Haven International, Washington

World Council of Indigenous Peoples, Hawai'i

World Wildlife Fund

Wyoming Outdoor Coordinating Council

Wyoming Outdoor Council

Wyoming Wilderness Association

Wyoming Wilderness Coalition

Wyoming Wildlife Federation

Yakima Clean Air Coalition, Washington

Yellowstone Valley Audubon Society, Montana

Earthjustice Offices

Headquarters
426 Seventeenth Street
Sixth Floor
Oakland, CA 94612
(510) 550-6700

Bozeman
209 S. Willson Avenue
Bozeman, MT 59715
(406) 586-9699

Denver
1631 Glenarm Place, #300
Denver, CO 80202
(303) 623-9466

Honolulu
223 South King Street
Fourth Floor
Honolulu, HI 96813
(808) 599-2436

Juneau
325 Fourth Street
Juneau, AK 99801
(907) 586-2751

New Orleans
400 Magazine Street
Suite 401
New Orleans, LA 70130
(504) 522-1394

Oakland
426 Seventeenth Street
Sixth Floor
Oakland, CA 94612
(510) 550-6725

Seattle
203 Hoge Building
705 Second Avenue
Seattle, WA 98104
(206) 343-7340

Tallahassee
111 S. Martin Luther King, Jr., Boulevard
Tallahassee, FL 32301
(850) 681-0031

Washington, D.C.
1625 Massachusetts Avenue, NW
Suite 702
Washington, DC 20036
(202) 667-4500

Earthjustice Environmental Law Clinic
  at Stanford University
Owen House
553 Salvatierra Walk
Stanford, CA 94305
(650) 725-8571

Earthjustice Environmental Law Clinic
  at the University of Denver
Forbes House
1714 Poplar Street
Denver, CO 80220
(303) 871-6996

Anderson, Frederick R. *NEPA in the Courts: A Legal Analysis of the National Environmental Policy Act* (Washington, D.C.: Resources for the Future, 1973).

Baldwin, Malcolm K., and James K. Page, Jr., eds. *Law and the Environment* (New York: Walker and Company, 1970).

Barnes, Phil. *A Concise History of the Hawaiian Islands* (Hilo, Hawai'i: Petroglyph Press, 2000).

Bean, Michael J., and Melanie J. Rowland. *The Evolution of National Wildlife Law*, 3d ed. (Westport, Conn.: Praeger, 1997).

Borrelli, Peter, ed. *Crossroads, Environmental Priorities for the Future* (Washington, D.C.: Island Press, 1988).

Bullard, Robert D., ed. *Unequal Protection: Environmental Justice and Communities of Color* (San Francisco: Sierra Club Books, 1994).

Chase, Alston. *Playing God in Yellowstone: The Destruction of America's First National Park* (New York: Harcourt Brace Jovanovich, 1987).

Dietrich, William. *The Final Forest: The Battle for the Last Great Trees of the Pacific Northwest* (New York: Simon and Schuster, 1992).

Durbin, Kathie. *Tongass: Pulp Politics and the Fight for the Alaska Rain Forest* (Corvallis, Ore.: Oregon State University Press, 1999).

————. *Tree Huggers: Victory, Defeat, and Renewal in the Northwest Ancient Forest Campaign* (Seattle: The Mountaineers, 1996).

Echeverria, John, and Raymond Booth Eby, eds. *Let the People Judge: Wise Use and the Property Rights Movement* (Washington, D.C.: Island Press, 1995).

Ekey, Bob. *The New World Agreement, a Call for Reform of the 1872 Mining Law*, 18 Pub. Land & Resources Law Rev 151 (Missoula, Mont.: University of Montana, 1997).

Fitzpatrick, Sandra, and Maria R. Goodwin. *The Guide to Black Washington* (New York: Hippocrene Books, 1999).

Frome, Michael. *Chronicling the West: Thirty Years of Environmental Writing* (Seattle: The Mountaineers, 1996).

George, Robert P., ed. *Great Cases in Constitutional Law* (Princeton, N.J.: Princeton University Press, 2000).

Gilliam, Ann, ed. *Voices for the Earth: A Treasury of the Sierra Club Bulletin* (San Francisco: Sierra Club Books, 1979).

Glidden, Ralph. *Exploring the Yellowstone High Country: A History of the Cooke City Area* (Cooke City, Mont.: The Cooke City Store, 1976).

Gottlieb, Alan M., ed. *The Wise Use Agenda: The Citizen's Policy Guide to Environmental Resource Issues* (Bellingham, Wash.: The Free Enterprise Press, 1989).

Greider, William C. *One World, Ready or Not* (New York: Simon and Schuster, 1997).

Hansen, David T. *Waste Land: Meditations on a Ravaged Landscape* (New York: Aperture, 1997).

Herring, Susan Tabor. *Taste of Homer: Sesquicentennial Cookbook and History* (Homer, La.: Homer Sesquicentennial Committee, 2000).

Ketcham, Robert Glen, and Carey D. Ketcham. *The Tongass: Alaska's Vanishing Rain Forest* (New York: Aperture, 1987).

Kirk, Ruth, ed. *The Enduring Forests* (Seattle: The Mountaineers, 1996).

Korten, David C. *When Corporations Rule the World* (West Hartford, Conn.: Kumerian Press; San Francisco: Berrett-Koehler, 1995).

Mander, Jerry. *In the Absence of the Sacred: The Failure of Technology and the Survival of the Indian Nations* (San Francisco: Sierra Club Books, 1991).

Marston, Ed, ed. *Reopening the Western Frontier* (Washington, D.C.: Island Press, 1989).

Michener, James A. *Hawaii* (New York: Random House, 1959).

Netboy, Anthony. *The Salmon: Their Fight for Survival* (Boston: Houghton Mifflin Company, 1973).

Patterson, Walter C. *Nuclear Power* (New York: Penguin Books, 1976).

Roberts, J. Timmons, and Melissa M. Toffolon-Weiss. *Chronicles from the Environmental Justice Frontline* (New York: Cambridge University Press, 2001).

Rodgers, William H., Jr. *Environmental Law* (St. Paul: West Publishing Company, 1977).

Sax, Joseph L. *Defending the Environment: A Strategy for Citizen Action* (New York: Alfred A. Knopf, 1971).

———. *Mountains without Handrails: Reflections on the National Parks* (Ann Arbor: University of Michigan Press, 1980).

Servid, Carolyn, and Donald Snow, eds. *The Book of the Tongass* (Minneapolis: Milkweed Editions, 1999).

Shabecoff, Philip. *Earth Rising: American Environmentalism in the Twenty-first Century* (Washington, D.C.: Island Press, 2000).

———. *A Fierce Green Fire: The American Environmental Movement* (New York: Hill and Wang, 1993).

Shoaf, Bill. *The Taking of the Tongass: Alaska's Rainforest* (Sequim, Wash.: Running Wolf Press, 2000).

Stone, Christopher D. *Earth and Other Ethics: The Case for Moral Pluralism* (New York: Harper and Row, 1987).

———. *Should Trees Have Standing? Towards Legal Rights for Natural Objects* (San Francisco: William Kaufman, 1974).

Tliden, Freeman. *The National Parks: What They Mean to You and Me* (New York: Alfred A. Knopf, 1951).

Udall, Stewart L. *The Quiet Crisis and the Next Generation* (Salt Lake City: Gibbs Smith, 1989).

Wenner, Lettie M. *The Environmental Decade in Court* (Bloomington: Indiana University Press, 1982).

Wilcox, Carol. *Sugar Water: Hawai'i's Plantation Ditches* (Honolulu: University of Hawaii Press, 1996).

Zinn, Howard. *A People's History of the United States* (New York: Harper and Row, 1980).

The text in this book was set in Century Old Style, designed for American Typefounders in 1894 by Linn Lloyd Benton in collaboration with T. L. DeVinne for the *Century Magazine*. The display type is Meta, created in 1984 by Eric Spiekermann as a custom design for the German Post Office. *Justice on Earth* was designed by Ingalls + Associates, San Francisco, and printed in four-color process lithography by A. Mondadori Printing Company, Verona, Italy. The paper is Symbol Freelife satin (recycled), 150 gsm.

Right: Baby green sea turtle, Hawai'i. *Frans Lanting/ Minden Pictures. Page 217:* On Fisheating Creek, Florida. *James Valentine. Page 224:* Mendenhall Lake, Tongass National Forest, Alaska. *Robert Glenn Ketchum*